The Amazing Story
of the
Tonelli Family in America

The Amazing Story
of the
Tonelli Family in America

12,000 Miles in a Buick
in Search of Identity,
Ethnicity, Geography,
Kinship, and Home

Bill Tonelli

Addison-Wesley Publishing Company
Reading, Massachusetts   Menlo Park, California   New York
Don Mills, Ontario   Wokingham, England   Amsterdam   Bonn
Sydney   Singapore   Tokyo   Madrid   San Juan
Paris   Seoul   Milan   Mexico City   Taipei

The excerpt from "Immigrants and Family Values" by Francis Fukuyama, *Commentary,* May 1993, is used with the permission of the author and *Commentary;* all rights reserved.

Map on jacket from the Road Atlas © 1994 by Rand McNally R.L. 94-S-25.

Library of Congress Cataloging-in-Publication Data

Tonelli, Bill.
    The amazing story of the Tonelli family in America / Bill Tonelli.
      p. cm.
    Includes bibliographical references.
    ISBN 0-201-62455-9
    1. Italian Americans—Biography. 2. Tonelli family. I. Title.
E184.I8T66   1994
973'.0451—dc20   94-6400
                                           CIP

Jacket design and Tonelli crest design by Michael Ian Kaye
Text design and maps by Karen Savary
Set in 10-point Clarendon Light by Carol Woolverton

1 2 3 4 5 6 7 8 9-MA-97969594
First printing, April 1994

This book is dedicated with love

to my father and mother

Willie and Sylvia (nee Funaro)

TONELLI

and to all who bear

the blood or the name

He stands strongest who stands alone.

IBSEN

Contents

Prologue: Who Are We?

We're a nurse who drops out of the sky in a helicopter when you've driven into a ravine in the Appalachian Mountains and are losing blood and consciousness fast. We're a running back for Notre Dame and the old Chicago Cardinals who gets captured in World War II, survives the Bataan Death March and forty-two months of cruel captivity, then returns not only to home and health but to the gridiron, bathed in glory. We're a high-school dropout from Iowa who gets fifty years for beating an infant to death; we're the number two official in the Massachusetts State Police; we're a nun in Joliet, Illinois, who devotes her life to counseling men behind bars. We're a little girl playing accordion in her father's restaurant who graduates from Vassar and becomes one of the top museum directors in America. We're a pair of first cousins in San Diego who fall in love, get married, and have two perfectly normal kids. We have a nightclub act in central Massachusetts where we sing while drawing caricatures of audience members. In 1936, Barney Ross knocked us out in the fifth round of a nontitle fight. We grow soybeans in Ohio, we're a psychic in Santa Rosa, we're a dentist in Green Bay. We started a successful business, then pushed our ex-boss into our swimming pool, and he broke his leg and sued us. We're the title character in a short story by William Dean Howells. We run a small hospital in Vidalia, Georgia, a Toyota dealership in Westborough, Massachusetts, the

The Amazing Story of the Tonelli Family in America

Department of Public Health in Grayson County, Texas, a crack house in Des Moines. We're a lawyer in Tampa, an electrician in the Bronx, a morning DJ in San Jose, the 1991 Sports Car Association of America rookie of the year, the director of Nevada Citizens for Perot. We stole twenty-seven handguns from a National Guard armory to feed our heroin habit. We're a star forward for the South Florida University basketball team, the president of the posh St. Anthony's Hall fraternity at Columbia University, the Minister of Justice of Argentina. We're a nine-year-old Korean girl in North Carolina, an eight-year-old Native American boy in Alaska, a two-year-old Jew in New Jersey. We live in a federal prison camp for women in Texas, in a log cabin on the Arctic Circle, aboard a sailboat somewhere in the Caribbean. We're Mickey Mouse.

We're the Tonelli Nation. Yes we are.

The Amazing Story
of the
Tonelli Family in America

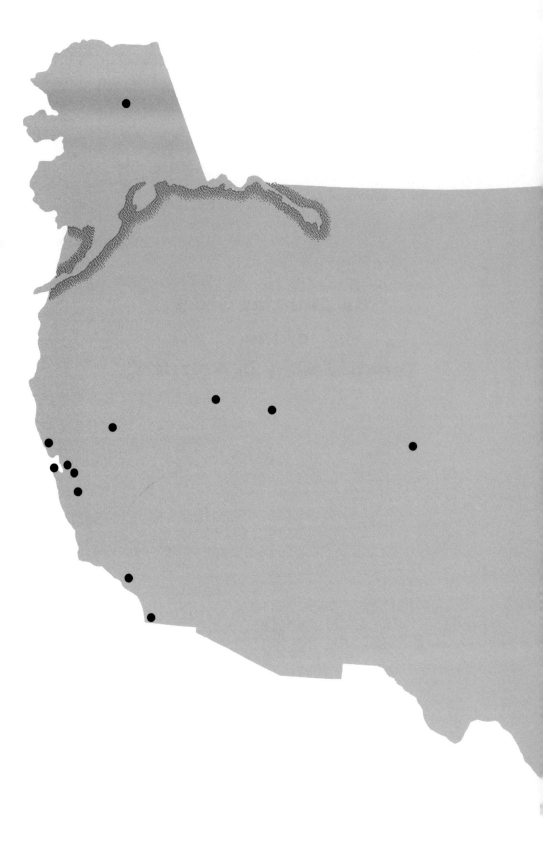

Part One

The Birth of a Nation
(Don't Tell the Citizens)

1.

Crossed Goats on a Bed of Linguini

Once upon a time—it was 1984, if you want to know, my thirtieth year as a Tonelli—I had the luck to open a piece of junk mail that changed the world.

Not *your* world, right, but mine, though even I didn't know it at the time. At the time all I knew was that I was about to become a $27.95 sucker thanks to an irredeemably cheesy appeal that began:

Dear Friend,

As you may already know, we have been doing some work relating to people who have the same last name as you do. Finally, after months of work, my new book, THE AMAZING STORY OF THE TONELLIS IN AMERICA, is ready for printing, and you are in it!

We have spent a great deal of effort and thousands of dollars to research through 70 million names and have located almost every Tonelli family in the United States. My new book features this valuable and extensive directory of Tonellis living in America, and it is as complete as possible.

Due to the uniqueness of the Tonelli name and the small Tonelli population in the U.S., it is economically impossible to produce extra copies after our scheduled publishing date. This is the first edition of the book, and it is certain to be quite a rare and valuable acquisition.

I believe this is the only book of its kind in the entire world, and you will want to have your own copy for you and your children. Each book is virtually handmade to order and will be serially numbered, registered in the owner's name, and accompanied by a Certificate of Authenticity. . . .

Would you fall for that? Look, I knew I was making an idiotic mail-order *acquisition*—it was practically a Thighmaster. And when the burgundy leatherette-bound, gold-embossed volume arrived, it was bad but no worse than I expected, with a spurious Tonelli coat of arms (crossed goats on a bed of linguini), some very generic advice on how to hang yourself from your family tree, and the only part I cared about, the complete directory of Tonellis in America.

Amazing! There's a Tonelli in Texas! There's a Tonelli named Abner! And, to my chagrin, only two Dr. Tonellis in the whole frigging country. How exactly *did* Miss Judy Tonelli come to reside at R.D. 1, Eleva, Wisconsin, and did she like it there? And why so many Tonellis (I shuddered to think) in Joliet, Illinois? Either they were prison guards or they were jailbirds living in a halfway house, I figured, and I couldn't decide which was worse. It went on and on that way, page after page of us—roughly three hundred and fifty Tonelli households in twenty-two states, a thousand or so individuals: Two-thousandths of a percent of the American population, give or take. The book simply listed names and addresses, but for some reason I was spellbound; reading it had the same effect as staring at a map—uncompromisingly quotidian at first, but capable of sucking you into a dream state.

At the time of this purchase I was living where I had

always lived, in the stout-hearted Little Italy of South Philadelphia. I mention this only because I believe now that my geographical circumstance was largely responsible for the weird hold this book had over me.

But how can I explain? Well, maybe this will help: Until I was in my twenties, I was unable to fully grasp the idea that *you may choose where you live.* How simple that concept seems now, but how inhuman, how futuristic, how absurd it sounded to me then. Even when it did sink in, I felt not liberated but vaguely horrified. Shaken, even. You mean you can just decide to live someplace and then live there, right? Without asking? And you make your choice on the basis of, what—nice weather? Righteous neighbors? Happening job? Mellow vibe? Unreal. All the possible reasons for choosing this place over that one seemed so . . . bloodless. I never thought this through, but in my soul I was sure: You were born in a place because *that's where you were meant to be.*

Of course, at that point in my life I don't think I knew anybody who had ever moved. I lived in South Philly because I was born there. My parents lived there because they were born there. And their parents lived there because . . . well, obviously, because the great sweep and clatter of history had intended to deposit them there. And the same set of facts held for just about everybody I knew, because just about everybody I knew was either the child or the grandchild of immigrants. So is it any surprise that in my unworldly worldview, ancestry, kinship, birthplace, and residence were four sides of the same coin? (Hey—I just invented the four-sided coin!) And that choosing one of the four seemed as possible as choosing any of the others?

As I say, I knew this in my soul, because had I devoted any of my brain to the subject, I would have realized how stupendously flawed my assumptions were. Clearly, people *did* move around. They moved around all the time. There were actually people living all over the country—I *knew* that—and in many instances they had gotten there under their own power. Still, something deep inside prevented me from connecting all the dots; I think that in this, in my sheltered little corner of an unimaginably big country, I was not alone.

Look, I know how quaint and backward all that sounds,

but the other way, the hypermobile, "Honey, IBM's transferring us to Atlanta" way—the American way—sounded just as screwy to me. Even worse, it sounded pathetic. How can somebody's attachment to the ground on which they stand be so superficial? Honest, how do they keep themselves from blowing away? People like that, I don't know, they're detachable, they're lightweight, they're . . . they're dust.

Of course, by now *I'm* dust, too. But back before I bought my Tonelli book, mobility seemed to be the kind of dangerously fickle behavior that only other people were foolish enough to indulge. Before I opened that piece of junk mail it never even occurred to me that there might be a bunch of strangers running around the country using *my exact name.* And there I suddenly was, faced with evidence that not only were there lots of them, but that they were living their lives wherever the hell they pleased. Mississippi! Utah! They were Tonellis, OK, but they were practically, to retrieve a common term of derision from my Italo-American youth: *Medigans.* Which, when pronounced in proper English, is: *Americans.* They were practically Americans. Well, no wonder I was amazed.

• • • That stunning realization disturbed me so much that for the next eight years, I gave it not one thought.

Aunt Josephine and Aunt Marie

2.

Horatio Alger,
Kiss My Ass

My Family Values

Interview with my father's sisters, Josephine (Tonelli) Garozzo and Marie (Tonelli) Cavaliere.
The interview took place in the kitchen of the house where my grandparents lived, where my father was born, and where my Aunt Jo continues to live.

Jo: OK, let's see, there were three brothers in Grandpop's family.

Me: When was Grandpop born?

Marie: May 1, 1889.

Me: And he was born in Nereto, in Italy.

Jo: Yes. And there were three brothers.

Marie: There was Joe, Pete . . .

Jo: And Uncle Joe.

Marie: *Two* brothers. And two sisters.

Jo: Yeah, two brothers and Grandpop.

Marie: And his sisters were Saveria—Sara, we called her—and Santa. . . .

Jo: Bill, another sandwich?

Me: No thanks, Aunt Jo, I'm OK. Now, there was some relative here before Grandpop came, right?

Marie: Yes, his older brother, Joe. Giuseppe. You know, your grandfather didn't want to come to America. He was put on the boat three times. One time he stabbed himself in the leg so they'd have to take him off. He came right out and said it—he missed Italy. He loved it here, but Italy was in his blood. After all, he was only sixteen years old when they shipped him over, and the reason they sent him was because his brother Joe had gotten into some kind of scrape in Italy—*I* think he killed somebody—and they didn't want their son to be here by himself. But Grandpop was very hurt, because once he came here his brother never bothered with him much or helped him. Pop always said that—"They made me come, and *then* . . . " He was very disappointed in his brother. Grandpop was a kid in this country, he was very green and didn't know anything, and his brother never wanted to have anything to do with him. Not that he needed Joe to support him, but Grandpop really had to fend for himself.

Me: And so that's why his brother came to America.

Jo: He came here to find a job, because there were no jobs. . . .

Me: Wait, that's not what Aunt Marie just said.

Marie: No, Jo, he came here because he was in trouble, so they sent him to America.

Jo: Well, I never heard that.

Marie: Jo, I'm telling you, I used to ask Pop all kinds of questions.

Jo: All I know is that Uncle Joe left a wife and a son in Italy when he came here, and he stayed twenty-five years. He only went back to Italy when his son was ready to get married.

Marie: He had no heart.

• • • OK, quite a bit has happened since my fateful book purchase, and I have to bring you up to date. But I love to hear my aunts talk—they kill me—so I thought maybe you would, too. There's something fierce and thrilling about where these two historians took their tale, about how Aunt Marie dispatched her uncle from the stage: *He had no heart.* Boom. Outtahere. It was the historian Barbara Tuchman who wrote, "History is character." *Women.* Still, it *was* illuminating to hear exactly why my forebears came to America—not, it would seem, due to any hideous privation, the motive that usually propels these immigrant sagas, but because my grandfather's brother, heretofore a bit player in my drama, was in a jam. Or so the hazy tale holds, but who knows? More relevant to me is that scene where my grandfather stabs himself in the leg to get off the boat headed for the land of opportunity. Jesus, would you say my psychogeographical legacy shows a little *ambivalence* where America's concerned? Horatio Alger, kiss my ass.

Anyway, where was I? Right, I bought the book, got the shock, banished the thought, and went on as before, a lifelong South Philadelphian, womb to tomb, sperm to worm. To this day, I don't want to hear about Brooklyn or Paris or Seattle or anyplace else: South Philly is the only place I ever want to be born and raised. South Philly made me. South Philly rules.

Even the experts agree. "The southern Italian perceived a strong social boundary between the world of his town or village and those of other towns or villages," writes sociologist Richard D. Alba, author of *Italian-Americans: Into the Twilight of Ethnicity.*

> The residents of other towns or villages were viewed as outsiders and strangers, even foreigners, and were the subject of ridicule: They are cuckolds, liars, or whatever. . . . Villagers took pride in their village . . . it was something intimate, familiar, where every stone, tree and

field was connected to this personal sense of history and
place. Thus, when southern Italians migrated to the
United States, they tended to settle where others from
the same place had settled, and their primary self-identi-
fication was in terms of their villages.

Do you see? I'm sociologically programmed to take a dim,
smirking view of anyplace that's *not* my birthplace, and for the
purely irrational, atavistic reason that I wasn't born in any of
those other places. A *very* flexible outlook on life, I know. *Very*
cosmopolitan.

Gazing into my past, I realize that even among my peers
I was in some ways backward (no modest achievement, believe me). Just one example: I sucked at driving. Which was no
surprise, since my father didn't know how to drive at all, and
neither did two of his three brothers. As a result, we lacked
something that's almost a requisite of full American citizen-
ship: Easy, mindless mobility. And it didn't bother us a bit, I'll
admit without shame. We didn't believe we were missing a
thing. We were already where we wanted to be. South Philadelphia had none of the aforementioned stones, trees, or fields to
connect us to our "personal sense of history and place," but we
did have some corner stores, churches, bars, fire hydrants,
schoolyards, and alleys that meant an awful lot to us. And with
the help of those homely landmarks, we all combined to create a
feudal peasant village about a mile and a half south of Independence Hall.

Like every Little Italy, it was superficially picturesque to
outsiders—*Yo! Rocky!*—but its inner life was comprehended
only slowly, only dimly, and even then only by us (barely). The
rich jumbles of personal and ancestral ties, the complex archi-
tecture of connections between individual, family, neighbor, and
neighborhood, the arcane hierarchies of *us* and *them,* all that
stuff ruled our lives. But we didn't waste much time analyzing
it: We lived by codes that were older than us all, old and—given
their murky, foreign origin—imponderable. We knew only that
in subtle and obvious ways, we were different from other people—that our passions, our suspicions, the conclusions to
which we jumped, what we valued, what we feared, and the

habits that we praised, what we'd say and would not say, how we loved and talked to God, were, by the standards of the America we perceived, otherworldly. I mean, we knew we were weird. We just didn't know *why*. It was as though our brains had been programmed elsewhere, then shipped here for final assembly.

Today, having read a thing or two on the subject, I know that Italian peasants came to this country equipped with ways that were distinctly un-American: they were fatalistic, they were clannish and suspicious of institutions (church *and* state), they were superstitious, and they were firm believers that calamity is always right around the corner. But they also had lots going for them once they reached these shores—white skins, ferociously strong family ties, the highest personal savings rate in the Western world, and the expectation that life is toil. All those attributes had evolved over centuries and served a highly practical purpose: They insulated the peasants from a long train of indifferent, sometimes brutal foreigners (Romans, Lombards, Normans, Germans, Greeks, Spaniards, Arabs, French, the list goes on) who invaded and ran the turf we now call Italy. Because those peasants had plenty of time to practice their survivalist manners—roughly from the birth of Christ to the middle of the nineteenth century—the code of conduct they made up was nothing if not stubborn. It was *so* stubborn that once it crossed the Atlantic, it found ample work here, protecting us from . . . well, it must have protected us from *something,* right, else why would it persist? It protected us from the indifferent, sometimes brutal foreigners *here,* from America and its bewildering, modern ways. And, of course, from bullshit like this:

> Now there came multitudes of men of the lowest class from the south of Italy . . . men out of ranks where there was neither skill nor energy nor any initiative of quick intelligence, and they came in numbers which increased from year to year, as if the countries south of Europe were disburdening themselves of the more helpless and sordid elements of the population.

Or so Woodrow Wilson wrote in 1902, ten years before becoming president of a country that was being built from the ground up by greaseballs and greenhorns. In 1914, a thinker named Edward Alsworth Ross chipped in with this, from a book titled *The Old World in the New:*

> It is fair to say the blood now being injected into the veins of our people is "sub-common." . . . You are struck by the fact that from ten to twenty percent are hirsute, low-browed, big-faced persons of obviously low mentality. Not that they suggest evil. They simply look out of place in black clothes and stiff collars, since clearly they belong in skins, in wattled huts at the close of the Great Ice Age.

Obviously, eighty years later enormous progress has been made. One example—today, we all look *great* dressed in black. And somehow—not solely by osmosis, either—we began acquiring that degree of skill and energy and initiative of quick intelligence. And a portion of that even filtered down to South Philly, and even to my humble block, and even to me. In other words, I was raised with the expectation that I would be as at home in America as the next guy (depending on where I'm standing).

But the giddy-dread sensation of reading the junk-mail book lurked in my thoughts, undigested, unabsorbed, floating to the fore at odd times. Once, while driving through New England (*riding,* I should say—my life has been blessed with female companions who are able and happy to chauffeur me like a pasha), I flashed on the memory that a great many Tonellis were listed in Massachusetts. There in the front seat, intoxicated by velocity, a vagrant dream seized me: Wouldn't it be something to get a car and, using only the junk-mail book as my guide, drive around the country to shake the hand of every Tonelli in America? I saw myself steering confidently up to the grassy borders of countless anonymous suburban tracts, leaving the engine on, hopping out, ringing the bell, and extending a paw of kinship past the half-open storm door to the astonished resident. (*"You're who? Wait—let me get the camcorder!"*) Then I'd race back to my wheels and peel out, on to my next visitation. Crazy! The obvious impediments to such a spree—I was still half-assed behind the wheel and thus hated driving; besides, the trip would require a luxurious amount of time and money—didn't occur to me, because I knew I'd never actually do it. To be honest, I didn't even want to do it. I only wanted to think about doing it. I never even thought about *why* I wanted to think about doing it. But clearly, the reason had to be a cousin to the fascination the junk-mail book itself had held: *So many ways to be a Tonelli, hundreds of them, thousands. . . .*

• • • After I had torn myself out of South Philly, those who knew of my chauvinism regarding the land of my birth would inquire (archly) about whether I missed the splendors of life there. "I love my mother," I would answer (elliptically), "but I don't want to live with her again either." It was a reply that revealed (to me, I mean) a hint of the depth and complexity of feeling that even an unlovely bit of real estate can inspire in its children.

But I left anyway, for the usual, cold-blooded reason—I get offered a job in New York, the job's good, the money's good, so I split in a heartbeat. I'm all talk. I'm *dust.* Which is not to say that I made my escape without mixed feelings. On the one hand, I knew that by unplugging myself from kin and corner I was simply doing, in a vastly safer, more orderly way, what millions of immigrants, the backbone of America, had done before me. So I was actually honoring their impulse to roam and prosper. Blowing off the people and places you love to chase a buck and personal fulfillment—that's what America's *about.* And anyway, by then lots of my peers were bailing out of the old neighborhood, either for the blissful autonomy of suburbia or points even more unthinkably alien. Our Little Italy was going the way of all the others—away.

But I also knew that I was being a selfish bastard, and that in abandoning my tribal home I had thrown away my right to mourn its passing. I was actually the one killing it. I was committing sociological suicide—*this* me was killing *that* me. Even sociology, it turns out, can be red in tooth and claw.

Anyway, I moved. Then—not that it matters, not that you care, only to record the story just as it happened—a completely practical impulse intervened in my life and pushed me toward an appointment that destiny, I think, had made for me eight years earlier. As I mentioned, Italians are world-class savers, a tendency I have witnessed up close—I know several people who have managed to overturn mathematical logic by saving more money than they've ever *had*. Once I asked my father what kind of advice his father had given him, and he could recall only one piece: "He told me, 'Save your money.' " Naturally, as the baby-boom grandson of immigrants, I stupidly squandered that sound instinct, until one alarming day when I realized I'd have to put *something* away. To that end, I thought up some free-lance editing projects that might throw a few grand in my direction. In August of 1992, I sent a long memo describing ideas for books that others would write and I would edit, in my spare time, to Richard, a literary agent I know. To end the five-page letter on a light note, I threw in a two-paragraph joke, prefacing it with the jest that I had one final idea to propose:

> *THE AMAZING STORY OF THE TONELLI FAMILY IN AMERICA*—The title is actually stolen from a book published by a shlock mail-order outfit trying to capitalize on ridiculous middle-class pretensions, trash like "gen-uine" family coats-of-arms and crests. . . .

I described how I came to own the volume, and then I wrote:

> Anyway, the plan would be to send a questionnaire to each household to get some basic (and some whimsical) information, almost like a Tonelli census. Then I'd hit the road—I'd visit as many Tonellis as possible, and I'd ask to stay for dinner. Then I'd turn the whole project, from the junk-mail book offer to the census data to the last Tonelli dinner, into a book. Big picture, it's about the meaning of the persistence of ethnic ties in the American experiment. Personally, it's about why I am absolutely crazy to know as much as possible about all those Tonel-lis, in large part for what it will tell me about who I am and how I'm doing. I want to know how many earn over $50,000, how many still cook Italian. I want to know what they wear and how they vote and how smart they

are and who they hang around with and marry and what being a Tonelli means to them and their kids. I want to take my picture with all of them. I want to know what Tonellis have contributed to America. I suspect that by the end of the search, the "Amazing" part of the title will be fairly deflated, but for some sick reason, that strikes me as the funniest part: Maybe the real subtext of this book is the idea that ethnic identity is persistent because it resolves the existential tension in ordinary people who desire to be, by some—any—definition, special. There is only one possible writer I can suggest for this book.

But I was only *joking*! Or at least I persist to this day in believing that I was. It's true that the addition of the questionnaire and the qualification that I'd meet as many Tonellis "as possible" turned the trip into a genuinely practical endeavor. And casting it as a book meant that, theoretically, there would be funding and a worthwhile (rather than nonexistent) purpose involved. Still, I laughed when Richard called to say that the last idea—the joke—was his favorite. And that he wanted to pursue it, and would I write a longer description of the idea, something he could show to publishers?

My first response (incredulity) was overtaken by a fleet shiver of terror (the driving, shit, the driving). But if Richard was so interested in Tonellis, who was I to deprive him? The longer proposal wasn't so long—maybe two pages—but writing it forced me to think in very precise terms about what it was I had been pondering off and on the past eight years, since that damn silly book showed up in my life. At one point in the expanded description, I wrote a two-sentence paragraph that instantly crystallized every thought I'd had on the subject thus far:

> I think I want to know the Tonelli Nation. But first I have to create it.

Huh! *A nation.* Never having considered statecraft as my one true calling, I had to stop a minute to figure out. . . . See, the nation thing *did* make a kind of sense to me, an absurdly self-aggrandizing but useful kind of sense. Like everyone else in this country, Tonellis once lived where they were supposed to live—*where they were born.* Then, for reasons I still don't completely comprehend, they allowed themselves to be swept up in something uncharacteristically fate-defying, a brain fever that shook the world—it was like a stampede, a real estate rush, a contagion of self-improvement unlike anything history had ever unleashed. At the start of the nineteenth century, America had a population of thirteen million; by the start of the twentieth, three times that many immigrants had claimed these shores. Imagine the cacophony, the confusion—this must have been one crazed country back then. Think of the current anxiety over American culture under siege by unclean foreign ways. Then consider that in Chicago, for instance, there was a year (1910) when 70 percent of its inhabitants were immigrants or their children. No wonder Woodrow Wilson and his buddies were so freaked out. It was as though a tidal wave had swept up all your tired, your poor, your young and restless, your ugly and stupid, your wanted for murder and deposited them on this spit of golden sand. They came from everywhere, but mainly it was a Europeasant diaspora, and so a Tonelli diaspora, too. We had flung ourselves to the wind, and it had taken us far and wide. Some of us went farther and wider than others, because the restlessness didn't go away when we hit America; it kept right on driving us, to points all over the map. (In fact, it hasn't stopped yet.)

Anyway, I imagined, we Tonellis *still* had lots in common—more, at least, than we had with our strange new neighbors. And then history paused, just to catch its breath. The immigrants were the generation of upheaval (though it stuns me to think of those stolid old paisans as agents of geopolitico-economic revolt, but they *were*). Their children, however, were born into such a state of culture shock that they were afraid to *budge.* It required all their attention and energy to find the balance between who they had been and who they were becoming. But that transition stage couldn't last forever, could it? Oh, it *seemed* like it could, and in fact, those funny hybrid customs, neither Italian nor American, did persist in certain places, South Philly being a prime example.

Elsewhere, though, Tonellis were marching into the future. Even from inside my bubble I sensed something like that was going on. But it took a volume of wisdom that could be purchased only through a junk-mail offer to open my eyes.

I didn't want to write a book that would undo the American Century, not exactly. But I wanted to understand what it was doing to me and mine in the only way I could:

I wanted to reverse the Tonelli diaspora.

First, I was going to find as many Tonellis as I could and, to the best of my ability, reunite them. (To wonder whether they *wanted* to be reunited never occurred to me.) I was going to look at them all at once and ask them how and why they got to wherever they were, and if they liked it there. I was going to deconstruct America and construct from the pieces—specifically, from the two thousandths of a percent to which I undeniably belonged—an imaginary nation. I was going to conduct a census and make personal visits, take pictures, and then draft a report—the State of the Union, only without the union.

Also, it dawned on me, I actually wanted to drive. A lot. I wanted to see some things. At last, *I* was restless, too.

Not that I imagined for a minute that this enterprise would ever come to pass. But then Richard shopped the Tonellis around, and a book publishing company actually bit. They put money on the table, too, perfect strangers expressing unmistakable monetary interest in the Tonelli Nation. Once that sunk in I thought, OK, it's now or never, so I went to my boss at *Esquire* magazine to see if it was even possible for me to take two months off (unpaid) to make this expedition. Before I spoke a word, I handed him the book proposal.

He read a sentence or two, and then he looked up and said, "I just ordered *The Amazing Story of the McDonell Family in America!*" And as he spoke I knew: I'm outtahere. I'm history. *Amazing.*

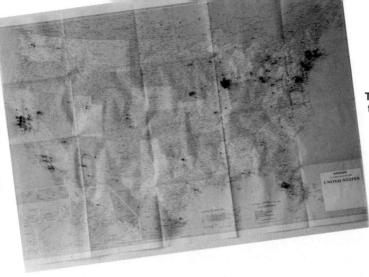

The Tonelli map of
the United States

3.

Little Red Map Pins

My Family Values

Me: In your family there were two adults and six kids, I know, but weren't there other people also living in this house when you were growing up?

Marie: Oh, we had so many people living with us. Anybody that came. Your grandfather was a generous man, Bill, a good man.

Jo: Marie, who else lived with us?

Marie: Aunt Mary!

Jo: Oh, right, Aunt Mary and her son, we took them in.

Marie: She was my mother's sister, but she got divorced.

Jo: Four people in one room—me and Marie with Aunt Mary and her son. Then, who else? . . . Oh, when Giustino died, his wife Ann and her two kids moved in with us, too.

Marie: And our four brothers all in one room. We had such a beautiful upbringing, let me tell you, Billy. We had no money, but it was beautiful. Hey, I'll tell you a story about your Peca side, your grandmother's side. This never came out. See your great-grandfather?

Me: You mean Grandmom's father?

Marie: Yeah. Now, he was in America before our grandmother came—

Me: Wait a second. What was Grandmom's mother like?

Both: Tough.

Jo: Tough as nails.

Marie: Your great-grandfather was the nicer of the two. Your great-grandmother was a tiger.

Jo: A tiger.

Marie: But then, she raised nine kids. Anyway, our grandfather came to this country before our grandmother did. And there was always a whisper in the family. We could never catch on, until we got older, and we heard—

Jo: Our grandfather had another son here.

Marie: We *think* he had another son here.

Jo: Not we think—we *know*.

Marie: And they never recognized him.

Jo: Well, Mom and her brothers and sisters met his son at school. *They* knew who he was.

Marie: Wait, what? Start over again.

Jo: They all knew.

Marie: OK, they all knew, and they used to whisper about it.

Jo: But our grandmother wouldn't have anything to do with the boy. They were not allowed to associate with him.

Marie: But Grandpop probably took care of him, because he had money. But the point is that now we don't know anything about this man, and it's a shame. Because he *is* our relative.

The Amazing Story of the Tonelli Family in America

> **Jo:** But our grandmother would have nothing to do with him.
>
> **Marie:** Grandmom was a tiger.

• • • I could listen to those two all day. So far, Aunt Marie has said that my grandfather's brother had no heart and my grandmother's mother was a tiger. It's starting to sound like *The Wizard of Oz.* My father used to tell me stories about his grandmother the tiger: When he was a kid they fought all the time, and one of their running battles was over the very Italian-American duality that's at the heart of these proceedings. Defiantly, he would bait the iron-willed old broad by proclaiming, "I'm an American!" To which she would reply, in broken English, "American? *Merda de cane!*" a sly pun meaning that to her mind, American equaled dogshit. Cracks me up, but it kills me, too, thinking of how all those poor children of immigrants were being pulled by the claws of history in two directions at once. My father had his grandmother yanking him from one side, and Woodrow Wilson yanking him from the other. A historian of the time quoted an immigrant who said that to succeed here, Italians had to show "a great interest in whatever is American and a high disdain for all that is Latin or glorifies the Latin life." An author named Leonard Covello wrote, "We were becoming American by learning to be ashamed of our parents." It was a bruising but efficient way of turning uneasy strangers into fervent citizens: First America shamed them, then it offered them a new way to be proud.

And so my father, along with millions of other men and women of his experience, strove with a purity of purpose I now find so moving to prove themselves "good Americans." And they succeeded, too, so why am I now compelled to drag up all this ancient greaseball grief? Back in the thirties, sociologist Marcus Hansen, who thoroughly studied the children of immigrants, coined this aphorism: "What the son wishes to forget, the grandson wishes to remember."

There is something depressing about realizing that even before you've discovered your innermost feelings, they've been isolated and dissected by sociologists. Educational, though, all the same. I just found a nugget of further enlightenment, again in the writings of Richard Alba, who observed that strong ethnic identification exists only in places where there are critical masses of members of the group in question. A condition that, in the second half of this century, prevails in only a very few places in America, but my weird birthplace among them. According to a study Alba conducted, 68.5 percent of Americans say they have had "no experience" of feeling curiosity about others' ethnic background. I am part of the primordial 2.6 percent who say they are curious about that "all the time."

I probably *could* survive without automatically calculating the ancestry of every individual I come across, but I can't help myself—I can't think of *me* without thinking of my ethnic background. Certainly, though, most people manage to identify themselves as . . . *themselves.* I look upon them with a kind of awe, because they seem to be, for the most part, sums of their own accomplishments, tastes, inclinations, hopes and dreams and fears. *Individuals.* Somehow, I got stuck absorbing way too much of my identity from dead people who weren't all that forthcoming when they were alive. Can anybody be said to exist outside the span of his own existence? I can: Hi, my name is Tonelli, and I used to be a peasant in Italy.

To which another part of me replies: We all used to be apes, too.

I just remembered something: I'm a little kid and my father and I are on the subway when I ask him, out of nowhere, "Hey, Dad, what does Tonelli mean?"

He answers, "Pliers."

Pliers . . .

● ● ● The birth of the Tonelli Nation takes place—in my head. As I mentioned earlier, the junk-mail book lists lots of us in Joliet, so, as an experiment, I begin my research for this book by calling the Joliet *News-Herald*'s morgue to see if they have any old clips filed under my surname. Sure do, Petra the librarian tells me, and a week and $14 (photocopying fee) later, a package arrives.

Jesus!

The Amazing Story of the Tonelli Family in America

The first clip in a fat pile is from 1965, with the headline RECEIVE SCHOLARSHIPS. There are two yearbook portraits side by side. On the left is a serious young man, mature in the way college boys tended to look back then. The guy on the right is younger, with a softer, more expressive face. Neither one looks anything like me, or even like each other, even though they're brothers, A. Duane and Ernest J. Tonelli, sons of Mr. and Mrs. Ernest Tonelli. They made the paper because A. Duane got $1,000 from the Douglas Co. (the aerospace giant), where he was employed at the time, to study toward a doctorate at USC. Ernest received a scholarship from Lewis College, where he planned to major in chemistry.

Photocopied onto the same sheet is a 1964 article with the headline BOARD STUDIES CHARGES BROUGHT AGAINST JOLIET FIREMAN TONELLI. It's about Karo—*Karo!*—Tonelli, who was the subject of a hearing because of his possible violation of department anti-moonlighting rules when he built a house for himself during his off-duty hours. The charges were brought by the city's fire chief, which makes it sound suspiciously like small-city politics.

Next, here's a short clip about Sister Theodore Tonelli, who, judging by her picture, is a sweet old nun. She was awarded the 1983 Charles Livingston Award for volunteer service from the Retired Senior Volunteer Program.

Hold on, it gets racier. From 1967, car stolen, two arrested—one of them, Charles Tonelli, age seventeen, was busted for grand theft for taking a car from a driveway and then crashing it into another car two hours later. On the same sheet there's mention of another scholarship won by A. Duane.

Here's an old item, from '52, just a photo of Derby—*Derby!*—Tonelli, local grocer, grinning and holding up a string of bass and catfish he caught in the Fox River. He uses crabs for bait, the caption informs.

Hey, good news: A. Duane was promoted by Douglas Aircraft in Santa Monica. But then, sadness: Derby, age fifty-seven, was badly burned in a flash fire when a spark from his cigarette fell into the glue he was using to lay linoleum at home. Lucky for him, his son-in-law, Fire Department Captain Henry Garovaglia, was in the house at the time; he snuffed out the flames that had engulfed Derby, who was reported to be in fair condition with second-degree burns to the face, arms, legs, and thighs. Henry was hurt, too. Same sheet, a year probation and six weekends in jail for young Charles Tonelli, who pleaded guilty to that car theft. Also on the same page, a clip from a year later, telling how Charles got into yet another scrape—he and a pal forced a cab to the curb, the cabbie got out with a tire iron, Charles pulled a knife, and the cops caught him.

Next page, Diane Tonelli, daughter of Derby, gets a BA from St. Dominic's College. . . . Karo quits the fire department two years after that trouble over his house, . . . and Charles Tonelli, twenty-four, who by this time is gainfully employed as a machinist with Caterpillar Tractor, shoots himself in the head and dies. His wife found the body on the garage floor. God, I feel so sad—I really was hoping he'd straighten himself out. . . . A. Duane's a newsmaker yet again—wrote a big article on a solar power unit capable of operating a space lab. . . . Young Nola Tonelli was named Daughters of the American Revolution Good Citizen for 1969, a rough year for good citizens, . . . and A. Duane's brother Ernest returns to the spotlight, as a winning candidate for a seat on the Joliet Township High School Board. By this time he's a businessman and teacher, with a degree in economics from the University of Illinois—guess he didn't major in chemistry after all—and owns ELT and Associates, financial planning and insurance. He and his wife Linda have three sons, and Ernest coaches Little League. Wow, surprise, here's A. Duane again. This guy must have had a press agent. It's an old clip, from '57, a photo of him with a scale model of an ocean liner he built entirely by hand, from pine, with a thousand portholes drilled and fitted with brass eyelets, took him three years—eight hundred hours—to finish. I bet he still has it, too.

By this point even *I'm* starting to worry about why I'm so fascinated. Mostly it's the thrill of seeing my name endlessly repeated in print—Tonelli Tonelli Tonelli Tonelli—and attached to total strangers. It's as though Joliet, Illinois, a town that has thus far in my life demanded zero attention, has suddenly revealed itself to be my personal parallel universe. I feel like an honorary citizen, and at this point I still don't know where

Joliet *is*. But I'm also caught up in the disjointed little drama that plays out as I page through the clips—A. Duane goes out in the world to find success and fortune while his kid brother Ernest, a hometown boy, coaches Little League and runs for the school board, and poor Charles, off to a rough start and then to a sad end, all against a backdrop of Derby and Karo and Sister Theodore . . .

One more clip, from '91, and judging by the headline it's the prize: "SURVIVOR" DOG NEAR END OF LINE. Charles Tonelli, seventy-seven, set traps on his property to catch vermin but accidentally caught a stray dog. He tried to free it but the dog was too crazed to approach, so he hit it in the head with a two-by-four. Even that didn't make the beast any more reasonable, so Charles got out his twenty-five caliber semiautomatic pistol and fired five shots, two of which went clean through the dog's skull. And the dog *survived,* a little calmer, too, but Charles got caught and was set to appear before a judge. If nobody adopted the dog, the article said, the pound would put it to sleep. Christ, Joliet's a tough town. Wonder what happened to the dog? *Have to find that dog.**

• • • I make a research trip to the Center for Migration Studies, on Staten Island. Driving back to Manhattan with its director, Dr. Lydio Tomasi, a scholar of global population shift, I'm explaining my book, telling him that my road trip will help me to create a portrait of the Tonelli Nation. He thinks a second, laughs, and says, "Then you'll be the king."

---

*I call the Joliet Animal Control Center and talk to Sharon Sherrell, who tells me the dog was adopted right away, by a guy who owned a construction company. And he named the dog Bullet. (I just made that up.) But his construction company went bust, after which the dog went to a new owner, in Elwood, Illinois. So the poor creature was saved, happy ending, except that three times in the past year it has run away from home and had to be picked up by the dog catchers. Two bullets through the brain and this mutt still won't behave. Sharon reminds me that Charles Tonelli was genuinely sorry after he shot the dog. She also tells me that she has a book that goes into the background of the Sherrell family, including a directory of Sherrells all over the country, etc.

• • • On a Sunday morning I buy the three- by five-feet Hammond Classic Map of the United States, pin it to a big sheet of foamboard, and hang it on my office wall. I stare at it awhile, then go back out and buy little red map pins. Using the junk-mail book and an atlas as my guide, I start putting pins into the map, one per Tonelli household, until I see that some cities can't hold all the pins they require. So I go back out and buy big red pushpins, each of which will represent five households. I spend the rest of the day marking Tonellis. When I finish, there's a cluster of red in northern California, one around Chicago, a small bunch in the middle of Iowa, and lots of red in New York and eastern Pennsylvania. Massachusetts is completely red. There's only one pin in Utah, one in Mississippi, and one in the middle of Alaska. (I worry about those lonesome Tonellis.) On Monday everybody who comes into my office asks what the map's about, and I explain how I spent my weekend. Somebody stares at it for a minute and says, "Very anal of you." I can't disagree. Somebody else looks, giggles, and says, "What a loser." I can't disagree.

• • • I could now write a short book on research strategies for the amateur genealogist. After my successful raid of the Joliet newspaper morgue, I begin calling newspapers all over the country, wherever there seem to be pockets of Tonellis. More than twenty papers send me bundles of clips. I also take advantage of the New York Public Library's research division. It's fantastic—essentially, the library subsidized my book by making a trained computer database researcher available to me, free of charge. Thanks to the excellent Sam Register, my research consultant there (who did all the actual work), I find mentions of Tonellis in hundreds of on-line computer databases and CD/ROM sources. The on-line gizmo is particularly magical: Sam would call up a publication, type in the key word for our search—*Tonelli*—and instantly the computer would tell us how many times the word appears in that source. (In TASS I found one article about a computerized archaeology exhibit involving an Italian journalist named Tiziana Tonelli.) Sam found my name more than a thousand times—in Dun & Bradstreet Market Identifiers, U.S. Copyright Office applications, Who's Who in the South, Latin American News, Tax Notes Today, on and on, each one more arcane than the last.

The Tonellis who turn up most frequently—the biggest "hitters," in the data-search parlance—are John Tonelli, a Canadian who had a long career in the National Hockey League, and therefore appears in hundreds of newspaper boxscores, and Edith Ann Tonelli, an art curator and museum director of some note (at the Wight Gallery, at UCLA), who has written and been written about a lot. I was prepared to find lots on him but am surprised and gratified to learn of her existence. Here's a brief digest of what else I learned:

• Aristedes Tonelli, of Standard, Illinois, is dubbed "the lost prisoner of Peoria." He was arrested in the 1930s on tax evasion charges, but through some mix-up, he was jailed in seclusion and never arraigned or tried. After a few months he sneaked into a courtroom, the error was discovered, and he was let off for time served.

• David Tonelli, a successful trucking company owner, quarry owner, and businessman in San Jose, was sued for $40,000 in 1953 for pushing his ex-boss into a swimming pool during a party, resulting in the fracture of the ex-boss's leg.

• Laddie Tonelli, a welterweight out of Marseilles, Illinois, went five rounds with Barney Ross in a nontitle fight in 1936 before Ross knocked him out.

• Joseph P. Tonelli, of Yonkers, appears in *Who's Who in America* as president of the three hundred fifty thousand–member International Paperworkers Union. He was the first big labor leader to back Jimmy Carter for president in 1976. He was also named to head the New York Racing Commission—my first Tonelli big shot.

• In the pages of *Vanity Fair,* I find a photograph of John Tonelli, president of the St. Anthony's Hall fraternity at Columbia.

• I find Tonellis serving as executive director of the Engineering Contractors Association of South Florida (Gail); starring, in 1975, on the South Florida University basketball team (Tommy); giving a demonstration of duck decoy carving at an aquarium in Chicago (Jay and Donna); and winning, in 1991, the Sports Car Club of America rookie of the year award (Peter). In World War II, Tonellis were shot down in a bombing raid over Berlin and receiving a Purple Heart (Vincent), wounded in action in Germany (Anthony), and in Belgium (Bruno). I find a Tonelli who holds the copyright for a song titled "Money, Won't You Come My Way" (Robert); one who authored a monograph titled *The Pharmacokinetics of Cefixime* (Alfred Paul); and one who was elected mayor of Dalzell, Illinois (Arthur).

• Uh-oh. In 1978, at age seventy, Joseph Tonelli the labor leader pleads guilty to embezzling a few thousand bucks from the union treasury and attempting to obstruct justice. He's even the subject of a three-part Jack Anderson column, which details Tonelli's attempts to get Bert Lance and Griffin Bell to stop the prosecution. He goes to jail for one year.

• I learn of the existence of several fictional Tonellis, among them the title character of a nineteenth-century German novel by Ludwig Tieck, *Das Leben der Beruhmten Kaisers Abraham Tonelli*; the title character of a nineteenth-century French opera by Thomas Marie Francois Sauvage, *La Tonelli*; and the title character of a nineteenth-century William Dean Howells story, "Tonelli's Marriage." (As artistic inspirations, the last century was a good one for us.) Howells's story begins:

> There was no richer man in Venice than Tommaso
> Tonelli, who had enough on his florin a day; and none
> younger than he, who owned himself forty-seven years
> old. He led the cheerfullest life in the world, and was
> quite a monster of content; but when I come to sum up
> his pleasures, I fear that I shall appear to my readers to
> be celebrating a very insipid and monotonous
> existence. . . .

A monster of content! I'll take it. In the twentieth century I find a police officer character, Lieutenant Tonelli, no first name given, in a made-for-cable movie, *The Sketch Artist,* screenplay by Michael Angeli; and a character named "Mrs. Tonelli" in a TV commercial for Mrs. Smith's Pies.

I'm puzzled at first when the database spits out this clip:

Civic Leader Diana Peters Dies at Age 46

HUNTINGTON BEACH: Diana Peters, 46, a civic leader and former superintendent of schools, has died of ovarian cancer.

Born in Joliet, Ill., Peters earned a doctorate in education from Northern Illinois University. . . . In 1990, she was named Woman of the Year for the 58th District by the California Legislature, and she received the Huntington Beach Soroptimist Woman of Distinction Award. . . .

But then I read:

She is survived by her husband of twenty-three years, Bruce; her mother, Margaret Tonelli; five sisters, and a brother, Karo Tonelli.

Karo! Last time I bumped into him was in those clips from the Joliet paper.

From abroad, I discover:

• Annalena Tonelli, an Italian lawyer who's devoted the past twenty years to treating Somalians with tuberculosis. She's kind of a junior Mother Teresa, judging by the long article in the *Washington Post.*

• Anna Tonelli (1763–1846), a renowned British painter

• Armando Tonelli, of Buenos Aires, author of *El Verdad Sobre de Rotary Club* (The True Story of the Rotary Club) in 1946

• Ideler Tonelli, Argentina's Minister of Labor under President Alfonsin

• Sandor Tonelli, a prominent Hungarian author and critic

• Leonida Tonelli, an Italian mathematician responsible for at least two innovations, the Fubini-Tonelli integral and the Tonelli-Picard method

• The Tonelli Mixing System, the first fully automated industrial cake-making technology, based in Italy but widely used around the world

• Giovanni Tonelli, who's also an editor-writer. He shows up in a 1947 article by William L. Shirer. Giovanni was alleged to be the front man for a fascist movement controlled by a former member of Mussolini's cabinet.

• Luigi Tonelli, same name as my grandfather, born one year later, a widely published Italian literary critic

And I know all this stuff without having talked to a single Tonelli! I hold hundreds of them, and scores of their life stories, all in my head. And not one of my . . . I mean *these* . . . Tonellis even knows I exist! At this point I'm tempted to keep the advance money and write a novel about a maniac who collects all this information over the course of years and then uses it to . . . to *what*? Can't think of a single practical use for this stuff, so I move to the next step in the birth of the Tonelli Nation. I conduct a census.

• • • These Tonellis have finally turned me into a total loser.

It's 7:30 P.M. on New Year's Eve, 1992, and I'm alone in my office, wetting stamps—more than eight hundred of them, almost a thousand dollars' worth. I'm also wetting envelopes—more than four hundred of them. I'm surrounded by heaps of the four-page questionnaires that every Tonelli household in America I could find will receive, about four hundred and fifty to start with. Here's the cover letter I'm sending.

December 31, 1992

Dear Tonelli Household,

My name is Bill Tonelli, I live in New York,
I am a writer and a Senior Editor at <u>Esquire</u>
magazine, and I'm not selling anything,
honest.

I am writing a book, however, and that's the
reason for the questionnaire in this envelope.

My book will be about Americans of Italian
ancestry and how they feel about their ethnic
background. It will be published by Addison-
Wesley Publishing Co. in the spring of 1994.
(I'm enclosing a copy of a letter from my editor there, to verify.)

The best way for me to research a book like
this, I decided, was to focus on one small
group of people, so that's what I'm doing:
Most of the book will be about people named
Tonelli. There are about five hundred Tonelli
households in the U.S., I've learned, in thirty
states, though mostly concentrated in Massachusetts, Illinois, California, New York, and
Pennsylvania. Most are not related to each
other, I feel certain, but for my purposes
that's OK.

I'm beginning my research with the questionnaire that's enclosed. It's only four pages long
and shouldn't take more than fifteen minutes
to complete, but it will mean a great deal to
my book if you'll help me and fill it out.

As you'll see, I'm asking the questions you'd
expect—about how you live, your jobs, your
eating and social habits, and how much (if at
all) you feel your Italian background in your
daily life. All the information will be confidential. I'll turn the answers into statistics, so
nothing you tell me will be connected to your
name.

There are two copies of the questionnaire enclosed. That's so I can gather information
from as many generations of Tonellis as possible. One copy is for the head of the household
to complete. The other is for that person's son
or daughter, if there is one living in the home
and he or she is old enough to fill this out.

Even though the information will be 100 percent confidential, in a few cases I'll want to
call and talk a little on the telephone. That's
why I ask for your name and phone number.
If for some reason you don't wish to give
them, that's OK. I hope you'll still complete
the rest of the questions.

You'll also find a stamped, addressed envelope
in this package, to make returning the questionnaire easier. I'm working on a tight dead-
line, so if you could complete this and mail it
back within a week of receiving it, I'll be
grateful. If you have any questions, please
feel free to call me. . . .

In advance, thank you.

Yours truly,

The Amazing Story of the Tonelli Family in America

You may have noticed that I didn't mention anything about paying visits in the letter. I just didn't want to scare anybody off so soon. Here's the questionnaire.

1. Which of your Tonelli ancestors first came here from Italy? (check one)

My father____   My grandfather____

My great-grandfather____   Don't know____

2. If you know, where in Italy did he come from?

_____

3. How many of your grandparents are (or were) of Italian ancestry? (check one)

All four____ Three____ Two____ One____ Don't know____

4. Are (or were) both your parents of Italian ancestry? (check one)

Yes____ No____ Don't know____

5. If you are or ever were married, did you marry someone of Italian ancestry? (check one)

Yes____ No____

6. Do you speak Italian? (check one)

Fluently____ A little____ A few words____ Not at all____

7. How far from your home does your nearest Tonelli relative live?_____

8. How often do you spend a social evening with a neighbor? (check one)

Several times a week____   Once a week____

Several times a month____   Once a month____

Several times a year____   Almost never____

9. How often do you spend a social evening with a friend? (check one)

Several times a week____   Once a week____

Several times a month____   Once a month____

Several times a year____   Almost never____

10. How often do you spend a social evening with a relative? (check one)

Several times a week____   Once a week____

Several times a month____   Once a month____

Several times a year____   Almost never____

11. How often do you spend a social evening with a sibling? (check one)

Several times a week____   Once a week____

Several times a month____   Once a month____

Several times a year____   Almost never____

12. How often do you spend a social evening with a parent? (check one)

Several times a week____   Once a week____

Several times a month____   Once a month____

Several times a year____   Almost never____

13. How far is your present home from your birthplace?_____

14. Have you ever driven across America?

Yes____ No____

15. Have you ever been to Italy?

Yes____ No____

16. How many cities have you lived in?_____

17. Did you attend college in your hometown? (check one)

Yes____ No____ Didn't go to college____

18. Do you own more recordings by (check one):

Frank Sinatra____ or Luciano Pavarotti____

19. Can you recognize more songs by (check one):

Madonna____ or Giuseppe Verdi____

20. Have you spent more time reading books by (check one):

Mario Puzo____ or Dante Alighieri____

21. Are you more familiar with the movies of (check one):

Sylvester Stallone____ or Marcello Mastroianni____

22. Which of the Godfather movies was your favorite? (check one)

*Godfather 1*____ *Godfather 2*____ *Godfather 3*____

23. As a general rule, do portrayals of Italian-Americans in movies or on TV offend you? (check one)

Yes____ No____

24. As a general rule, do you feel more comfortable with people of Italian ancestry than with those not of Italian ancestry? (check one)

Yes____ No____ Don't know____

25. How strongly do you think of yourself as an Italian-American? (check one)

Very strongly____   Moderately____

Slightly____   Not at all____

26. List three things that in your opinion make Italian-Americans different from other Americans.

_____

_____

_____(use back of page if needed)

27. List three character traits that are typical of the Tonellis you know._____

_____

_____(use back of page if needed)

28. When you have tomato sauce at home, is it (check one)

Homemade____ From a jar____?

29. If it's homemade, how did you learn to make it?
(check one)
From a family member_____ From a friend_____
From a published recipe_____ Other_____

30. If it's homemade, list the ingredients._____
_____

31. Have you ever been discriminated against because of your Italian ancestry? (check one)
Yes_____ No_____ Don't know_____

32. Have you ever been helped because of your Italian ancestry? (check one)
Yes_____ No_____ Don't know_____

33. Do you belong to a voluntary organization?
Yes_____ No_____

34. Do you belong to a political organization?
Yes_____ No_____

35. If you voted for president in 1992, who for?
_____

36. Would you vote for a woman for president?
Yes_____ No_____

I also ask for the normal demographic stuff—income, education, job, sex, and age. A similar questionnaire is going to a sampling of about fifty Tonellis in Canada, England, Switzerland, Germany, and Australia. I'm addressing them all by hand, on the theory that recipients will be less likely to trash these things immediately if there's a sign that a human being sent them. And so, tonight I'm alone with my envelopes for company, and the scariest part is this: I don't mind.

(Of course, I *do* have a party I'm going to in about fifteen minutes, but given the obsessive nature of this entire enterprise, there's something fitting about the picture of me alone on New Year's Eve wetting stamps.)

My mother waving *arrivederci*

4.

Emotional Agoraphobia

My Family Values

Marie: I told you this story before, right? A girl who worked with me, Marlene, she was Polish, and she was going with a guy named Tonelli, but I never associated it with us, because Grandpop had no relatives here, and—

Jo: Uncle Joe might have had some relatives here, because he was here twenty-five years without his wife.

Marie: Yeah, we think he farted around.

Jo: Yeah, I mean, I think he had a couple of kids. He must have had a lot of girlfriends, because I still say that one of those kids, over in Ambler . . .

Marie: Yeah, one of those kids. See, he boarded with this woman and her husband in Ambler, and the husband was kind of dopey. They were nice people and all, but you know what I mean. And they had two children and I swear to you, to this day, that one of them must have been Joe's daughter. Because Joe had the light coloring and so did the daughter, but the mother and father were very dark. We think—we *think,* we do not know. But the girl wouldn't have been named Tonelli, because in those days they used a lot of discretion. They never said anything [laughs]. It wasn't wide open! Anyway, this Marlene worked with me, and I'm sitting at my desk and it's Christmas time, and, you know, it's a sad part of the year if you don't have your relatives. My husband's cousin Francie, she worked at a home, you know, an orphanage where they had boys. Anyway, she called me and said, "Marie, I have this boy here. His name is Paul R——. He's nine years old, and he has no place to go for Christmas." I said, "Oh, my God, that's sad." Then she says, "But Marie, I'm looking over his records, and I see he's got a grandmother and a grandfather, Rose and Louis Tonelli." I says, "Well, gee, Francie, my dad didn't have anybody here." But anyway, to make a long story short, ten years go by, I mean, just to show you, I think God puts you in places. This girl calls me, her name I think is Sharon, and she says, "I'm Sharon R——, you probably don't know me but I was going through my husband's records"—he's nineteen years old now—"I was going through my husband's records from the home and your name was in them." I say, "Oh yeah? Well, what are you calling about?" She says, "I'm married to this fellow, and he's having a very bad time. He knows he has a sister somewhere and blah blah blah." OK, Bill? So when I heard that, I—*chickenshit*—I get real emotional. I say, "Oh my God, well, I'll see what I can do for you." And it hit me: I'm gonna call Marlene. By now she's married to that Anthony Tonelli, so I call and I say, "Marlene, you gotta tell me. I hate to do this, but I got this phone call and it's a very sad case." She says, "I'll have to see about it, Marie," but then she tells me: her husband has an aunt who was married before, she's remarried at this point, and the guy she's married to doesn't know—he knows she had one child, which was a daughter, but he doesn't know she also had a boy. I say, "Well, Marlene, something's got to be done. I can't let this rest. This is on my mind. I feel sorry for this kid. He's nineteen and he's still looking, and it's bugging him. He was only about a year and a half or two years old when they separated these two kids, and he still remembers." So I say to Marlene, "Well, go to the sister, find out what the hell—talk to *her*, don't talk to the mother." So Marlene says she'll do it, and sure enough, the girl wanted to meet her brother. And I invited them to my house, and they met. He was nineteen and he had two kids of his own already. Just to show you—he was looking for *family*. You know what I mean?

• • • Looking for family—right, Aunt Marie, I know what you mean. Do you see the pattern that's emerging here? A brother and sister are split apart, and his identity gets swallowed up in an institution. Men separated from their women father illegitimate children. And my poor grandfather comes over and gets blown off by his older brother. In fact, I learn only during these interviews that the third brother, Pete, also migrated to America. But my grandfather and Pete, for reasons unknown—and maybe for no reason at all—somehow fell out of touch. They fell out of touch to such a degree that my grandfather had to write to the Social Security Administration to find out where his brother was buried. Pete had a few daughters and one son, whom my father and his brothers and sisters knew well when they were kids. But then they all fell out of touch, too.

Immigration must have been hell on family ties—that's why the immigrants clung to one another so tightly: they *had* to, or else. The big peasant shift of the early twentieth century had the power to rend every fact of fate; the pull of distant real estate was strong enough to snap connections of blood and kinship that took centuries to create. And so the liberation that came with a huge new country where you belonged in no one place more than any other undid lots of family ties. Here's what I found in *Mountain of Names,* a terrific book on kinship in animals and humans by Alex Shoumatoff:

Early in the century the anthropologist Bertha Phillpots
advanced a theory . . . which has yet to be disproved:
kinship tends to be weak among people who have had
to travel a long distance to get where they eventually
settle.

It sounds sad to us—but maybe they *wanted* it that way?

● ● ● This will be remembered as a great moment in history, I
am certain.

The big day arrives January 12, 1993, when the first of
the census forms, around a dozen of them, show up in the
morning mail at the office. It's the first tangible proof that the
Tonelli Nation exists, that they will answer my call—now I
know how Jefferson must have felt. A nine-and-a-half-year-old
Tonelli girl, of northern California, filled out one of the forms I
sent to her father. Asked to list Tonelli character traits, she
writes: "Loud, eat a lot." Pretty cute! I open the envelope from a
Tonelli in Illinois, see where he's listed his sisters' names, and
suddenly I think: "Wait a second. . . . I remember you! Your
wedding picture was in the paper! Your sisters were brides-
maids!" Dino Tonelli, of the Bronx, sends me postcards of his
birthplace, a town in Italy called Mondolfo. Lots of expressions
of support for the project come in along with the forms. Here's a
typical one, from Albert Tonelli of Massachusetts: "I think
you're doing a *great deed.*" A sixty-six-year-old Pennsylvania
woman writes: "I am proud of being an Italian for they have
contributed much to mankind. Where there is great good—all
the Italian saints and contributors to mankind—there is also
great evil: the mafia. I hope and pray that you will show how
good we really are." Another woman writes: "Maybe we should
all have a party!" Those sentiments make it easier to accept that
lots of people just threw these things away. One lousy bastard
actually returned the whole package untouched, not one question answered.

My chest swells every time I open an envelope. I'm looking over the questionnaire from seventy-four-year-old Bruno

The Amazing Story of the Tonelli Family in America

Tonelli of Pennsylvania, and I remember that last time I saw his name, in a newspaper item, he had just been shot down by a German pilot in World War II. He made it back alive! Every morning my office becomes the site of a deeply transforming experience—I'm having five epiphanies a week.

Soon my coworkers begin stopping by to check out the forms, and their bemusement turns to something else: once they start reading, they report feeling some frisson of family sentiment—they're moved almost to tears, some admit (well, one). Even the stoics in the mailroom are affected—every day they drop a new batch of citizens on my desk, then linger a moment to stare into the map on the wall, noticing how expressive those shiny red pins have become, how all these Tonellis have given America a human face. I'm in a constant state of wonder as the nation I imagined becomes real, as I slit envelopes sealed by Tonelli tongues and Tonelli spit, and read Tonelli thoughts, written with Tonelli pens, in Tonelli hands.

A heretofore unknown (to me) Tonelli woman from Philadelphia writes this note at the end of her questionnaire: "I believe I knew your dad and mother. If you are the Bill Tonelli that I think you are, your grandmother and grandfather are buried two lots away from my mom and dad at Holy Cross Cemetery." Do you hear what she's saying? We're neighbors! I am dizzy with delight, I'm swooning, my heart is a balloon.

A twentysomething woman living in the Midwest limns the mysterious contradiction of how tribal love and hate coexist in one heart when she writes, as a postscript to a question:

> My Tonelli relatives are very lively, active, and energetic. The other side of my family is German and Irish, and they are much more conservative, quiet and restrained. The Tonellis were always the fun side to visit. They talked loud, laughed a lot, and ate lots of outstanding food. They were very outspoken. They hugged and kissed everyone. I could go on and on but you already got more than you probably wanted out of this answer. I do remember one bad characteristic that I think many of them had. I think they were fairly racist. It used to upset my mother a lot. Don't get me wrong: I love all of the

Tonellis dearly—old and young, they were all wonderful to be with.

Then the telephone starts kicking in. One day a writer I know gazes into my map and insists that I *have* to visit the sole Tonelli in Alaska. Good idea, but no way, I tell him—it's too far to go to find one lousy citizen. The guy's in the dead middle of the state.

At home that night, the phone rings and through an electronic scrim a faint voice asks, "Who is this speaking?"

I say, "Well, who is *this* speaking?"

And he says, "It's Stan Tonelli, in Alaska."

And I say, "Hey, I was just talking about you today."

He got the envelope and is kind of worried about how it was I found him, but he sounds friendly anyway. Funny, I'm thinking, that the farthest-flung Tonelli is first to call, but then he breaks some weird news. "I'm not really a Tonelli. I don't know if my father was Mexican or Italian or whatever, but he couldn't get a job, so he joined the Marine Corps. And he fought in the South Pacific during World War II and got malaria. Now, this is more or less how I understand the story from my second cousin. Anyway, he almost died from the malaria, except an Italian corpsman named Tonelli saved his life. And my father was so grateful he changed his name to Tonelli. I don't know if it's true, but that's what they tell me."

I don't know if it's true either—what was an Italian corpsman doing in the South Pacific helping an American soldier during World War II?

Stanford says he was born in northern California in 1957, and his dad took off when Stan was small, leaving Stan's mother to raise their three sons alone. Stan *thinks* his mother got further word about his dad, maybe even that he was in a plane crash and had plastic surgery, but she won't say much on the subject. "She got a hair dryer from Africa once, I think, and another time a bouquet of roses from Italy." Stan also says his father then changed his name to von Nuremberg, and he may have changed it again, too. Stan's two brothers, Paul and Brad, and their mother, Dr. Mary Jo (O'Dell) Tonelli, all live in Texas, which is where they moved after the old man took off.

I ask how he ended up in Alaska, and he says, "I had trouble dealing with people. No. I didn't have trouble. I just don't *like* people. I like peace and quiet. I'm three hundred miles from Russia. There's nothing up here but Indians and Eskimos." With his Native American wife and their son, in a log cabin, he lives a subsistence life-style, hunting, fishing, hauling water (no plumbing) and wood (for the stove), and working as a trapper, gold-mine laborer, and land-grading equipment operator when he needs cash. Lately he's gotten into raising musher dogs, too. We promise to stay in touch.

• • • Soon, the entire global telecommunications network is buzzing with Tonellis. At the office the morning after Stan's call, I hear from Renato Tonelli, of Jackson Heights, New York, who detects that the questionnaire is aimed mainly at descendants of Italians. He wants to know if Italian-born Tonellis can fill it out, too. (Sure.) Then he wishes me good luck. Five minutes later it's Paul, a morning DJ in San Jose, who just called to say hello and promises to give a copy of the form to his eighty-year-old uncle Bill. Sally, of Des Moines, gets me at home. Not only do we have the same name, but we work for different divisions of the same company, it turns out. She's not even Italian, but she married (and divorced) one of a clan of Tonellis in Iowa. As she's telling me her children's names a bell rings in my head and I ask, "Hey, is Teresa all right?"

"What do you mean?" she asks, and I explain that as she was talking I recalled a twenty-year-old newspaper clip about how her husband got into a car wreck and their daughter's throat was pierced by the gearshift. And Teresa's *fine,* Sally tells me—she survived the accident in good shape and is married now, with kids, living in Illinois. Sally says that her son Todd feels his Italian roots so strongly he's thinking about getting the flag of Italy tattooed on his arm. "I told him, 'You're one-quarter Italian and who *knows* what else!' " she says, laughing. And she says she'll make copies of the census form and send them to her ex–in-laws. Really, a nice lady: Tonellis helping Tonellis.

At five o'clock one morning the phone rings and it's

James Tonelli, of Adelaide, Australia, a young-sounding guy who's calling on his dad's behalf. They want to know how I found their address, but once I explain, he promises to fill out the form. Did I ever imagine there could be a Tonelli with an Australian accent? Why not? Next day Ruggero Tonelli checks in from Chicago; he came from Italy to work as an engineer for a company that makes jet engines, and he's just calling to say hello and to offer whatever help I might need. Jodie Tonelli Brown calls me from Seattle; her WASP husband has a family history book that was written on his tribe, so she'll be glad to have one, too, she says.

A completed form comes back from an eleventh grader living in Antioch, California. At the bottom he writes: "Dear Mr. Bill Tonelli, I would be very grateful if you would mention my name: Joseph Nello Tonelli." Done.

The phone rings at work one afternoon, and a man asks how I spell my name, so I spell it. Satisfied (I guess), he introduces himself—it's Tom Tonelli of Chicago. "This questionnaire is on the level, right?" he asks. "This isn't bullshit?"

"Nope," I say, "it's hard for me to believe, too."

"Well, I'm going to fill out the form and send it to you," he tells me. "My father and his brothers all got them too, but they threw them out."

Typical suspicious old dagos, I say to myself. When I get to Chicago, I'm gonna force those guys to sit down at the kitchen table and fill the things out while I watch. Then I'm going to make them pay me back for the stamps I wasted.

A Tonelli from Pennsylvania drew a big X over the question about income, then wrote: "As an Italian child, we learned: Never tell how much you make. Never tell how much you save. Never tell how much you carry with you. In answer to your question—none of your damn business!" I'm filled with admiration.

By my informal count, the most common answers to the question about what traits make Italian-Americans different are: outgoing, family values, respect, warm, love food, biased against other "extractions."

There's less consensus on the question about typical Tonelli character traits. My respondents' lists are all over the

place—dark-skinned, fair-haired, liberal, intolerant, philosophi-
cal, impulsive. (In one extended Tonelli family—my own—the
traits listed include outspoken, soft-spoken, shy, loud, timid,
express opinions openly.) Tonelli traits most often cited are: hard-
working, strong family ties, loyal, stubborn, loud, proud, clannish, funny, demonstrative. One respondent wrote: "Stubborn,
stubborn, stubborn," then crossed out the last one and wrote in,
"Proud." Several wrote: "I don't know any other Tonellis."

Older respondents tend to state their replies in honori-
fics; younger ones are less reverential. I compare the answers of
two men from the same midwestern state. The sixty-year-old
wrote: "Hard workers, proud, meticulous." The twenty-four-
year-old wrote: "Hairy, stubborn, big appetite." A woman in her
twenties, from New England, takes this unvarnished view of
the Tonelli character: "They think they know everything and
are never wrong. They believe in family values even though
they don't follow them. They feel they are the best at everything."

And the future of Tonelli cuisine is revealed by a twenty-
one-year-old woman from Pennsylvania, who, when asked for
her tomato sauce recipe, writes: "I haven't the foggiest idea. My
mom won't even let me in the kitchen."

One day I open an envelope and discover the most articu-
late Tonelli I have ever come across in my life. She didn't sign
her name, but her replies are breathtaking. To the question,
"List three things that in your opinion make Italian-Americans
different from other Americans," she writes:

> **1.** I don't know a single Italian-American who is es-
> tranged from an immediate family member. Communica-
> tion among family members is frequent. Even after the
> children are no longer living at home, family members
> are still aware of each other's dentist's appointments, job
> interviews, episodes of indigestion, etc.

> **2.** Activities and pleasures of independence from
> one's family are not taught or encouraged, and there-
> fore, sons and daughters often continue to live at home—
> and even take meals with their parents—until a later age
> than most adult children. So the trait, I guess, is emo-

tionally agoraphobic about establishing themselves in a world larger than the family unit.

3. Unconditionally loyal and supportive of other family members.

For the question, "List three character traits that are typical of the Tonellis you know," she writes:

1. After marriage, there does not seem to be a shift of allegiance from parents to spouse; the allegiance seems to remain somehow with the parents, especially the Italian parent. The character trait here is overdependence, lack of autonomy.

2. The family offers an enormous amount of unconditional support (financial, practical, emotional) during difficult times.

3. The downside of numbers 1 and 2 is that the family fills so many needs there is little need for outsiders. There is a somewhat socially debilitating credo that family members are the *only* people one can trust and depend upon.

Exactly! But if somebody this smart can't escape all that stuff, is there any hope for the rest of us?

I open a questionnaire and a little dream comes true. I learned of the existence of Kathleen Tonelli So, of Chicago, from her brother Terry's form, so I sent her one, too. I knew that she was married to a Korean man, but not until I got her form back was my hope confirmed—they have two kids together, two half-Korean Tonellis. There's a half-Indian Tonelli, too—Stan's kid, up in Alaska. I sent a form to a San Diego man named Juan Tonelli, praying that he's half Spanish, but it hasn't come back. And a newspaper clip turned up a Tonelli who plays for the Toronto Spitfires, a wheelchair basketball team. I still have to find an African-American Tonelli and a gay or lesbian Tonelli, but if I do, I'll have New World perfection—a culturally diversified, rainbow Tonelli Nation.

The phone at home rings one night with a collect call from Texas. A woman introduces herself, she's Carmella Clausi, maiden name Tonelli, and she says that she heard that her brother back home in Des Moines got a questionnaire, and can she get one, too?

"Sure," I say, and we begin to talk about her family. She asks if I sent a form to her half-brother, Bob Tonelli, who's in jail, and I say yes.

"I'm in like him," she says.

"*Oh?* You mean in jail," I ask.

She says, "Yes, in a federal prison camp for women in Bryan, Texas."

"How'd you end up there?" I ask.

"It's drug related." OK! A drug-dealer Tonelli! (By the way, in all my research, scouring newspapers here and abroad, never once did I come upon a Tonelli connected in any way to organized crime. All our criminals are disorganized.)

One Friday afternoon at work the receptionist rings me, choking back giggles. "Bill Tonelli is here to see you," she sputters, so I hustle out to the lobby, where a man in his thirties with a mustache is standing with an attractive, dark-haired woman. Two or three of my colleagues are also standing out there, grinning like goons. I introduce myself to Bill and his wife, June, and we head back to my office. He's an electrical contractor, and they were in the neighborhood on business anyway, so they figured they'd stop by and make sure I was legit. While we talk, a few more coworkers wander by, openly rubbernecking. When I get Bill's form back, there's a P.S.: "Your office mates made me feel like a celebrity!"

It goes on and on that way for two solid months, like a sixty-day trance—like a contact high. My head is swimming in a sea of Tonelli birth announcements, DWI arrests, wedding banns, and obits; high achievements and depths of disgrace and despair; opinions, tastes, statistics. I know about the living and the dead, the fictional and the real, the good, the bad, and the ugly, the historical, the apocryphal, the mundane. I don't discriminate: each fact seems precious. I've used the "siblings" question on the census forms to lead me to Tonelli women who have changed their names in marriage, and I've sent them questionnaires, too. I have also contacted a company called Ancestry, in Salt Lake City, and for $15 they conducted a computer search of all ninety-two million American telephone listings for Tonellis. That turned up some new ones that I added to my directory. Altogether, I know the names, addresses, and phone numbers of more than six hundred Tonelli households, many of which I've cross-indexed to show family ties. I also have two cardboard cartons full of newspaper clippings and database printouts, and I'm to the point where I have almost all of it memorized.

I thought life would forever deny me this distinction, but now it is mine: I know more about one subject than anyone else in the world. And *what* a subject.

• • • By the end of February, I've gotten back almost two hundred completed forms. Because my own extended family has stuck pretty close to home, I'm not surprised to find that none of the other Tonellis is even distantly related to me.

A fair number are able to say where their Tonelli ancestor originated, so I buy a big map of Italy, mount it on foamboard, and dig out the little red pins. When I finish putting them all in, a surprising pattern emerges. Almost all Italian immigrants to America came from the southern part of their country, which always was (and is) poorer, more backward, and more generally disadvantaged than the north. Southern Italian peasant culture *defines* what we think of as Italian-Americanness. My first realization, once all the pins are in, is that America's Tonellis are virtually all from northern Italy. I see also that my grandfather's hometown is *the* southernmost point of origin of American Tonellis. Crudely analyzed, this means that we Tonellis are of loftier stock than most other Italian-Americans. And that my family is of lowlier stock than all other Tonellis.

I'm also surprised to see that a majority of American Tonellis seem to have originated in one of three small rural regions of Italy. It occurs to me that some of these people *must* be related and don't even know it. I begin making lists—whose family is from Fano, whose is from Fivizzano—when it dawns on me: There's *no way* I can do this book properly without creating a total, multigenerational family tree that connects every Tonelli in America. I'm on the verge of turning this perilous corner in the conception of my book's goals when it dawns on me that committing myself to that path will add decades to my research, ensuring that this book is published only posthumously, and even then incomplete.

And anyway, I have more pressing concerns right now. I'm sitting on my office floor, a heap of questionnaires before me, and staring at my wall map of the USA. Now begins the logistical challenge—scheduling two months of driving and visiting. I figure I can see a Tonelli a day for sixty days easy, so now I only need to figure out which sixty and put them in geographic order. I imagine a rough oblong starting in New York, going south to Florida, west to San Diego, north to San Francisco, and then back through the heartland. I just have to assume they'll all want to see *me*.

By February, I'm so swamped by calls to Tonellis, asking if I can visit, that I'm losing sight of anything more profound than which exit ramp and when. Everything else about this journey is starting to get mixed up in my head. Is this about people and their names? People and their homes? Is it about America, ethnicity, geography? Driving? All the above? I no longer remember.

• • • I decide to certify my entrance into the ranks of good Americans by joining the American Automobile Association. For one thing, I don't want to end this trip stranded at midnight on some desert road, surrounded by rattlesnakes closing in, until. . . . Also, I need AAA's expert navigators to chart every mile of my trip with its fabled customized spiral-bound maps. No sense in leaving *anything* to chance. The day after I join I call the AAA office and say I need directions for a trip that will incorporate about thirty-eight stops from sea to shining sea and back. To my disappointment, whoever answers replies, nonchalantly, "Sure, just let us know where." My copilot, Mrs. Harper, calls a week later to say my maps are ready; I leave her office burdened by free AAA guides to cheap motels and eats in every state I'll visit, plus *two* map books with my course marked in green. Now I know how Columbus must have felt.

Every spare minute, I dip into my maps—that green line, taking that exit, in that faraway state, that's *me*. From the day I decided to make this trip, I've accepted the probability that it will end on some lonesome highway with me turned to grease under the thundering tires of an eighteen-wheeler. Now, even if I get killed, I won't get lost. I'm still convinced that the main talent required for driving is the ability to trust total strangers of unknown intelligence and motivations to steer several tons of metal around your ears at high speed without hitting you. But I'm ready to do it—I'm ready to trust America.

In fact, by this point, about a week before my departure, I've gathered so much outward momentum that I can't stop myself: One day I finally decide that if I'm serious about this trip, I *have* to go to the extremity of the Tonelli Nation. That night I call Alaska to ask Stan if it's OK with him, and he says sure, glad to have me, I can even stay with them (not that there's an alternative—there are no public accommodations in his village). I just have to get myself to Fairbanks, and he'll borrow a plane, pick me up, and fly me the rest of the way, about an hour into the bush.

"Oh, I guess everybody in Alaska has a pilot's license, right?" I say.

"Well," he answers, "if you watch enough people do it, you can pick it up easy—it's like driving a car." Oh, fuck.

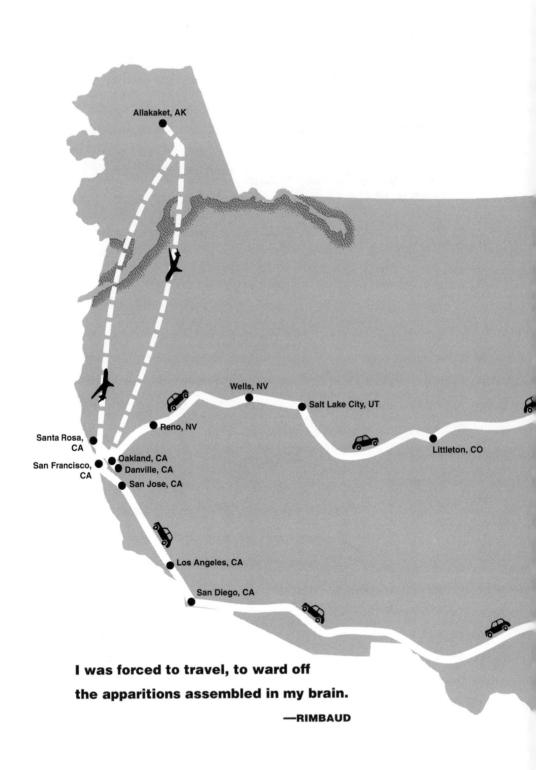

I was forced to travel, to ward off
the apparitions assembled in my brain.

—RIMBAUD

Part Two

Down the Side, Across the Bottom, Up the Other Side, and Over the Middle

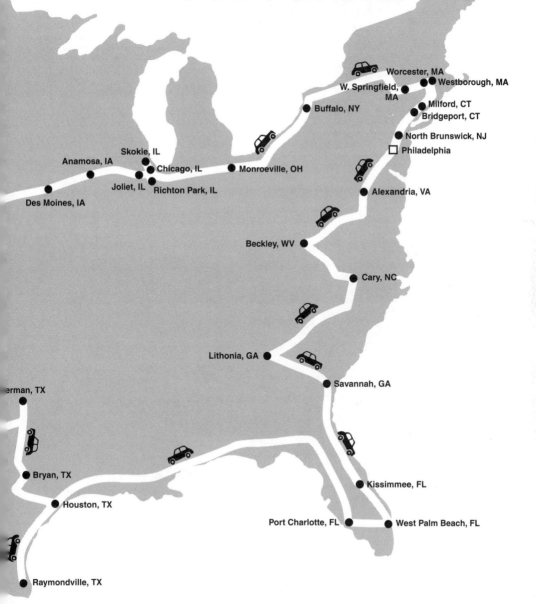

Ed and Debbie Tonelli
with Brian and Michael

Alan and Beth Tonelli
with Heather and Chris

Parking lot of the Mayberry Inn

Alyssa Tonelli

5.

Haunted by Rocky

 Do you care for your dead? I sure don't, except in my occasional, mostly ceremonial habit of pulling the grass that grows over my father's and my grandfather's tombstones and scraping out the dirt that collects in the letters of their names. But I have enough sense to feel ashamed that I'm not more attentive (though there's also some shame attached to being attentive *at all*). I'm sure there's a connection between relaxed cemetery protocols and waning ethnicity—in both cases, we disavow ourselves as creatures of history.

On the afternoon before my departure, I take my mother out to Holy Cross Cemetery for a visit. My father's been here for sixteen years, and today's the first time I notice there's a John Tonelli, no relation, buried five holes away. For some reason, discovering that makes me glad. Standing at my old man's grave, I say, "Hey, Ma, is it weird to look at the stone and know that someday your name will be there, too?"

"To be honest," she says, "I never really thought about it until you brought it up."

We leave the cemetery and return to my mother's house.

There, just hours before my leave-taking, we stage the scene that plays out every time I'm here. It goes like this: My mother and my grandmother each wait for a chance when the other's not around, then they sneak up on me with a folded ten or twenty cupped in one hand. For years, I fended off these touching but unnecessary acts of charity. Ultimately, though, their relentless, badgering pleas to accept my tribute from their modest life savings wore me down, to where I now automatically cup my hand, too. (Sometimes, lately, I cup my hand *first*.)

These scenes always remind me of what beasts we humans are—every living thing employs the same strategies to ensure the survival of the bloodline. If Darwin saw the three of us in action, he might predict that I'd use the money for roughage, or for a taxi instead of the lethal subway, thereby giving the family genes a greater shot at immortality. But I never do—I put it into a special fund I use to tip go-go dancers.

The eve of my departure finds me in the bedroom of my childhood, receptive to visitations from any appropriate ghosts, echoes or omens. Instead, I sleep.

• • • On this momentous morn I kiss my mother and grandmother good-bye, leave the fortress of my youth, and start the engine of my future. The car radio blasts open the first minute of the rest of my life:

> *Baby, this town rips the bones from your back*
> *It's a death trap. It's a suicide rap. . . .*

But what *is* it about Americans and home? For every "Home on the Range" there's a "Born to Run," maybe two, and always more romantic. Everybody (except for the natives and those who were forced to come) is here because they were sick of their homes. So everybody moved, and *still* everybody's sick of their homes. I mean, where else can you live?

I escape via wildly romantic Interstate 95, drive south three hours, and I'm barely on the road when I'm off it, in

Alexandria, Virginia, the home of my first victim, Alyssa Tonelli. This driving stuff's a breeze—I get lost only once, and barely, before I find her anonymous, blocky little building and her apartment, near the laundry room.

Then I ring the bell and the door swings open and I'm face to face with—a stranger. A perfectly nice, hospitable stranger, one who's gracious enough to welcome and indulge the curiosity of—another stranger. Well. What did you expect? She doesn't look like me or sound like me; had we passed on the street, we would have exchanged not a glimmer of recognition. As I walk inside her apartment, I am struck by a small panic— the thought that what we have in common is a barely significant thing: A suffix. We have the same suffix.

So. We sit at her kitchen table and eat cookies from a box. We talk. She's twenty-eight, grew up just outside New York City, her mother is a Hawaiian-Filipino-Portuguese mix. Her mother was her father's second wife; Alyssa has a half-brother she's never met, owing to the bitterness between him and their father after the marriage ended.

"Until I was eleven or twelve, I used to send letters to my half-brother. I used to write, 'I don't know if you know I exist,' or, 'You don't have to talk to Dad. You can talk to me.' Or I'd write that I was really curious about him and his family. Or I'd send newsy letters, like, 'I got a gold star in school today. . . .' I'd even tell him, 'Just let me know if you're getting these, or if you want me to stop.' I sent pictures, too. He never wrote back, though."

She has a nine-year-old son by a fiancé she decided not to marry: "I was nineteen and I wanted to give him up for adoption, but my mother said no to that, so I said, 'OK, fine, I'll be his sister and you be his mother.' So he calls me Mom, but I'm really like his big sister."

She works as an administrator but has also been a law student and a teacher in Mexico. She's kicked around everywhere, she says—Eastern and Western Europe, China, Africa, went to school for a while in Russia, accompanied an emerald buyer to South America, and now she's waiting until she can get six months off before she goes to Australia.

"As long as I can remember, I knew I wasn't in my place," she says. "Of course, I haven't *found* that place yet, where I'm really content or ready to settle down."

And that's about all I remember.

Wait—that's *it*? My first actual contact with a citizen of the Tonelli Nation yields, what—six paragraphs? No way can I sustain a respectable voyage on this kind of transaction. Even if I do meet fifty Tonellis, that's . . . a three-hundred-paragraph book. I'm sunk. None of this is Alyssa's fault, of course. I think I'm still not quite sure of what I'm after, or why I want to talk to people just because they have my name. If I think on our time together, I can take some meaning from things she said. There's something affecting about a little girl sending unanswered letters to a brother she's never met, something that speaks of the power of blood ties. And the part about her travels, and that final quotation, seem to add up to the kind of geographical restlessness that's at the heart of this book. Still—pretty slim pickings. It's way too early to worry, but back in the car, driving south on 95, I remember that just before I left New York an experienced reporter I know wondered, "So, once you meet these people, what are you going to *ask* them?" Not until then did it occur to me: *I had no idea.*

I find a cheap motel in Charlottesville, Virginia, check in, and, first night out of South Philly, I'm haunted already— *Rocky V* is on HBO. I've never seen this one, but what happens is he learns that the beating he took in *Rocky IV* scrambled his brains, so he can't fight again. Then his accountant steals all his money. (Rocky's moronic brother-in-law Paulie gave the thief power of attorney. *Family.*) So Rocky is forced to move Adrian and their son from the big fancy house in the country back to South Philly, where he'll take over the stinking gym Mickey left them when he died. The squalor! The hopelessness! This movie's climactic fight takes place not in a ring but in the street; when Rocky wins he's swept up by his neighbors and borne away on their shoulders, a champion again, even if only in the eyes of his loyal downtown paisans. The movie ends on the art museum steps with Rocky and his son practically ecstatic—broke, unemployable, washed up in South Philly, but ecstatic. At one particularly low point in their reacquaintance with the old neighborhood, Rocky yells to his wife, "Yo! Yo, Adrian! Did we ever leave this place?" Big dramatic pause, then she shrieks back, *"I don't know!"*

Well, *I* know: Months ago, I sent a letter to Stallone requesting an interview for this book. I explained that I wanted to discuss the fact that Rocky Balboa is the only South Philadelphia Italian I've ever heard of with *no relatives.* I wanted to know what connection Stallone drew between that and Rocky's ambition to distinguish himself as the genuinely singular, one of a kind, world heavyweight champion. I got a call back from a publicist at Rogers and Cowan who was instructed to say that while Stallone still loves the Rocky character, he considers it part of his past and won't talk about it any longer. If even a big dope like Rocky can outgrow his beginnings, what's *my* problem?

• • • Up early Monday, on the interstate, then off it in White Sulphur Springs, West Virginia, for gas. I'm running a little ahead of schedule, so I ask the pump jockey where to go for breakfast. "I'd try Granny's," he says. "It's clean and it's got good eats." He really said that! I find Granny's, a homey little diner, and the waitress really does have bad teeth! And a sweet disposition! And the biscuits really are fine. There's a hulking trucker a few stools away, my first road kill. I open with a sure-fire conversation starter: Where's the interstate on-ramp? He's got ex-wife tales to tell—how, when their daughter was nine years old, his wife informed him that the girl wasn't his. How his wife once gunned the engine of his vintage Mustang until she ruined it—and he forced her to rebuild it herself. How, when he was on a run to California, his wife sold that same car without telling him, and for thousands less than it was worth. Honest, to a total stranger he said all that! No wonder country music sounds the way it does. This trip is going to be *great.*

The Amazing Story of the Tonelli Family in America

• • • Can Italians live in West Virginia? I didn't think so either, but here we are, not quite black-lung Appalachia but in smoke-less coal country, the city of Beckley, with Ed and Debbie Tonelli and the boys, in the house Ed's father built himself back in 1952. It's early afternoon, but Ed's shift as a helicopter flight nurse doesn't start until later.

Ed's father was born Amerigo Giovanni Tonelli, in Affin-ity, West Virginia. His name was Americanized—ironic, consid-ering what it *was*—to Okey. But *he* wasn't Americanized, not entirely. "I guess his biggest luxury was eating," Ed says. "He grew his own lettuce, and he'd mix the oil and vinegar himself. It wouldn't be anything for him to go through two heads of let-tuce and three loaves of bread in the course of a night. He used to get my mother's sister in New Jersey to send him a special kind of olive oil. He made his own wine, too. I remember when I was a kid, squashing grapes downstairs with my feet. I'd be purple up to here. Then me and my cousin would steal some of the wine, and we'd end up drunk as monkeys. And he'd eat that real hot salami, and polenta. And he used to smoke these little black cigars . . . DeNobilis, and Parodis. I can't find them any-where now. And capocollo? Prosciutto?"

It cracks me up, hearing *prosciutto* with a West Virginia twang.

"He even had his own machine for slicing it. I used to *love* that stuff."

Ed doesn't eat much of that stuff anymore.

Debbie, who's from nearby Oak Hill, says, "I remember, as a joke to my friends at nursing school, I'd say, 'I'm going to find me one of those hot Italian guys.' And then I met Ed. And his family was *very* different from mine. In my family nobody raised their voices and nobody fought with each other. Then I came over here one day, and everybody was yelling at each other, and I was like this," she says, putting her hands over her face. "But I learned to speak up. In my family if you screamed at someone, you wouldn't speak for months. With them, they'd be in each other's faces screaming one minute, then they'd be laughing two minutes later."

"Hey, there's something I want to show you," Ed says as he leaves the living room and disappears down a hall.

While I wait I'm wondering, Have I found what I'm looking for? The panic that followed my first Tonelli visitation is absent, but I'm not completely convinced that this session would have gone much differently had I accidentally visited the people next door.

Ed comes back with a large framed black-and-white photo of a mountain town, his grandfather's home, he tells me. Neither of us can read the Italian written on it well enough to figure out which word is the town's name.

Because I have to make North Carolina by nightfall, Ed and I sit down to eat by around three. I'm about to have my first Tonelli meal, the recipe for which appeared in a cookbook published by their son's school to raise money. I'm looking at the page right now: Debbie Tonelli's Stuffed Cabbage. The recipe was handed down by Ed's mother, who was Hungarian. It's fantastic.

• • • My new favorite country song (I don't know the title) has the lines:

Now I lay me down to sleep
I pray the Lord my soul to keep
If I die before I wake
Feed Jake
He's a good dog. . . .

Weather's funky heading southeast out of here on Interstate 77: Every ten minutes it goes from overcast to drizzle to downpour to sleet, then back again. And I have to contend with that instability while navigating the vertigo of mountains and valleys—through my windshield it's one morose picture postcard after another. From the start, I figured my big driving tests wouldn't come until L.A., the Rockies, and Chicago. Two days out and it's already white knuckle time.

The Amazing Story of the Tonelli Family in America

By evening I make it to clear skies and Mount Airy, North Carolina, birthplace of Andy Griffith and supposed inspiration for Mayberry. I pull over at the Mayberry Inn, which has lots of Andy and Barney memorabilia and a woman behind the desk who'd look like Aunt Bea if Aunt Bea had been in shape and worn a sweatsuit. Dinner at Ray's Starlight Buffet (steak, potato, two vegetables and lemonade: $9.52 plus tip); waitress looks and sounds like she's fifteen. "I'm from Covington, and I know people say it's small up here, but it seems big to me," she says. Her husband moved her here, they're in a trailer, saving to pay off their car and bankroll a move to Texas. "There's nothing going on, no opportunity, in Covington. That's why I came here. But I hope we go to Dallas. I'd *really* be lost there, but that's where I want to go. I just want to move someplace where there's . . . opportunity." The way she says that word, you finally hear something: It's used only by dissatisfied people. Which means the land of opportunity must also be the home of the culturally malcontented. This country is made for people who like feeling lost, lost in a sea of opportunity.

(Hey, wait a second—is this going to be one of those road books where every offhand little thing a small-town waitress says when she's refilling your coffee is made to take on profound meaning about the soul of America? No way.)

• • • "I had just two requirements—it had to be a place I wanted to live, and it had to be a place I could do polymer research." That's not the waitress, that's Alan Tonelli on how he came to live in the woodsy Loch Mere residential development in Cary, North Carolina. We're in the heart of the so-called research triangle, where, it is said, there are more Ph.Ds per capita than anywhere else in the country.

What's a polymer? I did ask, but a five-minute explanation later all I can say is that they're big, complicated molecules. I ask Al to draw one for me, and the sketch looks like an overhead view of six bald men standing on a train platform.

I first found Alan in *Books in Print*, where I learned that he's the author of *NMR Spectroscopy and Polymer Microstructure: The Conformational Connection*. He worked as a research scientist at Bell Labs in northern New Jersey, then took early retirement and got a job teaching at North Carolina State. It's a long way from his origins, in the Italian part of Al Capone's hometown, Cicero, near Chicago. Alan grew up in the bosom of his extended clan (his parents' families lived across the alley from each other), then went to Kansas to college—"My parents dropped me off and I loved it. It was great"—where he met a girl of the Midwest, married, had a kid, divorced, then remarried, another Italo-American, Beth, from New Jersey. They have a son, Chris, and a daughter, Heather.

(When I showed up at their house earlier, there were two girls playing outside the house, one of whom was Asian. So of course I assumed the other one was theirs, but I was wrong: Heather Tonelli's Korean. "Beth wanted a girl," Alan says, "and I told her, 'We're not going to just *try* to have one,' so we adopted.")

Over dinner (chicken, pasta, salad) Al falls into his tales of Cicero—boyhood adventures of crawling through abandoned buildings and warehouses alongside railroad tracks, BB-gun battles, a paper route that included a strip joint on the edge of town. It's heady, romantic stuff, especially for seventeen-year-old Chris; his life as a professor's son in Ph.Dville will never bring him any closer to the grit-and-tumble romance of his roots. He's heard the tales so often and loves them so well that he can finish his father's sentences.

After dinner Al works the Dustbuster while Beth straightens the kitchen. They mention the Korean Culture Camp that nine-year-old Heather will attend in the summer, an ethnic refresher for adopted children. She's gone before— "When you go in there on parents' day," Al says, "you really have to look around for a minute to figure out which one is yours."

Beth peers into the refrigerator and asks, "Are you taking a lunch tomorrow?"

"I don't know," Al says, "what do you have?"

"Pepperoni or turkey."

"Yeah, I'll have turkey."

• • • New favorite country song: "Bubba Shot the Jukebox." He shot it because it played a sad song.

This is only the fourth day of driving and I already find myself falling into road trance, a state of highway-induced meditation. Today, with just three Tonellis under my belt, Route 1 inspires the thought that being part of a family requires a lot of sacrifice. Not the parental kind, which will always be necessary as a practical matter for reproduction, but filial sacrifice, which is harder to make these days because it has become more or less voluntary. You have to sacrifice moving to where you really want to live, for instance, or getting divorced—you have to ignore *lots* of interesting impulses to be genuinely part of a family.

In a pretty famous book titled *Sociobiology,* Edwin O. Wilson wrote:

> . . . What is good for the individual can be destructive to the family; what preserves the family can be harsh on both the individual and the tribe to which the family belongs; what promotes the tribe can weaken the family and destroy the individual. . . .
>
> If each family worked out rules of behavior on its own, the result would be an intolerable amount of tradition drift and growing chaos. To counteract selfish behavior and the "dissolving power" of high intelligence, each society must codify itself. Within broad limits, virtually any set of conventions works better than none at all. . . . When conformity becomes too weak, groups become extinct.

As I understand it, the overall point of Wilson's book is that sometimes social behavior echoes the biological. Which doesn't sound all that earth-shaking to me, but he got lots of his

scientific peers in an uproar. Still, even one of those who dis-
agrees, Stephen Jay Gould, who's famous for being smart, con-
ceded: "Families with no tradition for sacrifice do not survive
for many generations."

Albert and Pearl Tonelli

Ed Tonelli at
Disney World

6.

Not Too Many
Guineas Down Here

Is it a harmful geographic stereotype to suggest that southerners are a little bit *poky*? I pull into a gas station in Lithonia, Georgia, and when the skinny, pinched lady behind the counter sees me approach, she scurries away. That leaves me to ask directions of her coworker, a fat woman who turns at the sound of my voice, revealing a gaping tracheotomy hole in the pit of her throat. She begins to grunt and point her response, but I wheel away and corner the first woman. Sulking, she says, "Yuh goda road foah. . . . "

"OK," I repeat. "I go to Route 4—"

"Yuh goda wheah the road *foaks*," she snaps, exasperated. "Then go rat."

I eventually find my way, head down a country lane, then turn in at a rustic-looking mailbox carved with my last name. Funny to see it way out here, within sight of Stone Mountain. There's a good-looking, slender blond with a tiny black poodle waving me in, so I park and get out.

"C'mon, I have to hug you if you're a Tonelli," says Denise, wife of Rick, who's not home from his engine repair

Rick, Denise, and
Craig Tonelli

Edward Tonelli

Enrico Tonelli

shop yet. She's a former dancer, born in Akron, Ohio, moved with her family to Atlanta, met Rick when they lived in Miami. She's effusive, bubbly, just the opposite of Rick, who comes home and tells me, once we're settled in the living room, "See, I'm just the opposite of you. I've *never* been interested in my family history."

"And I don't understand that," Denise says. "I'm a Heinz 57—Jewish-German is my strongest suit—but if I was Italian, I would want to know *so much.* Like his mother's father—he came over here and moved to *Mississippi!* To be a *farmer!* Trying to speak English with an *Italian-Southern accent!* I *mean!* All I knew about Italians was from movies and TV, and then I met Rick and his family, and they're not huggy or touchy *at all.* I had to teach them to hug and kiss hello and good-bye. That's not what I had in mind *at all!*"

Rick Tonelli's a friendly but taciturn guy who was born in Connecticut. When he was a baby, he says, "My father just visited Miami once and he came back and packed us all up. He loved growing things, and in Florida he could work his garden all year long. I met Denise there, and her folks were living in Atlanta, and we came up here to visit quite often, but that gets *old.*"

Anyway, Rick's father died at age forty-six, when Rick was sixteen, which had been the last time Rick saw either Connecticut or any of his extended family there. But a few years ago, Rick was approaching forty-six as his son, Craig, was about to turn sixteen. And Rick started to feel a little haunted by the similarities. So . . .

"So . . . we went on a trip to Connecticut to see my father's brother, my uncle," Rick says over an excellent dinner (chicken, sweet potatoes, apple sauce, corn with peppers, asparagus, fruit salad, pie and ice cream, and coffee). "We call him Lolly, but his name's Alexander. It was really something I wanted to do. Denise and Craig came with me, too. That was different, because usually we'd go to the beach for our vacation. But I really *wanted* to do it. And we stopped in Virginia to see my sister, something else we never do. But I really wanted to see my uncle. And it was our best vacation ever."

"Rick was concerned," Denise says. "But we discussed it and said it might be our last family vacation with Craig, and we were worried that Craig might rather have gone to the beach. These were people Craig and I had never *met,* and here we were dropping in on them. But I knew how much it meant to Rick, and I would have crawled on broken glass to make that trip."

"It seemed so funny," Rick says, "because we had never been around any Tonellis, and we pull up to my uncle's house and there are the cars, with plates that say TONEL-1 and TONEL-2."

"You have to understand," Denise says, "on that trip we heard all these things that Rick never knew, and he sat there for two days and listened to his Uncle Lolly tell stories about the old days, and Rick laughed and cried at the same time."

Rick squirms at the mention of crying.

"Yeah," he says, offhandedly. "It was a good trip. . . . "

"And we were in stitches for two days," Denise says. "And I cried and Rick cried—"

"Yeah," he says, heading her off at the pass, "this uncle of mine is so cool. He's just a little bitty sawed-off runt of a guy. And he told all the stories about the old days, about him and my dad growing up. When they were kids, Lolly stole their stepfather's car and took it out for a ride. When he brought it home, he knew his stepfather was going to beat the crap out of him. Now, he and my father slept in the same bed, but when Uncle Lolly went to bed that night, he made my father move over to the side *he* usually slept on. And when their stepfather came into the room, it was dark, so he just reached in and dragged my father out of the bed and beat *him*. And Dad never said a word.

"Anyway, we drove to their town up there, got a motel room, and then we called my uncle and said we were coming by. And when he heard about the motel he went crazy—'Whaddya mean you're in a motel, we have all this room. You're staying with *us!*' Now, I hardly knew these people. I hadn't seen my uncle for thirty years, since my father's funeral. But the second night, we stayed with them. We even slept in their room."

"Oh, God, remember?" says Denise. "The rosaries?"

"Yeah, I have a great family."

"You're lucky," Denise says.

"Yeah, I can't complain. And if we had more time, we would have spent that there, too. And our son also loved it."

"Well," Denise says, "he's very proud."

Rick shrugs. "He's more interested in family and that stuff than I am."

"He's *proud,*" Denise says.

"Well," Rick allows, "I am, too."

Craig comes in from his job at a convenience store. He's eighteen, a gregarious kid of the New South, baseball cap on backwards, about to join the air force.

I ask, "Do you come across many Italian kids at school or anywhere?"

"Hmm," he says, thinking hard. "Well, I know *some,* but—"

"How about Brent?" Denise says.

"Yeah," says Craig. "*He* is. He's my real good friend, too.

But I just don't think of him as being Italian." Then he grins and turns his cap around, and on the front it says: Italy.

• • • Leaving off Tonellis for a minute, have I told you about the knife fight I witnessed when I unwisely wandered into a bar in the bad part of Macon? Or about the breakfast in a McBee, North Carolina, diner with a tableful of barley farmers? How about the altercation in a hotel lobby with the mayor of Blackshear, Georgia, or the time I sat up all night drinking coffee with a whore at a truck stop in Rogersville, Tennessee?

Forget about it—none of that stuff happened. What am I, crazy, barging in on strangers trying to have a peaceful meal? Talking to criminals? This is a scary country—once you're out there on unfamiliar turf, you're on constant lookout for trouble, maybe some homicidal hillbilly clan, or some cretin with a shotgun who'd just *love* to mess you up, Yankee. It's going to happen to me sooner or later, I bet. I think growing up where I did left me immune to the poetry of the open road and the stranger just around the bend. I don't trust open roads *or* strangers. I'm reading *Blue Highways,* William Least Heat Moon's tale of his aimless trip along America's back roads, and this guy's talking to *everybody.* Nobody gets away untalked—every conversation becomes a transaction, and every transaction is recorded. I just read a passage where he discusses *the size of the local reservoir* with a codger in North Carolina. It's the longest discussion of reservoir size I've ever read. It ends with the old man saying: "I'm not atakin' sides, I'm just atellin' you, but there's people who say there was plenty of water in that old reservoir. They say, 'Who needs a bigger reservoir?' "

I say: *Who cares?* Anyway, it's not all that easy, finding the true heart of America. Down on Route 16 in Georgia I hit a roadblock—very dramatic, state troopers dressed in black standing on the highway by their squad car, lights spinning, directing us onto a country road that goes through the town of Dexter. There's a sleepy little main drag, so I figure I'll stop for coffee and a bite of real American scenery at the Dexter Café. Regular Meals, Short Order, the weathered sign says, but there's a piece of loose-leaf paper taped to the door: Closed due to illness. Then I figure I'll visit a truck stop that's just ahead, but when I get close, there's a white jeep zooming up my ass, so I zoom, too. I think about stopping when I see a sign that says, Bloomingdale 5 Miles, just because all my New York friends will find the idea of a hick town in Georgia with the same name as the department store so amusing.

Instead I keep driving, get to town, time to kill, so I find a bartender to kill it. Kirk pouring—tall, skinny, streetwise, Irish, I make him. Born in New York, then to Atlanta as a kid when his father's job moved.

"So, what are you doing in Savannah?"

I tell him.

"No kidding? What's your name? I love it. Hey, Rachel, listen to what Mr. Tonelli is doing here."

I tell Rachel.

"You got a publisher to front you money for this?" Kirk asks. "He's got a sense of humor. How many Tonellis live in Savannah?"

"One," I say.

"Yeah, not too many guineas down here. You ever eat the Italian food in this town? Don't. Sucks. *All* of it."

• • • The taped calliope music is blaring, and the carousel at the big mall in Savannah goes round and round, but it's deserted except for an obese woman clutching her little daughter to a pink horse. At 7:00 P.M. even the spectators' benches and chairs are empty, except for me, waiting for Enrico Tonelli to show. I met his kid brother Ed, the flight nurse, back in Beckley, West Virginia, their hometown. Enrico's the thirty-nine-year-old CEO of a small private hospital near Vidalia; he's spent most of his adult life away from home, in Virginia and Washington.

Here comes a mild, handsome man in a suit, and since we're the only ones there, it isn't much of a guess. We decide to find a restaurant, so we get back into our cars and drive to a seafood chain place on the river. Enrico seems a little subdued, maybe because he recently separated from his wife, who's also from Beckley; she recently moved herself and their three kids back to West Virginia. As the chirpy young hostess marches us to our table, it strikes me that this is the first time I've visited a Tonelli anyplace but home.

"It's just like every five years I have to move on," he says. "I'm just not settled. I'm *not* settled. I guess when you get near forty you kind of change. I'd *like* to get back to West Virginia, but I want to stay in hospitals. Two years ago I took the law-school boards. Maybe I'll be a lawyer. I don't know. I used to want to study oceanography, but somehow I let my father talk me out of that. He said I was watching too many Jacques Cousteau shows on TV."

I wonder what life must be like, living in the South with a name as vividly Italian as his. When I ask, he smiles.

"Enrico is so formal," he says. "And here in Georgia people are pretty informal. My brother calls me Rick. That's what most people call me. My dad called me Ricky. A girlfriend I had in college was the only one who consistently addressed me as Enrico."

At the mention of her, his eyes go a little dreamy.

"I tell you, this woman was such an influence. She was what I wanted, in terms of intelligence and sophistication. She told me one time, after she met my parents, 'Are you *sure* you're not adopted?' I said, 'What do you mean?' And she said, 'Because you're so different, so much more worldly in who you are, in what you want. You're just nothing like them.' And she always played up the Italian thing a little. After all, she was the only one who called me Enrico. But she was also the only one who saw anything special in all that. She told me, 'You're Italian. You're very . . . *passionate*.' "

• • • Back on Interstate 95 heading toward Florida, I pass a big flatbed truck carrying half a house—siding, windows, half a peaked roof, the standard deal. I'm still trying to figure this one out when I catch up with the truck hauling the other half. These babies are all over the South; from the corner of my eye I catch one coming onto the highway, and at a certain angle I can't see the truck at all—just a house zooming in on me. What's it like, to live in a house that's seen more of the country than you have?

• • • I get to the parking lot (Chip 'n' Dale section, Row 9) early and ride the monorail to the Magic Kingdom's gate, where Ed Tonelli and I have agreed to meet. Last night the whole East Coast got snowed under; even the towns I visited in North Carolina and Georgia were punished in my wake. In Florida we got off easy with hurricanes, tornadoes, flooding, thunder and lightning, death and destruction (the latter mostly of flimsy mobile homes, which lived up to their name). The weather's still grim—is there anything sorrier than watching entire families in Mickey Mouse T-shirts and short pants huddle morosely against the cold, spitting rain?

Time for Ed to show, but where is he? There's no way I was going to pass on meeting this guy, not once I saw on his questionnaire that he works as a custodian at Walt Disney World, a place I'd never seen until today. When I called to ask if he'd show me around, he agreed in a second but had a request: "Do me a favor and bring me some provolone," he said. "I buy it down here and it tastes like plastic."

So I'm feeling like a latter-day immigrant myself—shivering at the gates to the Magic Kingdom with a chunk of stinking cheese in my bag. Wait a second . . . there's a three-foot-tall employee in a jumpsuit uniform walking my way. *Please* Jesus, let this be Ed. Imagine, a midget Tonelli. Nope, there he goes. An hour later I'm still hanging, as miserable as any eight-year-old on the premises, so I call Ed's apartment from a pay phone, and he answers. Could I *really* have failed to spot the only man in Disney World in a green M*A*S*H T-shirt and shades? OK, so he's on his way back, but I'm pissed, until I see this jolly little guy in oversized, impenetrable black goggles striding toward me. I'm wearing a thick cotton shirt and denim jacket and I'm freezing my nuts off; he's in a T-shirt and jeans that ride perilously low on his hips, and he looks as comfortable as a duck. Gotta be. I'm happier already.

"My mother brought me down here to visit for the first

time about nine years ago," he tells me. We're in a theme restaurant just inside the gate, having a big breakfast—Daisy Duck's Eggs. "We got hold of one of those cheap package deals, like a couple hundred dollars. And when I got here, the magic hit me. I got impregnated by that pixie dust. I came back to visit every year after that. Well, some years I missed, but then other years I came twice. I always knew this was my place down here." Finally, two years ago, at age thirty-seven, he made the big leap—he applied for a job at Disney World and got one. Back home in Connecticut, he'd roam from security guard job to dishwasher job to janitor job. "I took sick days all the time. I had the worst attendance record ever. And here, as of now I've got nineteen months of perfect attendance. I'll never go back to Bridgeport again, not for a funeral or a wedding, not even my own. It's part of my past. It didn't hold much for me. It's a dirty, violent city. I couldn't see myself doing anything positive in that town."

Another reason for staying away is that practically his entire family has abandoned Bridgeport—his parents have retired in Florida, and his sister's in L.A. Only his younger brother stayed in their hometown, stranded by the American dream of mobility.

Now breakfast's out of the way, and he's ready to begin the grand tour. Because I've vowed that three hours is my limit, Ed determines that we'll squeeze in only two of the big parks, the Magic Kingdom and Epcot. First we head over to Splash Mountain, the log plume ride, which is dear to Ed's heart since part of his duties involve scrubbing the big plastic logs that carry customers down the mountain. He also cleans one men's bathroom, which he includes on my tour, and a ladies' bathroom and a baby-changing room, which he does not.

We wait in line, then climb side by side into our bobbing log; in the darkness of the mountain's innards, I hear Ed laughing at every one of the robot animals' jokes, even though he's heard them a thousand times by now. He's heard them so often that he's telling B'rer Rabbit's jokes along with him. Slowly, we're rising to the peak of the ride's big dramatic drop, but instead of gripping the rail with all his might—like *me*—Ed throws his arms up in the air and braves the final, splashy fifty-foot plunge.

The rest of the tour goes by in a gray, drizzly blur. From my end it's just what you'd imagine if two strangers, men in their thirties, mysteriously found themselves together on a rainy Saturday afternoon at Disney World. But Ed, thank God, remains chipper, on top of the world. I'm forcing him to spend his day off at work, but he doesn't mind. He's still in love with his personal promised land. We travel through some kind of pirate thing then zoom over to Epcot, and all I remember from there is a ride through the history of the world as narrated by the voice of Walter Cronkite, and a walk through a series of pavilions devoted to various foreign countries. "Here, let's go this way," Ed says, stepping from Norway into Mexico. "I want to take you through Italy."

Then he leads the way into a Georgian-looking building where something called "The American Adventure" is about to be performed. We join the crowd under the rotunda just as the Liberty Singers, a crew of collegiate weenies dressed in a motley of colonial and antebellum costumes, parade in and begin to croon: "This is my country, land of my birth. . . . "

"Hey, Ed," I suggest after about twelve seconds, "why don't we skip this and go somewhere we can talk?"

"No, we have to stay for this," he says urgently. "This is really beneficial. I know you think it's a drag. But since we're cutting it short, I don't want you to miss the best parts."

Now I feel guilty—he's right, I *do* think this is going to be a huge drag, but I didn't want to make it obvious. Chastened, I file right behind Ed into the auditorium.

The show isn't as bad as I expected—it's a lot worse. It's hard to understand the point of making robot actors so lifelike that they're almost human when it's so cheap and easy to use humans in the first place. I'm squirming through a half-hour of the Ben Franklin robot and the Mark Twain robot tossing prefab homespun one-liners back and forth; if I hear the words *freedom* or *liberty* once more I might strangle poor Ed, I think. In the darkness, as the final crescendo of platitude swapping cranks to life, I scribble in my notebook, *This is fucking inane!*

I'm carving in the exclamation point when the lights go up. Ed turns to me and says, "Doesn't that make you proud to be an American?" I'm so torn—between thinking that Ed's gone a little goofy on this place, and thinking that his quest to find a hometown he can love makes him the wisest man I know—that all I can do is nod.

• • • Back on 95, and motoring down to Palm Beach. A bartender asks where I'm from; he's an electrician from Maine. "I worked for a company there five years, but then they ran out of work, and they couldn't see any more coming. My brother was already down here working for an electrician, and I got a job there too. Yeah, so far I've met only two people who were actually *from* here. You know what they say about Florida— nobody's born here and nobody's buried here. I've been here a year, and I still haven't seen a cemetery."

• • • Ed Tonelli and Albert Tonelli have never met, but they have lots in common (even beyond the obvious).

They're both natives of Massachusetts, sons of poor immigrants, and achievers of worldly success and official position unusual among men of their generation and beginnings. Ed was the second-highest ranking officer in the Massachusetts State Police and the state's assistant secretary of public safety, and he's part owner of a car dealership; Albert had a prosperous restaurant-banquet hall and has a long list of civic involvements, including his service as head of the local draft board during the Vietnam era.

Both men also married non-Italian women, which is not inconsistent with their offspring's confident trajectory into the world outside what I normally (and maybe stereotypically) think of as the Italian-American experience. Ed's three daughters went to Vassar and his son, to Williams; Albert's three daughters, all handsomely educated, include Edith Ann, the museum director whose name appears in *Who's Who* more than any other Tonelli's.

And both men are enjoying genteel retirements in Florida: Ed, who's sixty-seven, near Palm Beach, within sight of his country club; and Albert, who's seventy-six, in a placid, tropical setting on the Gulf Coast.

When Ed opens the door of his condo, he's looking at his watch and grinning. Standing behind him, his wife, Dorothy, laughs and says he's just shocked to find another Tonelli who's prompt for appointments. He looks like a lawman—tall, lean and tanned, like a cowboy hero, one who's hung up his badge and discovered golf.

Of the many news clips I found on Ed, the one I remember best was about when he was chief of security for a golf tournament back home, and a drunk, naked woman had to be removed from the country club pool. He laughs when I mention it. "I heard what was happening and went to the pool," he says, "and when I got there, I saw these cops poking at her with boat hooks. So I told them to stop, to do nothing, and then the guy who was running the tournament came over and said to me, 'Are you *sure* you're handling this properly?' I said, 'Look, if you don't think so, *you* do it.' My idea was to move the spectators away from the pool, and once nobody was watching, the woman would come out. And she *did*."

Anyway, he's that kind of guy, cool and confident. He's got what looks like a pretty great life now—golf four times a week, winters in the sun, makes furniture as a hobby. It looks like the great generic American golden years fantasy.

"It was tough back in the old days," he says. We're talking about when he first joined the state police. "When I went in, there were two hundred state policemen. I was only the second Italian, and there were probably a hundred and ninety-eight Irishmen. I started to smoke guinea stogies in the squad car, just to make *sure* everybody in the barracks knew I was Italian. Back then you'd hear radio transmissions where they'd describe suspects—'Four men, looked like Italians. . . . ' And it cost you at promotion time. If you were Italian, you *must* be in the mafia. My brother, Arthur, was a successful businessman—he *must* be in the mafia. And so I *must* have been protecting him.

"Our kids have *no* idea about discrimination—*none*.

The Amazing Story of the Tonelli Family in America

They're . . . I wouldn't *dare* say anything of an ethnic or racial nature in front of them. Oh, no," he says, smiling. "My daughter Jodie majored in Italian and has gone to Italy several times, and she speaks and writes it. She considers herself to be Italian, and so does my son, Julius. But Jill and Judy, no. We kid around about it a lot in the family, particularly with Julius. Like, if he does something stupid, I'll say, 'Well, there's the Polack in you.' " (Ed's wife Dorothy is Lithuanian.)

"But back then," he says, of the old days, "you always had the feeling that if something didn't happen properly, the fact that you were Italian had to be one of the reasons."

"Was there some promotion you wanted but didn't get?" I ask him.

"Sure," he says. "The last one. Colonel. I was promoted to major, but then the appointing authority jumped a guy over me. Colonel was the highest rank. And I always felt, maybe, one of the unsaid things . . . "

We let that hang there.

• • • I find Albert and Pearl in their bungalow, which is shaded by the thirteen fruit trees out back. It's lunchtime, and though he made his life on the staples of spaghetti and tomato sauce, he and Pearl and I sit at a thoroughly nineties table, laden with tuna, cottage cheese, fresh fruit, raw vegetables, and a pitcher of water.

It's hard to imagine two people any more relaxed, but when I ask about his childhood, Al says, "I was always aggressive. I went to work cutting pork chops when I was nine years old. And I started the restaurant at twenty-one. My father had a stroke when he was forty-five, but he had some land, and I swapped it for the restaurant. It was rough. We had the place but no cash. You never knew if you were going to make it. But finally it did well, yes, and that's why we're down here. But it took a long time. And then I lost two and a half years when I went into the service."

"Yes," Pearl says, "when Al left, all his suppliers forgot us."

"That was during the war, when there was a quota system," he says. "We got screwed by our suppliers. The Budweiser guy took care of us, though. He was Italian."

"Oh, right," Pearl says. "He *was* Italian."

"Yeah, and the New England liquor guy took care of us, too. He was Jewish, but he was all right."

The fact that Al is Italian Catholic and Pearl is German and Protestant was the cause of some discomfort back when they got married, he mentions. She nods, adding that it took quite a while, and some persistence on his part, before she decided to accept his proposal.

"But I got a tattoo with her name, Pearl, before she even agreed to marry me," Al says, grinning.

"He always said that if I didn't marry him, he'd have added the word *Harbor*," Pearl says, laughing.

One last thing Ed and Al have in common. While they're both genial and supremely contented in retirement, there's an unmistakable steeliness beneath that. For men of their generation, they showed uncommon fearlessness when it came time to tackle non-Italian America head-on. Could their origins in New England, the crucible of the rock-ribbed Puritan ethic, have something to do with that? Maybe, but one thing's for sure—to go from rags to riches (and Florida) requires guys like these, men who are a little angry about the old ways and eager to break with them.

• • • From Gainesville I check in at work and find a message to call a heretofore unknown Tonelli woman of New Jersey. She sounds excited when I phone, and no wonder: For the past sixteen years, she says, she's been playing detective, trying to figure out the shadowy circumstances of her birth and upbringing, and she's about to crack the case (she thinks). She believes that when she and her sister were infants, they were either illegally adopted or kidnapped by a Mr. and Mrs. Tonelli. She says various documents show three different dates of birth for her, but there's no birth certificate or adoption papers. Also, she and her sister, who's a few years younger, have baptismal certificates from the same date, which *does* sound kind of screwy. She says her father was a mystery man—cut all contact with his relations, never left the house, once moved the family into an unfurnished apartment in the middle of the night, made his daughters play on their swing set and kiddie pool in the basement. All of which leads her to suspect that he was either on the lam or in the Witness Protection Program. No happy memories of Dad. "I carry his name," she says, "but I don't mean to."

Her sick old mother insists she's got it all wrong, but she's not buying. Her father is gone; once he died she got into his Social Security records, which show he was born in a midwestern city. She called some Tonellis there out of the phone book, and one of them suggested that she contact me. I'm in the middle of telling her I don't know what to tell her when she asks my age. I answer and she says, "This is the closest I've *gotten*! I mean, *you* could be my brother." I think she means this hypothetically, until her expectant silence goes on way too long, so I assure her that's unlikely. We agree to meet once I'm home so she can show me all the leads she's collected over the years. She sounds pretty determined to get to the bottom of things; her sister's sickly, she says, and they wonder if it's something that runs in their blood. "Plus, my body keeps growing tumors, what's *that* about?" she wonders. "It *must* be genetic."

• • • Getting out of Florida takes forever. I had no idea it's so wide across the top—Pensacola's so far west it's in the central time zone. I spend the night in a gentle, scenic little town on Mobile Bay called Fairhope, Alabama. Next morning I breakfast in a luncheonette where there are eight young rednecks at a nearby table, one of whom stops on his way out and says, "Are y'all any kin to Eric Trizziano? Because you look like you could be his brother or somethin'." I tell him no, and he says, "Well, y'all look like you could be from the same patch."

Hey, I think, we *are*. This is what I respect most about southerners—they're the only other ones who still believe that you grow in your own patch of land, like a turnip.

I take Interstate 10 west through the southern edge of

Mississippi and Louisiana and ignore the turnoff for New Orleans with regret, since I've never been there. But no Tonellis live there, despite its large Italian population. (Louisiana is where eleven Italian immigrants wrongly suspected of killing a crooked police chief were lynched by a mob one night in 1891. The specter of this injustice looms in the Italian-American consciousness . . . not at all.) I keep driving past signs that announce this bayou or that one, and I wish I could stop—I've never seen a bayou. I don't even know what one *looks* like. From the elevated highway all I can see down there is water.

Paul Tonelli

Outside Federal Prison Camp, Bryan, Texas

7.

Eyetalians Believe in Fat Girls

Finally feel like I'm on a trip. It's Texas.

Down, down, down Route 77, and this gradually becomes an unfurnished planet. It feels like the road to the end of the world; a sudden realization that it's been fifteen minutes since I've seen another car is slightly spooky. We're into the cows and cactus zone, which will stretch all the way from southern Texas to western Nevada. For the first time on this trip, it's warm enough to drive with the window down and the radio loud. It feels as though—*snap*—my leash has broken at last.

A sudden complication arose yesterday when the warden of the prison camp in Bryan, Texas, pulled an about-face and decided that I now can't visit Carmella (Tonelli) Clausi, the dope dealer from Iowa who had called me on the phone. I employ practically every rest area pay phone from Beaumont to Odem, frantically pulling what slender strings are within my reach to undo this fast one. At one point I get himself on the phone, and here's what he tells me: "Well, sir, I don't think one Tonelli more or less is going to make much of a difference to your book."

Stacy Tonelli

Brad and Brenda Tonelli with Rachel and Joshua

There's also a potential complication: I'm heading south a whole day out of my way without actually knowing whether Paul Tonelli will be home and happy to see me. He doesn't have a phone, so I mailed a postcard from Florida alerting him to my arrival. His census form was lively for several reasons: For instance, to the question, "Have you ever been discriminated against because of your Italian ancestry?" he checked *yes,* then wrote in the margin, "Dumb-ass chicken fuckers!" It was also intriguing because I received it after I'd talked on the phone to his brother, Stanford, in Alaska, who filled me in on the weird route by which his family acquired the Tonelli name. And Paul hadn't mentioned that at all.

Raymondville is way too small and poor for the motel chains, so I find a room at the Tall Palms, which offers a sweet old mush-mouth lady owner, a sentimental horsehair sofa, a fringed lampshade, and TV with remote control (but no phone). Paul's house is two minutes away—everything in Raymondville is two minutes away—on a shady street of bungalows. I knock and then I'm facing a pleasant-looking, dark-haired man of about forty wearing a mustache, shorts, a T-shirt, and, when I introduce myself, a look of bewilderment. The postcard never made it; I think he's in shock. When he recovers he says it's a good thing I showed when I did—he was about to go fishing down in Port Mansfield, on the Gulf of Mexico.

I've never been fishing in my life. Let's go.

In his station wagon, Paul says he's been down here in south Texas about a year, teaching earth science and history in a junior high school. "What happened was, one night I was watching TV and there was a commercial with a toll-free number looking to fill teaching positions, so I called and left my name and address on the tape. Then I got a package of information in the mail from a school district in the Los Angeles area. I said no to that, but I ended up on a national listing of teachers, and Raymondville called me. And they paid real well, and it was a chance to get out of the forest. . . . " Wait, *what* forest?

"Oh, before here I lived in Jacksonville, Texas, in a house on sixty-five acres that my grandparents owned. I planted two hundred pine tree seedlings there, and along with the trees came assorted life forms, so I had created my own little world, in a way. But *limited*. I had to drive two hours to Dallas if I wanted to see anything. And then I'd be, like, 'Look—people! Humans! *Girls*!' Once in Jacksonville, when I was a computer operator, they put me on a weird shift, and I went two months without ever talking to another person. I was in Jacksonville for ten years, but even then you're never really accepted. I was always an outsider, or at least I felt like one."

Not that life's a whirlwind now. He still doesn't have a phone, his mother and a brother live a fourteen-hour drive away, and his girlfriend's way up in Tyler. He says he doesn't really have friends among his neighbors or coworkers, and anyway, most of Raymondville is Mexican and poor. And sparsely settled. And isolated.

"Between here and Kingsville, there's nothing," he says

when I ask about the area. "Between here and Harlingen, it's blank. From Harlingen to Brownsville, it's just desert. And from Brownsville to McAllen, it's . . . nothing."

By the time we pull up to the deserted pier, it's dark out. Paul loads my hook with shrimp, shows me how to get it out into the water, and there we are, side by side, two trolling Tonellis in the Texas night. Suddenly the rod bends in my hand—something's out there pulling on it real good. Paul's giving me counsel, and I start to reel it in, but then my line goes slack, sonofabitch. Even worse, as I pull it back I tangle it into a spectacular knot around my reel, and it takes Paul five minutes to fix the mess. The rest of the shrimp disappear into the deep without another serious scare. We're walking back toward the car when out of the darkness I hear Paul singing, in a quavery drawl:

"The stars are bright, and shine at night—"

I look up—Jesus, he's right, the sky is gaudy with stars. And the black part is *so* black. Outside of a planetarium, I've never seen a night look this real. I'm stopped dead in my tracks, I don't want to move: the fish, the sky, the Gulf of Mexico, Paul and me, all fated to come together on this day, it feels like magic, like a miracle.

"—deep in the heart of Texas. . . . "

• • • A story in this morning's paper reports that three of the country's ten poorest cities are in this neck of Texas. I read this over eggs, bacon, biscuits, and salsa at the Casa Blanca restaurant, where I am the only person who isn't speaking Spanish. Paul says that 90 percent of the kids he teaches are from migrant-worker families in town just long enough to pick cotton, sorghum, rice, and wheat. Then they move on. Does anybody really believe the kids have a chance to break the cycle? (I know, nobody wants them to.)

Last night after fishing, Paul had two things he wanted me to see. He put a cassette into his VCR and there in the credits of a cheap Italian thriller called *Dawn of the Living Dead* are Bob and Steno Tonelli. And he produced a photocopied letter:

The Amazing Story of the Tonelli Family in America

Dear Tonelli:

I received your name and address from the phone book at a local university. I hope you don't mind me writing you, but being a Tonelli myself, I am very interested in the existence of other Tonellis too.

A brief history of me includes moving to Texas from California in '66. Graduated from college and currently teaching in south Texas. Therefore I feel isolated down here in the flatland prairie, and would like to know a little more about you.

If this letter reaches you, please write back and try to include the following information:

1. Any Tonellis in the film industry?
2. Tonellis of the U.S., Italy
3. You, your family
4. Photos

I hope this letter makes it to you, so try to write soon.

Sincerely,

Paul Tonelli

It's . . . amazing! Scary, too, how Paul and I were struck by the same loony impulse at about the same time (he says he sent his letter out just a few weeks before getting mine).

We're two buds on the road today, to Brownsville (the nearest big bank), Matamoros, Mexico (shopping for Paul, sightseeing for me), and South Padre Island (for the beach). We have lots of time to talk in the car, and I keep waiting to see if he'll mention how his father appropriated the Tonelli name. I ask what it's like being Italian in a place like Texas.

"Being Italian down here, you stand out," he says. "Like a sore thumb. It's like a basket full of white eggs, and you're the only one that's colored. You should hear the way they pronounce it—'TOE-nelly? Toe-NELL-er? Whut kinda name's *thayt?*' I tell them it's Japanese. Or they'll say, 'Isn't that Italian? Are you in the mafia?' I say, 'Well sure, buddy, how'd you guess?' When you're around educated people, it's all right. But you have to remember that most of Texas is illiterate. From one to fifty, Texas's educational system is rated thirty-seventh. So it's near the bottom of the barrel. But it's exciting, though, when you come across somebody else of Italian origins, because they're so few and far between. But when you do, you connect like a magnet."

"Do you come across many?" I wonder. He thinks a moment then shakes his head.

"Just randomly. In college I knew a few. Or if I go out to an Italian restaurant and meet the owner. I didn't really feel much interest in it until just a little while before I got your questionnaire. I started to wonder if there were any other Tonellis in the world, or where they were, or how many. I guess I started to wonder one time after I was talking to my girlfriend, Lana. I was complaining when I lived in Jacksonville that they're all inbred there, that the only way to get anywhere there is to marry somebody's brother's aunt's daughter's sister or something like that. So she said—now *how* did she put it? She said, 'Paul, you have to find your own kind.' "

• • • We cross the footbridge into Matamoros, a baroquely depressing border town, and stop at a vast indoor bazaar. I buy something I've desired since puberty—a switchblade knife, a cheap but nasty little black and chrome number ($12). Once I get it I can't think of a single possible use for it. Then, since I've already made one embarrassing purchase, I feel free to buy a silver and malachite ring with the big initial *T* ($8). We pick up some cigars and duty-free liquor, then wander through the open-air marketplace. A brave little urchin in rags trailing two even smaller urchins offers me a bargain, five packs of chewing gum for a dollar instead of the usual four (brave because she then gives me three and quickly marches away). Amid all the dust and the commerce we come upon a guy stationed at a cardboard carton desk. For $2, his sign advertises, he'll write your name on a grain of rice. I take his little notepad, write *TONELLI* on it, and order two of them, one for me, one for Paul.

Then we cross back into America and return to the car. Back on the road, I ask Paul if he remembers his father, and he says no, he was too young when the old man took off, leaving the family in northern California. "The whole neighborhood I lived in was Italian," Paul tells me. "If I'd stayed there I probably would have ended up marrying some Italian chick—'the girl next door.' So it was a little like culture shock, moving to Texas. It was like going back in the past. I had a ten-speed bike, and there were kids here who rode their horses to school. I don't know how my mother chose Texas—I don't know if she threw a dart at a map or took the best job offer or what. She's from St. Louis, I believe. Then when I turned eighteen I said, 'I'm outta here. I want to see the world.' " But though he's lived in three or four places since, they've all been in Texas.

I ask him, "Can you really feel Italian in the middle of Texas?"

"Yeah," he says, "the olive skin, the name, my taste buds, just the whole culture you can identify with. It's just *there*. It's genetic. See, I never did pretend I *wasn't* Italian, even though the odds were against me. I never did renege on it."

"OK," I say, "but what does being Italian really mean?"

"I don't know," he says. "You know there's *something* there, but you don't know who or what or how. It's hard to find meaning when you don't have any information. You can't just pull it out of the sky. Being a history major, you know Italy is rich in heritage, and you know there had to be some Tonelli somewhere who came across to New York Harbor. It's not like being Billy Bob Smith who grew up in Jacksonville, Texas, and never left the city limits. What kind of heritage is *that*? When I looked it up, I learned that the Antonelli family owned one-third of Italy and were in the ruling class, so you and I are part of that. But then again, it could all be an illusion. Could be that it don't mean *shit*. But you know it does. But then again, it's hard not to wonder.

"When you've got other Tonellis around you, you've got security. You're not the only fish in the sea. That's why what *you're* out here doing, it's like . . . an answer. It's like, 'Well, well, I thought I was the only one.' I always thought it would be neat, if you wanted a wife and you wanted to keep the bloodline going and didn't want an American wife, I'd go to Italy and find one. Long, flowing brown hair, big tits, really pretty. Traditional. Like in *The Godfather,* he went over there and found the prettiest girl in the village and fell in love."

He asks about my family back in Philadelphia, and I give him the rundown—parents, sisters, cousins, aunts, uncles, Sundays at Grandmom and Grandpop's, the whole drill.

"That sounds kind of neat," he says, grinning. "Tell 'em all I said howdy."

• • • After an hour or so on South Padre Island—it's a sunny afternoon in the middle of spring break, so it's mobbed, but Paul managed to find the one stretch of beach that's deserted—we split for a barbecue restaurant just off the highway. It's huge, and we're the only people here under retirement age. Every long table is filled with oldsters in their golden years costumes—juvenile ensembles of short pants, T-shirts, and sneakers. They're mostly in groups, relaxed and laughing like kids in a junior-high cafeteria. "Winter Texans," Paul says, indicating the captains and first mates of the Winnebagos and Airstream trailers that clog the right lanes of every highway in the American south and west. No wonder nobody stays put—you couldn't find Grandmom and Grandpop to visit even if you wanted to.

I'm blowing Raymondville tomorrow morning, so when Paul and I get back we begin our good-byes. He's got an armload of souvenirs for me: A bag of oranges for the road, a bottle of herbal wake-up pills, a shot glass with the logo of a liquor store he used to manage, a Dallas Cowboys mug, a whole box of Black Cat firecrackers, three jars of hot peppers he grew and put up, Mexican chewing gum. Then he goes over to the wall and pulls down a final gift, one I try to dissuade him from parting with, but he won't hear it. Of all the souvenirs I collect on the trip, this one's my treasure: It's an oil painting Paul did, a picture of a blustery, gloomy dawn on a lake, and a bird, its head bowed, its wings beating against the wind, struggling to land.

• • • "We're one of the top local bands, which doesn't mean too much." This is Stacy Tonelli, the drummer for a rock band called Southside Groove, at home in the Houston apartment he shares with his girlfriend, his snake, and his lizard. "It basically means we don't suck but we're not signed." He's nineteen, green eyes, jet-black (dyed) hair to midback, handsome, a student at the Art Institute of Houston, the only child of Terri, who's also here, and Don Tonelli, who lives on a sailboat that's somewhere in the Caribbean right now. Don's from Chicago, moved here for an engineering job with Terri, who was pregnant with Bryan (Stacy's real name), "but Don was always interested in the water," Terri says. "It's all he ever talked about." After they divorced, which was when Stacy was four, Don took the sea as his home. "He pretty much always wanted to take off," Stacy says. "My grandparents hate it, but I don't—I respect him for doing it. If it was what *I* wanted to do . . . "

"He takes after his father," Terri says.

"No I don't," says Stacy. "I *really* don't think I take after him."

Stacy sees his grandparents in Chicago and talks to them often on the phone, but that's it for contact with other Tonellis. (On his questionnaire, where I asked for "typical Tonelli traits," he wrote, "Hard-headed, free spirits, somewhat loners.")

"Do you have much sense of being Italian?" I ask him.

"I take people as they are," he says. "I don't care what their nationality is or anything like that. Sometimes if I'm dealing with somebody who's Italian, he'll say, 'Oh, you're Italian, too,' so that's pretty cool. Italians have some cool attitudes—cook, eat, party. There are some bad sides, too—no, I was just thinking about the mob, but all I know about that is from movies. I'm not really into religion or roots or the Bible," he says, "or other trendy things that start wars."

• • • It's out of my way, but I decide to spend this Saturday night in Austin. Check into a motel, head back out in a taxi, and find that Sixth Street's a zoo due to the rodeo and a music festival in town. I wander, exhausted, in and out of cowboy music bars, and seriously consider getting a tattoo, a sure sign that I should lie down. My taxi home has a pilot and a copilot—a chubby, frizzy-haired woman driving and a stick-skinny old boy in the front seat with her.

"So, where you from?" he asks.

"New York."

"You Joosh?"

"Nope, Italian."

"Thailand!?"

"Nope, Italian."

"Ohhh. You married?"

"Nope."

"Well, I wanna give you some good advice. Get yourself one of these," he says, throwing an arm over the driver's back. "Get yourself a fat girl. I'm telling you! Nothing but good has come to me since I found this one. I mean it—money, a boat, nothing but good. Eye*tal*ians believe in fat girls!" We stop at a light, and they both turn and grin at me.

"What brings you to town?" she asks.

I'm in no condition to give these two the whole song and dance, so I mumble something vague.

"He ain't telling you nothin'!" he yells gleefully at her. "He's an eyetalian from New York. *He* ain't got time for all this happy bullshit. He's just in town to do a job. Do it right so he ain't have to come back and do it agin." He turns and winks at me. "Ain't that right?"

"Right," I say, and after that nobody says anything.

● ● ●

I woke up as the sun was reddening; and that was the one distinct time in my life, the strangest moment of all, when I didn't know who I was—I was far from home, haunted and tired with travel, in a cheap hotel room I'd never seen, hearing the hiss of steam outside, and the creak of the old wood of the hotel, and footsteps upstairs, and all the sad sounds, and I looked at the cracked high ceiling and really didn't know who I was for about fifteen strange seconds. I wasn't scared; I was just somebody else, some stranger, and my whole life was a haunted life, the life of a ghost. I was halfway across America, at the dividing line between the East of my youth and the West of my future, and maybe that's why it happened right there and then, that strange red afternoon.

Or so Jack Kerouac was inspired to write, but then Kerouac didn't have to spend all his time with Tonellis, did he? (Although, significantly, he made the protagonist of *On the Road* a guy from Jersey named Sal with a brother named Rocco.) Look, Jack, *I* was far from home, haunted and tired with travel, in cheap motel rooms I'd never seen, halfway across America, so on and so forth. But believe me, for better or worse, to my credit or detriment, on my road I *always* knew who I was. I wished like hell I didn't—I wanted to feel that transcendence, that sense that I had become as strung-out as the roads I drove. I wanted to give myself the slip, to escape who I had been, to grow big and boundless and deathless. "You cannot travel on the path until you have become the path itself," Buddha is said to have said. *I* wanted that, too.

But it didn't happen. It didn't happen. It didn't happen.

• • • It smells like popcorn in here, and it looks like a daycare center cafeteria. There's a handsome young family—he in black cowboy hat, starched white shirt, jeans, and snakeskin boots; she in tasteful sweater and tights, pearls, shampoo-shiny blond hair; two little girls in pink dresses—at a round table. They could pose for a truck ad. Here comes another tall, frosted-maned Texas beauty, Houston Junior League, my guess. Nearby, a pair of young lovers dressed for a date—Mexicans, judging by their dense black hairdos and brown skins—sit head to head, whispering. They're next to another family, an older couple, middle-aged woman and teenager, playing pinochle and eating chicken from a tinfoil package. The big room is crowded with similar scenes; against the wall, kids are playing with crayon-colored plastic toys. From the open doorway comes a breeze and the sounds of a playground.

This ain't *Hud.*

But all the women are prisoners, mostly here on federal drug charges. A uniformed guard enters the visitors' room, leading a blond-haired woman, fiftyish, in a green sweater and jeans. Turns out Carmella Tonelli Clausi has no idea of how close I came to being denied permission to get into the Federal

Prison Camp for Women in Bryan, Texas, but she's not surprised to hear it. When I ask her why she was sent from her
hometown, Des Moines, Iowa, to serve her time in Texas, she
says: "It's the Feds." She shrugs wearily. "To get you away from
your family."

She's had a rough life so far. When she was two, the
youngest of ten children, her father left her mother. "We lived
across the street from him," she recalls, "but I never saw him. I
used to go to the body shop he owned, to visit my brothers—
they all worked there—or to the restaurant he owned, to see my
sister. And he always had to ask who I was." Her first husband
was a drug addict who beat her (after they divorced, he committed suicide). Her second (common-law) husband was the boss of
the drug operation that landed her here.

"See," she says, "somebody told me the police were watching my house. I got a call, it was a man, and when he told me, I
said, 'Yeah, *right,* you're gonna *tell* me that you're watching me?'
So I kept doing it. Then I sold to a friend, and she was wired. That
eyetalian stubbornness. It was stupid. But my family stood by
me. A lot in here, their families desert them, but not mine."

All but her father, she means.

"I write to him, but he doesn't write back. I call him, but
he won't take my calls. He's still my father, though. He might
not think I'm his daughter, but he's still my father."

● ● ● "There's a friend at work, he's an Italian guy, who saw
this old black-and-white gangster movie, and the gangster's
name is Pete Tonelli. And sometimes he'll call me Pete—like, 'Ey,
Pete, I'm-a gonna get you.' " We're at home in late morning with
the soft-spoken and friendly Brad Tonelli, his wife Brenda, and
little Joshua and Rachel (daughter Blake's at school), on a quiet
street in Sherman, Texas, just north of Dallas. Brad doesn't go
to his job as a machinist until the afternoon.

"There's lots of times at work we'll be on our coffee
break and one guy'll say, 'Well, I'm Dutch, and . . . ' or, 'I'm German. . . . ' And I just say, 'Well, I'm half Irish and half Italian.'
Yeah, family descent comes up a lot at work. One old guy, he

The Amazing Story of the Tonelli Family in America

was German, and he used to kid me all the time. He'd call me a wop and laugh, and I'd call him a kraut. There are lots of people who don't know who they are or where they're from. I feel lucky there's something in me that's not just plain American. I'm lucky I'm not a Smith or Brown or whatever. You ever try looking in the phone book for a Smith?"

Like his brothers, Paul, who I saw down in Raymondville, and Stan, who I'll see in Alaska, Brad doesn't remember much about his father, who took off when he was small. "There are things my mom told me about him, but I kind of discount it because I don't know both sides." What kind of things? "Oh, that he was lazy, or that he thought he was more important than his family, and if he got some extra money he spent it on himself. I refuse to believe it, because if somebody tells you about somebody you don't know and then you meet that person, then it's totally different. I don't believe anything she says about him, even if it *is* true. I just don't know the other side of the story.

"I'd give anything to have known him, though, growing up. I think my life would be a complete one hundred eighty-degree difference from the way it is now—the way I view things, the way I feel about things. I don't know what kind of guy he was, but he would have given me guidance in the ways to deal with the world. I feel kind of passive—if somebody provokes me, I just say screw it and walk away. Whereas maybe I would just tear into 'em. But I have to blow it off—I have my own kids to raise now."

We're beginning to wrap up our time together—I have a lunch date with his mother—when he reaches under the sofa and pulls out a red photo album. Kind of shyly, he says, "This is just some stuff I confiscated." Together we sort through the memorabilia of his lost father's life—a yellowed newspaper clipping announcing the wedding, a plush red Easter card his father sent his mother, black-and-white snapshots of a handsome, curly-haired man. We're staring at one of the pictures when Brad says, "Put some glasses on him and he looks just like you."

We stare some more.

After a minute he says, "Sometimes I wish I looked more like my dad."

● ● ● There's a rare form of meningitis on the loose in Grayson County, Texas. Five people have caught it so far, and one of them died last night. There's not much in the literature on this strain of the disease. The most detailed account Dr. Mary Jo O'Dell Tonelli could find was of an outbreak just after World War II, among soldiers billeted in extremely tight quarters. When she talked to the current victims, she found they were all patrons of two very popular country music dance halls. And in clubs, as Dr. Tonelli, the director of public health in this county, points out, the music is loud, so people have to shout. And they smoke, so they tend to cough. Which is why, before we can go to lunch, she has to write a press release warning Texans about these two clubs.

I ask her, "Won't the club owners be mad?"

"Well," she says, "that's *their* problem."

The matriarch of the Texas Tonellis has got some grit, and I'm not surprised. When I sent her the questionnaire, she returned it to me promptly, untouched, with a terse note explaining that she acquired her name from her ex-husband and kept it only for the sake of her sons. When I telephoned from Florida to ask if I could meet her anyway, she cut me off, saying, "Do you know Jerry Tonelli?"

"No," I replied, "never heard of him," and attempted to finish my request when she interrupted again.

"Are you *sure* you're not one of Jerry Tonelli's bastards?"

Yo! Maybe she felt she had beat me up enough at that point, because she finally said we could meet.

When we settle into a restaurant near her office, she says, "I'm sorry about that business on the telephone. I was irritated. It's the one era of my life I don't like thinking about. It was a mistake, and I don't like making mistakes. I only wish I hadn't changed my name back then, because I am always in hot pursuit of other O'Dells. It's an interesting family—they're hard-working, straightforward people," she says, giving me a cool-eyed stare.

She was born and raised in St. Louis and went to undergraduate and medical school in Texas. "It was the first time I was ever away from home, and I loved it," she says. She went to

San Diego for an internship, where she met an ambulance driver named Jerry Tonelli. Then she was offered a job in northern California, so they married and moved there in 1951.

"I didn't really have the opportunity to meet his family before I went to San Francisco, and I don't know if it was because he didn't *want* me to, or if I just didn't think of it. He had met mine—my mother and dad and sister came out, and he met them then. Yes, it *was* odd that I hadn't met his, but I was too involved in my work to think about it. I was tired of working, and I wanted to get on with my life, and I think I saw this as a way."

They lived in northern California with their three sons—Paul, Stanford, and Brad—until the marriage ended, when the youngest boy was still an infant. What went wrong? "Well—" she begins, then stops herself. "Look. It's a story. It's a story. He had a neat personality. No depth. But a good personality, good with people." He owned a fish store, but she says he neglected it until it went under. She was the breadwinner.

"That didn't sit well with me," she says. "I didn't want to support him. He was a rascal." She pauses and smiles. "Good-*look*ing rascal, though."

After they split up she moved herself and the boys to Texas, where she'd found a job. That's when she found out the other unpleasant surprise about her life as a Tonelli.

"There was a green wooden box that he kept his papers in, and I think it was something in that box that first let me know his name wasn't really Tonelli. He never *did* tell me that Tonelli wasn't his name, but an aunt of his told me later that there was a man named Tonelli, and Jerry admired him so much that he took his name. I think also that he didn't want to go through life with a Mexican name. Then, a few years after that, he moved to Germany and changed his name again, to von Nuremburg—something like that, spell it any way you want. I only found that out when I went to get VA benefits for my son Paul's education. And I think he's changed it since then."

Lunch is over and she has to get back to work. But I think she's worried that I might still feel bad about what my name means to her.

"Tonelli is an honored name in Sherman because I've made it that," she assures me. "Still, I'd give anything for my name to be O'Dell. So you can understand why when you called I wanted to slam down the phone. But you should be proud of your name," she says, giving me that cool stare but smiling now, too. "We should *all* honor our names."

• • • Speaking of names, here's an article I clipped from the *New York Times* about new trends in surnames, which should be a contradiction but isn't. The piece opens with the tale of Elise Goldstein and Baruch Browns of Toronto, who were married six years ago and at that time discussed what they'd name their future children. "We absolutely wanted a family name," says Goldstein, a rabbi, but they wanted to create an alternative to using his *or* hers. So they took the "Gold" from her name and the "Brown" from his, mixed them together, and came up with "Sienna" as the surname that eventually got affixed to little Noam and Carmi (*Noam and Carmi?*). Browns, who is a calligrapher (figures) and a school administrator (yikes), says, "Ocher, or those other muddy-yellow color names, didn't seem like nice names." Wait—are they naming people or crayons? This is kooky behavior, I realize, but it's useful as a sign of where we're heading: Someday, maybe everybody will have *nice* surnames—meaningless, ethnicity-less, ahistorical, nice surnames. I always assumed that whatever else happened to our connection to the past, our names would persist to the very end, vestiges of our historical selves. So maybe the end *is* near. The article also tells about Melanie Graves and Michael Versace, of Virginia, who got married and chose a new surname for themselves—Rios, his mother's maiden name. The new Ms. Rios likes the fact that in Spanish it means *rivers*; "My whole spirit loves rivers and always has," she informs.

Farther down, a child psychologist named Bernstein says that even though long, hyphenated names are tough for children, he doesn't condemn the practice. But as another, possibly wiser psychologist—Dr. Salvatore Didato—points out, "Anything that deviates from what is customary is going to raise questions among the peer group. This could be an opportunity for attack, for teasing or ridicule."

Yo, Sal, why so touchy? "We didn't believe in the whole patriarchal tradition of women giving up their names and automatically giving the father's name to the children," says a Ms. Ledbetter, of Florida, who was interviewed along with her husband, a Mr. Skylar. "We thought it would symbolize our relationship if we came up with a new name." Their choice: *Skylab*. That's a joke, but not much funnier than the actual selection they made for their children—*Skybetter*. The reporter asks, isn't it confusing for the members of a family to have different last names. She replies, with chilly logic: "All our names are in the phone book." That's why we'll always need names—so people can find our numbers. Finally, there's Sally and Peter Rabinowitz Solis-Cohen, of Philadelphia, who say they'll let their kids choose from the array of surnames they have to offer. The children, she admits, "may have problems . . . but we haven't closed off any options for anybody." He states, "It'll be a challenge for the next generation. But we're blessed with being able to make choices in our society."

Blessed with choices . . . By this point I'm practically slipping into a coma—just when I've absorbed the idea that *where* you'll be is a matter of choice, I discover that *who* you'll be is, too. Someday we'll all be as insipid as cavemen. It's a new world out there, I accept that, but is it brave or brain-dead? Or are they the same thing?

• • • I now have to cross half a continent—Dallas to San Diego, fifteen hundred miles—without a Tonelli to see. These are the Days of Driving, on asphalt by 9:30 and keep it there (except for lunch and a leak) until dusk, at which time I select my cheapskate motel and call it a day. Interstate 20 through west Texas is benevolently unscenic and so provides no distractions to pure motion. If there's a beauty of the interstate, this is it. We're never more graceful than when we drive—in cars we become as fluid as fish, swerving and darting, shimmering and swift. The eighteen-wheelers are pushy and blind as whales, the Winnebagos look goony as blowfish, my car has a nose like a shark's. There's a rhythm of the road, and it's different every day—we move for hours at a time in schools, sensing who will set the pace, who will pass and when, who will fall behind. A flash of red metal zooms past, chased by a black one and then a white one—three mint Ford pickups with smoked windows, identical in all but color, blowing the rest of us away. They must be doing one hundred twenty; in a second they're gone.

I've been reborn as a driving robot, but in my mind I see my office wall, and the map hanging there, and a dirty, microscopic blue Buick crawling over the paper, crossing Texas, New Mexico, Arizona . . . Abilene, El Paso, Las Cruces, Tucson. . . .

Whew! Poetry in motion! That's another beauty of spending day after day alone in a car—no annoying other voices to stop you from attaining incandescence. I've been gone almost three weeks, and actually anticipated suffering from company deprivation, so I arranged for a conjugal visit right about now. The beautiful Lisa (half-Italian—but it's the culturally dominant parent, her mother) flies to Tucson and rides shotgun (map light) west. We motor along scenic Route 86, two hundred miles of tan dust, through Why, Arizona, and into Gila Bend for the night. I'm getting a wild taste of aimlessness, and having no practical purpose for being here is liberating—finally, for the first time in my life, I'm nobody, nowhere, for no reason. We ingest magic mushrooms and buy two six-packs of Coronas from the chubby, laughing Mexicans at an open-air store (they began laughing when I drove off the curb instead of using the driveway). The tape deck is cranked, Joe Ely singing "The road goes on forever and the party never ends," and all four windows are down. She remembered the Polaroid—that's us, beneath the buzzy fluorescent light hanging over the picnic table by the desolate Burger House, then cruising the 1.9-mile main drag of town over and over, stoned by the night and the mad idea of finding tramps like us, whoever *us* is, here, wherever *here* is.

It's lucky in a way that two days later, by the pitiless light of southern California, we're our old selves again, bickering like starlings. And so neither of us is totally sad at having to part—her for home and work and waiting, me for the road, the journey, the voyage, America, Tonellis.

The Amazing Story of the Tonelli Family in America

Mike, Beatrice, and Ginette Tonelli

Debra Tonelli

Lori Tonelli and
Barbara Tonelli McNicol

Bill Tonelli

Edith Ann
Tonelli and
Jonathan

8.

Reeking of Ethnocentrism

Because it feels selfish to keep all this Tonelli bonding to myself, I've invited two who have never met to have dinner with me tonight in a restaurant in San Diego.

Lori Tonelli, originally of northern California, shows up first—a middle-management-looking woman in her early thirties, blue suit, buttoned-up white blouse, modest necklace. She lives with her fiancé, Walt. Barbara—Bobbie—(Tonelli) McNicol, born in Michigan, in her forties, kind of a spunky glint in her eye, comes in a minute later.

"Wait, before we get started," Lori says to her, "I want to see if you have the Tonelli nose." Bobbie doesn't, at least not *that* Tonelli nose. Still, there are similarities: Turns out both women are computer programmers, both live in the same part of town, and both were called "Toenails" in school.

"This is scary," Bobbie says.

They both had WASP mothers, too. "My mom's family didn't want her to marry a damn wop, they said," says Bobbie. Her first husband was Hungarian, her second one's a Scot.

I knew this was going to be bracing if only because of

what Bobbie wrote on the bottom of her questionnaire: "Some of these questions, especially those regarding tomato sauce and the arts, seem silly. Those related to differences in Italian-Americans and family traits seem so ethnocentric that they offended me. I don't see Italian-Americans as different from any other Americans, and I attribute my family's traits to genes, not ethnic background."

"I thought it *reeked* of ethnocentrism," she says when I bring it up over dinner (I had fish; she had lasagna). " 'How do you make your tomato sauce?' *This is the nineties!*"

Now Lori, who has heretofore expressed no objection to the census form, says, "I was offended by the question about which Godfather movie was my favorite." (Unimaginable, she hadn't seen *any* of them.)

"Yeah!" Bobbie says. "Like I'm going to see a movie just because my grandparents were Italian! My sauce is *Ragu*—if I can't nuke it, I don't eat it."

I listen attentively, without offering a reply, but I'm thinking: *Jesus—southern California.*

"I think that in my family I'm the only one who dated out of my race," Lori says. "I dated a black guy. I was engaged to a Japanese man. I went out with an Ecuadorian guy. My father and brothers were definitely against it. But my sisters just joked about it—like the Thanksgiving I brought my black boyfriend home, my sister was carving the turkey and she said, 'So, Lori, you're having dark meat this year?' "

"I *never* classify people," Bobbie says. "It limits your thoughts. I personally bristle at being classified as Italian, because that comes with preconceived notions of having to be a certain way. My mom was real careful not to makes ethnic jokes or snide ethnic remarks. She raised us not to think in terms of stereotypes."

Lori says, "I remember once I said to my grandmother, 'I'm Italian,' and she said, 'No, you're American.' "

I pounce on this. "Then you *have* thought of yourself as Italian," I say.

"I *do,* but only because the world defines me as that."

"So doesn't that have *anything* to do with who you are?" I ask.

"No. Not a bit," she replies. Soon dinner ends, and Lori and Bobbie exchange phone numbers.

"Well, this has been more fun than I thought," Bobbie says. "I was a little apprehensive, to be honest. And my husband felt left out."

"Actually," Lori says, "Walt felt a little bad about that, too."

• • • I'm in a living room in Escondido, just outside San Diego, listening to a burly, thick-fingered exterminator play the most delicate, lyrical, sentimental melody on his piano. He composed it, and I taped it as he played, and his wife and I applauded when he finished. Then Beatrice and Mike Tonelli and I sit at the kitchen table.

Beatrice: I came out here from the Bronx on vacation when I was eighteen, with my mom. We took the train from New York, traveled all around and came to San Diego and stayed at Mike's parents' house—my aunt and uncle's. And Mike and I met and fell in love, and I went back home and told my father I was moving to California, and we got married. Married for twenty years.

Me: Was anybody upset about it?

Beatrice: Oh, we had a lot of . . . *your* parents more than mine.

Mike: My dad, he was all against it. My parents didn't want us in their house *at all.*

Me: How exactly did it happen?

Mike: When they came out to visit, my dad told me to show my cousin around town. So I did. And we fell in love.

Me: But didn't it occur to you that there would be trouble?

Mike: Sure it did.

Beatrice: Yeah, it did, but it didn't stop us. But it's not like we grew up together, or really knew each other before that.

Mike: We had met once—I was eight or nine and she must have been five or six—in New York. If we were raised around each other, it probably wouldn't have happened.

Me: How did your father find out?

Mike: He caught me writing her a letter. He grabbed it and read it, and, oh boy, was he mad. *Sheee.* Plus, she started crying at the train when they left, so my dad and mother and her mother kinda went, "Well, what's going on *here*?" My dad told me, "You can't marry your *sister*." I said, "She's not my sister," but he said, "She might as well be, she's my brother's daughter." Then my dad said, "Oh, she's not gonna come back and marry you anyway. You have nothing to offer. You're just a janitor." And I was so tired of hearing that from him—you're just a janitor, she's got a good education and good job out there, she's not coming back—so I said, "What do you mean, Dad? What about *this*?" [Reenacting the nonverbal part of their exchange, Mike looks down at his lap, so I do, too, and then we're both staring at his crotch, which is pumping up and down off the chair.] Oooh, he almost sent me flying. "*You talkin' about my brother's daughter?!*" I said, "Yeah, I got plenty to offer, Dad." He was really pissed.

Me: How did you break the news?

Beatrice: On the train home I told my mother that we had fallen in love and I wanted to come back to California.

Me: Was she mad?

Beatrice: I'll tell you, my mom was upset when I was going out with this Puerto Rican guy, and I guess we were getting serious. She grabbed a kitchen knife and told him, "Your name is on this. If I see you with my daughter again, this is going right through you." So she wasn't that radical about Mike.

Mike: My father used to joke around, "My poor brother, one daughter married her cousin, one daughter married a Puerto Rican, and one's shacked up." Cousins getting married is real common in England, though, right? That's royal blood, isn't it? She said she wouldn't have married me if the priest back there hadn't OK'd it.

Beatrice: Well, I had to be married in church.

Mike: But I didn't think the priest would OK it.

Beatrice: Fooled you, ha-ha.

Mike: And a year later my father said it was the best thing that ever happened to me. And at the time they had told me they'd rather see me marry a black person.

Mike and Bea saw a geneticist before they married, and he gave them the OK to have kids. They have two perfect daughters, Ginette, who's fifteen, and Sabrina, eleven.

As I'm packing to go, Mike says, "Yeah, Italian is the only nationality there *is*. And if there were more of us, this would be a better country. I only wish I was pure Italian. My mother's German. I used to tell my dad, if you had married an Italian girl, I'd be a concert pianist today. I don't even *tell* people I'm half German."

Then, as I'm walking out the door, Beatrice says, "Oh, wait—did I tell you that *both* my dad's parents were Tonellis?"

"Mine too!" says Mike.

• • • Sunday morning I head north up Route 5, to L.A., where I'll stay with the beautiful Michelle, who's half Italian, half Lebanese, and from South Philly. She and I go way back. Last time I saw her we were in Washington at a dinner party with Bill Clinton, Barbara Bush, quite a few members of Congress, a former vice-presidential candidate, an aged baseball god, a Supreme Court justice, and about three thousand members of a national political-cultural-philanthropic-fraternal organization of Italian-Americans, mostly middle-aged and older, prosperous-looking businesspeople and professionals in tuxedos and gowns.

Michelle and I were there purely out of curiosity, and because I got the tickets free. All night long, serious, important matters were addressed; vital information was exchanged. The prevailing spirit in the room was we're-all-successfully-assimi-lated-so-no-Vito-Corleone-impressions-please. We were with it.

Then it began to unravel. We left the vast ballroom and headed for the bar in the hotel lobby. We settled into a table for two and ordered drinks. I looked up and spotted Big Mike.

Though we hadn't seen each other in a long time, Big Mike and I go way back. When I was a kid reporter, he was a hometown character, a kind of freelance presshound with a dizzy client list of teen idols, saloon crooners, athletes, and smoldering starlets of both genders. Everybody downtown knew who he was, and I knew him a little. So I got his attention and reintroduced myself. Big Mike faked a happy heart attack, kissed me, squeezed Michelle's hand in both of his. We invited him to join us; he said he was waiting for an attorney named Catherine whom he had met earlier, but sure.

We were drinking and smoking and talking when he looked up and saw the woman wander into the bar. He called her over, and when she arrived I realized, *I* know Catherine—in fact, she and I go way back. She grew up around the corner from me, and our baby sisters were best friends for many years. Small world, everybody agreed, and Catherine sat, too.

For a moment, Big Mike lost his giddy cheer. He was still boiling over something he'd read about Columbus in a maga-zine. "Do you believe this?" he appealed to me. "This guy calls Columbus a thief, a slavemaster, a this, a that. But where would we be without Columbus? We'd be sitting around in . . . *Thai-land!*" (Except he pronounced the *th*.) Then Big Mike picked up a pen, wiggled it like Groucho's cigar, and giggled, "And I'd be the Thighmaster!"

The mood of the table brightened just in time for the unexpected arrival of another South Philadelphian, a former city councilman, who was with a friend. Mainly through their involvement in politics, Big Mike and Catherine and the coun-cilman all go way back. We stole some empty chairs from neigh-boring tables, and the six of us sat and drank and smoked and talked, but we hadn't said much when we heard a loud, sur-prised man's voice call Big Mike's name. The man, a physician, and his wife approached the table, and then Catherine yelled in shock—the doctor was her cousin. Obviously, they go *way* back. Somehow we squeezed in more chairs, for them and for a couple they had met earlier, a man who owns a bakery in South Philadelphia and his wife.

With these additions the noise level at our table was increasing geometrically, and we could barely hear the handsome congressman, whose district includes South Philadelphia, when he stumbled upon the group, recognized several of its members—they all, needless to say, go way back—and began shouting hellos, shaking hands with the men, and kissing the women. He had two guys with him, so there were suddenly thirteen of us at what had been, just minutes earlier, a quiet table of two. We were drowning out every conversation in the room. We'd dragged over so many armchairs that the waitresses could no longer make their way around us, so they began using alternate routes and frowning conspicuously. Bedlam.

At this point I remember wondering: What does it mean that at an event celebrating how completely we Immigrant-Americans have entered the ruling class, we're all huddled together like a tribe? It's like they say in southern Italy and think in southern Philadelphia, *Moglie e buoi dei paesi tuoi*—marry and buy cattle from your neighbors. Whether we think so or not, whether we want to or not, we all go way back.

• • • It makes perfect sense that the most sublime incarnation of Tonelli-American, the absolute vanguard on the trajectory from *then and there* to *here and now,* the ultimate synthesis of the blood and the dream, is a woman, a southern Californian, and half German. (And so tall, slender, blond, blue-eyed, graceful, beautiful, successful, brainy, warm, and an expert cook.)

A few blocks from the beach in Venice, behind a wooden gate with a cutout heart, is where I find Edith Ann Tonelli—Dee Dee—who is forty-three, educated at Vassar, and until recently a steady entry in *Who's Who* as the director of the Wight Art Gallery at UCLA, one of the best jobs in American museumdom. She grew up in western Massachusetts and is the daughter of

The Amazing Story of the Tonelli Family in America

Albert and Pearl, whom I had visited for lunch at their house in Florida.

We sit down with cappuccino while her second husband, Robert, looks after their blue-eyed, blond-haired adopted son, Jonathan.

"As soon as my grandparents died," she starts in, "we stopped hearing Italian spoken. My father wanted us to speak English only. My sense was that my father wanted us to be American. He wanted us to be able to 'pass.' But I really didn't have a sense that I *was* Italian until I went to Vassar. That's when I started not telling people my last name. And my first name, Dee Dee, was like Buffy, anyway. So I *could* pass. But I was from sort of a lower-middle-class Italian-American family, and I didn't know anything about politics and connections. I knew I didn't have as much money as the other girls at Vassar, but I didn't know about networking and all that. I had been president of the student council in high school and head of this and that, so I just walked into Vassar and said, well, I could be president of this, too, and I just went about it in the way I had done it before. But it was like everybody already had their connections, and I was like this wild card. Of course I lost the election, but that's when it began to dawn on me about Vassar.

"And then, for Easter vacation, I went home with a friend to Connecticut, you know, Darien, that kind of thing. We're having Easter dinner, but there's a lot of tension at the table. Her brother was supposed to be home, and a place was set for him, but he's not there. This very proper WASPy family, and finally the mother is about to burst into tears, and her husband says, 'Please try to control yourself,' and she says, all teary, 'I can't believe our son's going to do this to us.' Anyway, it turns out that the son was engaged to an Italian girl and they were totally upset. They even used phrases like *'I can't imagine—we'll have greasy-haired grandchildren.'* The whole thing. And of course they didn't know my last name. They just assumed I was one of her Vassar friends. And I just sat there at this dinner table, and then my friend bolted from the table and grabbed me and said, 'Well, we're done eating.' She was totally terrified. And I think she was nervous about having me as a friend, too. I mean, this was the way she had been brought up, so while she liked me and was embarrassed by her parents, she was also nervous about me. And that was hard for me. So that was my first year at Vassar, and it wasn't fun and games. The ethnic stuff was pretty heavy there. This was in '67."

"All that 'ethnic stuff' was just what your father hoped you would transcend," I say.

"Yeah, and he was delighted that I could sit at the table with these people and that I could be at Vassar. I've always felt I was the son in the family, the one who was more independent. I mean, I'm the one who got up and moved away. My sisters both went back home. They tried to move away, but they had real emotional difficulties doing that. But my dad wanted a son. My mother and I have talked about that. I was the one who played the accordion, and I was the one who took over the restaurant he owned and learned to cook. I had always been by his side there. I was his sidekick. I learned to do everything the way he did it. He really in some ways had hoped I would take over the restaurant. And my first husband and I did, for a while, help out there.

"I had met this sort of WASPy Princeton guy while I was at Vassar. It was like my mother's dream come true—Steven Fenwick. Blond hair, blue eyes. The only problem was that when I came home with him, he had a ponytail and didn't wear socks. It was '68, and we were both, you know, radical, and civil rights, and feminism. So it didn't *quite* fit the dream. But we were wonderful companions, marching on Washington together. I kept my name, too. My parents just couldn't figure it out, especially my mother. She was horrified. For years she wrote to me as Mrs. Steven Fenwick. He loved my family. He didn't have much of a close family. Even after we got divorced, he would call my mother to talk. He says he still misses the Tonelli stuff, you know, on the holidays."

I ask, "Did you keep your name for feminist or ethnic reasons?"

"It was feminism, but it was also about ethnicity. I said, 'I'm not going to hide this. This is not something to hide.' I had tried that already at Vassar."

The Amazing Story of the Tonelli Family in America

"Wait," I say, "you actively tried to hide it?"

She smiles. "Initially, I tried to have girlfriends who had money, but it clearly didn't work for me. It was hard for me to accept their values and the things they said. Their upbringing was pretty straight and traditional, conservative, politically. They were different—just how they dealt with other people, or whether they wanted to associate with people who were ethnically different than they were. As long as I played their game, I was OK—I was smart, and in the arts, and they related to me in that way. And I didn't look different than they did. But there were always these comments, like how the clubs they belonged to didn't allow different people. My first husband's club at Princeton was still restricted—they had black waiters only, and certain rules. When I started at Vassar we had demitasse after meals and you had to wear a skirt. I think I bought into it the first couple of years, trying to get into that world and denying a lot about my background. I didn't bring people home for holidays. I was ashamed. I was embarrassed. When I first brought Steven, my ex-husband, home, I really tried to warn him, these were real family types: they ate and they drank and didn't worry about manners so much, and they didn't worry about the way things looked.

"The irony of my life is that I became so conscious visually, with studying the arts and everything, and I grew up in a house that was very chaotic and—now I have white walls and not much around the house because I need that. I grew up with *lots* of stuff, and I love going home, I embrace it, but for a while there . . . I would go to other people's homes and see they were very different, and part of it was economic, but part of it was just style. There was a different style, our home was like—as long as the food was good and everybody was having a good time, who cared what the china looked like? So I was beginning to operate in different worlds, and I wasn't sure I could bring all of me to them. And that's an issue I've had in a lot of my life. Could I be as Italian as I want to be? Even now, becoming a psychologist, in some ways it has been a chance for me to just be who I am. Part of what that world's *about* is accepting the whole being. So I'm required as a therapist to bring all of who I am to the room, and I need to accept everyone around me. And it's kind of a relief to me, in some ways, because both being a woman and being an Italian in my career has not always been an advantage."

"And when did you accept who you are?"

"I don't remember," she says. "It was late '68 or early '69, one of the marches in Washington. I went in a big busload of people. Antiwar, or civil rights—maybe it was Cambodia bombing? We used to go to marches fairly regularly. And I was on this bus, and then we were in Washington sleeping in the parks, and one time we were all around the Washington Monument, and everybody broke out singing 'We Shall Overcome.' Like two hundred thousand people. And I looked around and saw every kind of person, and it was something really powerful, and I was part of that something, and it seemed important to accept all these people as well as myself. My attitude toward who I was was that I wanted to accept *me*. Because here's the place where we all come together. There was something about that experience, I remember. I sort of re-accepted myself. Coming from a little town like Westfield, we were *all* accepted. We were all ethnics. Then at Vassar it was different. But halfway through there, I realized it was *OK* to be different. That I wanted to accept that I *was* different."

"Was that a big deal for you?"

"Yeah. Yeah. It was emotionally difficult. When I went to Vassar, I remember sitting in the library—Vassar has one of those big gothic libraries—and I said, 'What am I *doing* here?' I felt like if they ever found out who I was, . . . I felt like I had sneaked in. Even with my blond hair and blue eyes, I had that sense of not belonging. And I'd never experienced feeling like an outsider. To walk into that and feel the power and the strength—you walk into the gates of Vassar and it says 'Do Something Significant'—to realize what that power structure's *about*. So I felt like I couldn't be who I was if I was going to succeed. And my parents wanted me to succeed, and *I* wanted to succeed. I had to get out there in the world and really *do* something. It was hard. I had never been away from home. I didn't even get to sleep over at other kid's houses. My parents kept us close. Being away from home wasn't comfortable for us. But I had this feeling that I had to get away, which was different from what my sisters felt. It hasn't been easy for me to be away from my family. There's something I miss. But there was something else, too. Part of the reason I got married so young the first time—I got married four hours after I graduated—was because I needed a way to get away from home that was legitimate. I decided that if I was going to make it on my own, I had to be away from my family. I made that decision then, and I continue to make it. There was so much difference between their lives back home in Westfield and what I wanted for my life. It was pretty political. It took me a long time to reconnect with my family, with my parents, just with the whole scene. I didn't go back to my high-school reunions. I couldn't deal with that environment. And after I got away, it amazed me that I could go back to these people living the way they had always been. For me the war had happened, but even my sisters—their lives were so little touched by the things that were so important to me. So it was hard to reconnect."

"But in a way," I say, "isn't that estrangement from your origins what your father had hoped for himself?"

"In some ways I think, yes, because he married my mother. I think that for him, that meant marrying up. My mother—I've actually heard her say that she married down. Her family, at least, felt that way. I don't know if she felt it. It was the feeling that marrying an Italian was not the kind of thing— she belonged to the riding club, and her mother's expectation was that she'd marry an appropriate person. And I think my father felt very proud of marrying my mother. I never heard him talk about it, but I know *his* family wasn't very happy with the choice either. Partly because she's not Catholic, but also because she's from a totally different world. She's a sweet woman and very accommodating, so they grew to love her, but I think it was unusual, certainly unusual in his family.

"She didn't even want to date him at first, and she said he convinced her that it couldn't hurt to go out with him once. And then when he wanted to marry her, she didn't want to be married to him, and he said, 'Look, I'll wait as long as it takes,' and it was six years later that they finally got married. I think there was something in his mind about making life better for himself, for his family. I don't know how consciously, or what his dream really was. He joined the riding club; he somehow got into the club that she belonged to. That was *definitely* not something that somebody from his family would normally have done. And sort of sadly, I think he was very disappointed when I left the museum job at UCLA and started my new career in psychology, because I think he liked that I was in *Who's Who,* that I was making good out there, and I think he felt that somehow my career was gone once I got remarried and adopted my son. It's a little bit sad for me to know he felt that way. He never said so to me, but he said it to my sister, 'Well, her career's shot to hell.' I sensed I was doing something a son wouldn't do. And I do feel that I'm the one who carried the name for him, because he didn't have a son. I live his dream, in some ways."

"What dream will you give to your son?"

"I think that what's been translated to me, in my life, is that what's important is making a contribution to life bigger than just your own life. Whether it's the Tonelli name or what, it's bigger, and I think *that's* what will come down to my son. Even for me there was definitely a feeling that we should go out beyond our own families. It's who *I* am, but it's connected to what my father wanted, too. The values I got from him—he saw me as the hope. If there was going to be a son in the family I was going to be the one. That's the thread in my life. That's something I've never been without."

"But all the ethnic stuff," I say, "won't your son feel that it's like an alien culture?"

"No—he's probably going to feel the Italian part of his life as some warm, wonderful, family side, because Bob's side is kind of cool—he's Russian and Austrian. His parents were divorced, and they're a very fragmented kind of family. It's not like going home to my family, where everybody's there—screaming. We took Jonathan home last Christmas, and he was like—it's a *loud* family—and they were so happy to see him they were yelling. He was totally shocked, and he just looked at me and started to cry. Bob's first experience with my family was tortellini night—it's one of our own traditions—and he said it was like walking into a Fellini movie. Tortellini night is usually two or three days before Christmas. It's when we make the tortellini for Christmas Day, and everybody who can be there comes, and usually we all end up drinking champagne. Aunt Anna makes the dough, and everybody sits there and cuts and makes tortellini. Bob worked the crank machine, to get the dough thin enough. It's a big event, and I always try to get back in time for tortellini night."

"Yeah, I guess, but really, your son will have only the 'fun' aspects of ethnicity."

"I think it's going to be sort of an interesting thing in his life. He's not going to grow up in the compound, like we grew up, where it's so different outside the home than inside. He's going to grow up in a fairly straightforward, middle-class environment. Except that I insist that we do sort of traditional things. Mostly food things. I try to do as much as I can. The other thing is the feeling of being home and eating and being with people, as a social thing. My husband didn't grow up that way—eating, to him, was something you did to live. It's taken him a long time to feel comfortable to finish dinner and just sit there awhile. He's usually up and washing the dishes, and I'm just sitting there talking to Jonathan. The kitchen is the center of this house, and I'm sad about our new house, that the kitchen isn't quite like this. We really live in the kitchen. I want my son to grow up with as much of that as possible. It's one of the things that makes me sad about living in southern California, that he'll be so far away from the rest of the family. Actually, it's one of my dreams that in our new house we'll build guest quarters, and my parents can live there two or three months a year. Bob's business will keep us here, it seems, but we'd both move back to the East if we could, I think."

"Still, your son won't have any real attachment to all the ethnic stuff."

"No. If I had had a biological child, he might have had more of that. But it wouldn't be the way I had it growing up. The fact that he's got my father's name in the middle of his— Jonathan Albert Tonelli-Raylove—will be of some curiosity to him. But he might just become Johnny Raylove. But I doubt it. I think the Tonelli thing will continue to be a part of him. But it makes me a little sad, that we get farther away from the good parts of our ethnicity, that we somehow become so blended."

"But that's the process of Americanization, isn't it?"

"Right, and that's certainly the way my father sees it. Some people come here and want to stay the way they are, but I don't think that's the way my father wanted it to be."

• • • Still in L.A., out to dinner with Michelle and John and Elissa (all originally of South Philly), Richard and Paivi (England and Finland) and Eve (the only native at the table). Michelle, John, and Elissa can't imagine living in Philly again. Neither Richard nor Paivi can imagine moving back to their homelands either (they both wish they were in New York). Eve, though, can't see herself ever wanting to move from the place of her birth. Lunch next day with Margy, also an L.A. native, who lives up the block from her sister and also can't imagine being elsewhere.

• • • "I was the perfect little Italian-Catholic girl until I was eighteen, and then my folks must have thought that a spaceship came down and switched bodies." This is Debra Tonelli, who is sitting in the living room of a condo in L.A. with her husband, Matt Brown, an accountant of Czech-Norwegian lineage. "Then I went to college, and it was a whole new world. The Doors, the Vanilla Fudge—I saw Hendrix *twice*."

From personal experience as well as from research, I can say that most Tonellis weren't exactly rocking with the zeitgeist during the decade of love. So isn't it funny that the two who were most deeply affected by the 1960s are both female, both now living in L.A.? Debra has probably lived more places than I've *been*. Since she was born forty-two years ago in Bridgeport, Connecticut (her brother is Ed, the Disney World Tonelli), she's lived in a hippie commune ("But I only lasted two days, then this guy rescued me and I moved in with him"), and in Denver, where she went for a vacation from her first husband and ended up staying ("cashed in my return ticket and only went back to sign the divorce papers").

She has coppery hair and blue eyes, and she's wearing a purple shirt and jeans. Debra's a jewelry maker and an artist; in fact, she was one of the workers on Christo's "umbrella" project. "I've followed his career since I saw *Running Fence* in an art history class and was blown away. It was my dream to work with him someday. And then Matt saw a little article in the *Times* about the umbrellas, so I called the reporter and got the office number, and I sent in an application. I even had to write a little essay on who I was and why I wanted to be involved. And then I was picked, and it was *amazing*. The camaraderie! There were these three little towns up in the hills, and we'd walk around in our T-shirts, and it was just like we all *knew* each other. It was this bond! It was like Woodstock. In fact, I called my mom and said, 'I forgive you for not letting me go to Woodstock.' In *fact,* I called Matt on the night after we finally opened the umbrellas, and I said, 'Matt, I can die now.' And I was in tears."

Before L.A., Debra and Matt had been living in Nutley, New Jersey. "We were standing out on the terrace," Debra says, "and I told Matt, 'I *really* don't want to be here when these leaves fall.' Plus, Matt was leaving his job, so we could choose where we'd live. He wanted to go to Denver, and at one time I could have done it. But I don't do winter anymore. And he had business contacts here, and although I had never been here before, I said, 'Yeah, yeah, let's *go*.' "

And it's going fine, they say, except for the distance from her family in Florida and her brother Paul, who still lives in Bridgeport. "I'd be a lot happier if I were around them," she says. "They're my closest friends, aren't they, Matt?"

"They're a great support group," he says. "With my family, it's a whole bunch of individuals, and I think I always sought out friends or girlfriends with families that would just draw me in. I'd seek out these emotional, affectionate families."

"He admits he has more fun with my family," Debra says.

"Yes, when I visit my family it's very pleasant and loving but nothing to write home about."

"We just sit there in the living room and eat bad food," she says, grinning.

• • • I'm closing in on Alaska. I can feel the chill; it's a pretty drive from L.A. to San Francisco, but all I can think about is *tundra*. Back in Texas, Paul Tonelli mentioned something about his brother Stanford having to shoot a wolf that was getting too close to the cabin. Or maybe it was a bear—maybe it was a wolf and a bear. And when I told Stan's mother, Dr. Mary Jo, that I was going to Alaska, she wondered about whether or not the ice had broken, something like that—whatever it was, it sounded dangerous. Until now, all my road worries have concerned either a driving fatality or an ambush by crazed trailer-park desperadoes. But now I'm heading into nature—the scariest thing of all. All my life I've felt safest among my own kind. And nature is *nobody's* kind.

Because I have an early flight tomorrow, I pull into a fancy airport hotel in San Francisco, my poshest accommodations thus far. Back in February I talked on the phone with a semi-retired pharmacist named Bill Tonelli, who lives just minutes away, so I call to invite myself to dinner. His wife Irene says fine, come on over, as long as I don't mind whatever potluck meal she can throw together.

But first it's lunch with the lovely Sandra, whom I've known since we were teenagers. She moved from South Philly out here with her boyfriend about two years ago, loves it now, gets along with her family back home better than ever, doesn't miss much. "But people out here really look down on you if you're from the East," she tells me.

"Sandy," I say, "they're *all* from the East."

"Yeah," she says, "but they try hard to forget it. When they ask me where I'm from and I say Philadelphia—*South Philadelphia*, I always include that—they're like, 'Oh.' Hey, did you see Al Pacino on the Oscars the other night? He was so great! Did you hear how he said he was from the *south* Bronx? I *loved* it!"

• • • Guess what qualifies as potluck at the home of Bill and Irene Tonelli? Crabmeat cocktail, homemade ravioli, roast pork, potatoes and stringbeans, salad, a good California red, and dessert. We're at the table with our hosts, plus their son Randall, his wife Pearl, and Bill's sister-in-law Elsie, widow of his late brother Dino. I'm getting the royal treatment—it still surprises me that people will be so sweet and eager to you just because of a coincidence of surname. Every time I call my mother from the road she marvels at the hospitality I'm finding, until finally I ask her, "Well, if *you* got a call from somebody with your maiden name who was doing a book like this, wouldn't you invite him for dinner?"

"Ohh, I *guess* I would," she replies. I know how her mind works.

"Well, if you had gotten one of the questionnaires like I sent, would you have filled it out?"

"Hmmm," she says. "Maybe—*if* I saw some credentials." I'm not buying it—my own mother would have blown me off, no question. In fact, *I* might have blown me off.

Anyway, *so* relaxed is tonight's dinner (and so preoccupied am I with tomorrow's flight into oblivion) that I'm barely taking notes. Let's see: Bill's the dean of a family dynasty of pharmacists and a genial, active guy—Lions Club, three or four professional organizations, two religious ones, a member (with his son) of the Italian-American Social Club, and an officer of both the Sons of Italy *and* the Stella d'Italia. His father mined gold out here, then went into the bar business in San Francisco after the earthquake of 1906; his two brothers also settled in California, and everybody's had big, successful families. I'm always automatically impressed by anybody of my parents' generation who went to college. It seems unthinkably progressive to me.

At the end of dinner, Irene informs me, "Those potatoes we had tonight were Bill's mom's." I know that Bill is eighty, so

I begin some quick arithmetic when Irene says, "Oh, *she* didn't grow them. But when she died, twenty years ago, I went over to her yard and picked some potatoes and brought them back and planted them in *our* garden."

Dog and outhouse

9.

Justin, Annie, and
Stanford Tonelli

Losing My Place

I can't even consider the possibility that I sub-consciously wanted to miss my flight to Alaska, but I just did—*by ten minutes*—which means I'll have to spend a night in Fairbanks before mush-ing on to my final destination. I call Stan from the airport in San Francisco and wake him up with the bad news. He groggily advises me to stay at the Wedgwood Manor Motel, and also to go to Big Ray's for my wilderness outfit. I'm a spooky flier, so I buy something diverting, *Rabbit at Rest*, to read on the plane. Updike's creation is the ultimate American road warrior—from the first installment to this one, whenever Harry Angstrom's family ties start to strangle him, he jumps in a car and takes off like a burglar. Unfortunately, the entire be-ginning of this book is spent waiting for Rabbit to have his heart attack, so it only intensifies the flight dread.

I get to Fairbanks expecting to find a city, and instead it's an oversized frontier town, lonesome, wide-open spaces covered in dirty ice. The airport's so idle that the motel van can practi-cally come inside the baggage check to get me.

The driver (born in Wisconsin, moved when his soldier wife was transferred here) recommends the Klondike Inn for

Stanford

Justin

dinner and the Lonely Lady topless bar for nightcaps. The Klondike is raucous and noisy, lots of good-natured thumping and cuffing going on. I've never seen so many beards in one room. I sit at the bar next to a tough Indian-looking guy and watch the darts league. The Indian turns out to be Mexican, Cruz, a regular who introduces himself and the barmaid, then disappears into the kitchen so he can make an informed reply to my request for a dinner recommendation (the steak). He met an Alaskan woman in Mexico, came here to visit, and she got him a job in timber. "I've been here one year, Beel, but I'm going back to Mexico. Too cold! This winter we had eighteen straight days thirty below. Cold! Also, not so many women."

One such specimen, in her middle years, spots her son walking in with two young guys in Russian military hats. Turns out they're boxers, in town for the amateur bouts Saturday night. Only the Russians speak Russian, and that's all they speak, so there's lots of signing and overenunciation. The mother yells at the soldiers, "ARE-YOU-GO-ING-TO-BAR-WHERE-WO-MEN . . . ?" then motions with her hands as though she's removing her breasts. The answer's yes; they show up at the Lonely Lady about fifteen minutes behind me. Sure enough, the topless ladies act lonely, and they're not the only ones.

Next day I'm up early and off to the Bakery Restaurant for breakfast. My waitress stares, then says, "I'm sorry, but you look just like my first boyfriend. It's like déjà vu. Are you *sure* you're not from Massachusetts?" Funny, in a state where everybody goes to get away from people, everybody's starved for connections. Sheldon, the motel's assistant manager, runs me into town for my wilderness outfit and the bottle of Canadian whiskey Stanford has requested. Sheldon's family moved here from Minnesota when he was a baby, "but I left for good four times now. You can only take this place for fourteen or sixteen years at a pop." His wife's from Iceland; they had one date in Fairbanks before she left for New York, then she sent him $900 for a plane ticket so he could visit. "I called a friend of mine and said, 'Hey, I just got this money, do you want to go to Vegas?' She asked me where my wife was, and I told her Long Island, New York, and she said, 'Well, you better be careful, that's probably mafia money.'"

(In *Ethnic Options: Choosing Identities in America,* sociologist Mary C. Waters reports that *100 percent* of the non-Italians she surveyed think of the mafia when they think of Italians. As a kid, I'd hear the old-timers complain that all non-Italians thought all Italians were mafiosi, and I'd laugh—it always sounded like such a defensive belief. And then I discover—*they were right.*)

I buy Stanford's jug and a carton of cigarettes easy, but in Big Ray's I might as well be shopping for outer-space wear—I have zero idea of what I'm looking at. With help, lined Timberland boots are a cinch, as are manmade fiber long underwear, insulated gloves, and a very cool black dog musher hat. Think I need something to protect my ridiculously inappropriate bottle-green suede Italian car coat. I'm about to buy a two-piece trash-bag-green rubber rainsuit (suspenders included) when a quick call to Stan dissuades me: He points out that it's not raining.

Two big headlines in the morning paper concern a race car driver killed in a small plane crash and a local story about a snowmobile supposedly possessed by evil spirits. (A year ago its accelerator stuck, killing its original owner, and it almost did the same thing to its second owner a week ago. The villagers fixed the problem: they set the machine on fire.) Lively omens, but what do they mean? Cab to the airport, a big fat driver with a long beard complaining about the forty-below winters. " 'Course, if we had milder winters and warm summers, we'd be up to our armpits in people. We'd be . . . *California!*" That's Alaska: A place where California is the symbol of overcrowded, uptight civilization gone amok.

As things turned out, Stan decided against flying into Fairbanks to get me (*thank you, Jesus*), so I had to make other arrangements. The woman at Frontier Airlines suggested I get to the airport an hour early, but the departure area is an office the size of a restroom, and the plane is parked right outside the door. They just want you to get in a full hour of dread before you take off. Good thing I skipped the rainsuit and hid the dog musher hat in my bag—when I walk inside I find a roomful of Indians in mallwear (leather jackets, sweaters, jeans, and Reeboks). A minute before we board, a Pizza Hut guy rushes into the office. "Hey, you barely made it," says a man who takes delivery of one large pizza. I assume he's going to eat it on the flight, but instead he belts it into the seat next to his. I knew Stan's village, Allakaket, was *out there,* but until I witnessed how you get a pizza delivered, I had no idea.

I hate these little airplanes—I hate any plane where you can sit in the tail and still read the dials on the dashboard. As soon as we're high, I open my eyes and see black land, white snow, frozen lakes and rivers, and miles of jagged mountaintops—no roads, no buildings, nothing human. After fifteen minutes we run out of land, too, and the rest of the hour it's solid white outside. We start our descent, and I can't see anything down there. We're about to land, and I can't see anything down there. We hit the ground, and I *still* can't see anything down here. Wait—there's a barn. A few log cabins almost totally buried in snow. Some people on snowmobiles.

"Who are you waiting for?" an Indian woman asks me. "Stanford Tonelli," I say.

"Stan's out running his dogs. I'm Annie. Come with me." At this point I would normally think to ask, *Annie who?* but in-

stead I grab my bags, climb behind her on the snowmobile sad-
dle, and off we zoom over a path of solid, bumpy snow that
winds past the scattering of log cabins that makes up the village, population around two hundred. I'd have a thousand im-
pressions to report right now were it not that all my concentra-
tion is in my knees and ankles, which are squeezing dents into
the snowmobile, trying to keep me from bouncing off into the
void. Shit, I'm really here. Shit.

• • • Well, the thing about Alaska is that it's actually not so
scary once you're inside. Of course, the ratio of inside to outside
is so small, it's not worth thinking about. Every time you turn
around up here, on the south slope of the Brooks Range, you
see some awesome vista, but you think: *I am a fucking dot.* Still,
my corner of the one-room cabin is homey and A-OK, near the
wood stove, with a curtain around the bed, a reading lamp, and
several small toys (the bed belongs to Stan and Annie's eight-
year-old, Justin). The whole cabin is maybe twenty by twenty
and also holds Stan and Annie's big bed, a sofa, a kitchen table,
some chairs, cabinets, the stove, two TVs, a Nintendo and VCR,
and a deep freeze. Once I'm settled in, Annie and I go outside to
wait for Stan. On their little piece of Alaska there's an outhouse,
a shed, and an oil drum, around which, half-buried by snow, I
can make out a few disconnected animal heads, forelegs and
tails, and some scraps of gray fur—spare parts. Improbably,
there's also a streetlight.

Did you imagine that Alaska would be so *quiet*? Jesus,
when the ravens fly overhead you can actually hear the
whoosh, whoosh of the air pumping under their wings. (That
the birds are as big as cats may have something to do with it.)
Soon the silence is broken by another weird animal noise—
something between barking and screaming bloody murder. I
look down the path, away from the village, and see these dogs,
smaller and scrappier than I pictured, dragging a sleigh
through the snow, and standing heroically at the helm is Stanford . . . Tonelli of the North.

Annie helps him unhitch and chain the dogs to their
stakes, which encircle the cabin, and Stan and I say our hellos

and how-was-the-trips and all that. He's a lean, good-looking guy, mid-thirties, laconic but friendly. He asks if I saw any caribou herds as I flew in, and I say no, but the truth is that it never occurred to me to look. It's my first lesson in survival out here: Pay attention to everything, because everything must count. Fifteen minutes here and I already feel like a useless city boy, so once we go inside I give Stan the bottle *and* my switchblade. Stan likes the knife, flicking it open over and over; *every* man has wanted one since puberty, I bet.

After Justin comes home and we polish off a meatloaf, Stan's friend and neighbor Philip drops by, and we men crack the half-gallon of Canadian Mist. Up here everybody drinks it cut with 7-Up or water—it's called a "mix." The whole idea of me being here amuses Philip, I can tell. When the subject turns to New York he asks, "Hey, Bill, tell me—did you ever sit in on a mafia meeting?"

Justin wants to go to the high school basketball game tonight, and I offer to take him, so the three of us pile on Stan's snowmobile and we're off. Stan deposits us at the gym, which is new and modern, we pay a dollar each to go in, and Justin immediately disappears with his school buddies, leaving me alone on the bleachers, the object, I suddenly realize, of sizable curiosity. One little Indian kid, maybe four years old, stops dead in her tracks, astonished, when she sees me; then she cracks up laughing. Another one races by, touches my hand, and keeps running. It's like I'm suddenly on the wrong end of a National Geographic TV special.

It's between periods, so I step outside for a smoke and am soon ambushed by around a dozen giggly Athabascan Indian schoolchildren, all of whom are shouting the same questions: "Who are you? Where are you staying? Where are you from?" They laugh helplessly at the sound of my name: of all the moments I envisioned this trip might bring, did I ever imagine one of them would consist of me standing on the steps of a gymnasium, on the Arctic Circle, surrounded by a mob of Native American schoolchildren chanting, "Bill Tonelli! Bill Tonelli!"? (Sure I did.)

Then one little girl demands of me, "Guess my name!"

"What's it start with?" I ask.

"*H!*"

"Ummm . . . Heather!" I try.

"Heather?!"

"Harriet?"

"Right! Guess how old I am!"

"What's it start with?"

"*E!*"

"Eighty!"

"Eighty? *Eleven!*" Everybody else takes their turns, too— by the ninth round it's like we've invented a new sport. I've never seen kids so completely lacking in self-consciousness and neurotic shyness. In the middle of all this, a little girl walks up and crooks her finger at me; when I bend down, she touches the end of my nose and says, "Beep!"

The basketball game ends and Justin and I go outside to wait for Stan. The gym is clearing out fast, and the darkness deepens. My thoughts, naturally, run to calamity: What if Stan forgot us? In my mind, it's McCabe and Mrs. Miller Time; one false step and you're permafrost. So I pull Justin out of his group of buddies wrestling in the snow and tell him we're going to a house maybe fifty yards away to call Stanford at home. Like any kid, he's willing to go along obediently with whatever fool-ishness an adult suggests. We walk maybe twenty steps into the night when I look down at him and it hits me like an electric shock: *I grabbed the wrong kid.*

Well, look, I've known him for all of three hours at this point. Plus he's bundled up in a hat that covers half his face. Plus, to my eyes, these Athabascans look more alike than not. I see it all in a flash: Millions of miles from home and reliable legal counsel, in the middle of the most alien environment I've ever known, I have just kidnapped a small boy.

• • • OK, as it turns out I did *not* grab the wrong kid. But honest to Christ, for a second there all I could think of was how those other villagers torched an innocent snowmobile. We make it to a telephone, call Stan, and he comes to fetch us straight-away. As we pull up to the cabin, I notice that the streetlamp is broken.

"Hey, Stan," I say, "your light's out."

"I know," he says nonchalantly. "I shot it."

What next? I feel like I'm sinking fast, drowning in differentness—I'm losing my place. Stan, Philip, and I have one more mix together and talk about the strange paths that bring people to Alaska. "See," Philip says, "for me it's very simple. I was born here. I live here. I die here."

Well, *that's* a feeling I know well, but I'm too far from home to make the connection. And I feel like I'm about to die here myself, so I go to bed. From outside the curtain Stan says, "Uh, Bill, if you hear any noise during the night and it's a bear, the gun's over here." Got it, Stan—if I hear a bear I'll shoot myself.

• • • The trick to sane traveling, I think, is to give yourself over to the experience while always remembering who you were before you got there. And I was somebody who doesn't shit in a closet, so even before I arrived in Allakaket I made the decision that I would not use the outhouse. There is, however, something completely exhilarating about waking up, walking two steps out the cabin door, whipping it out in the brisk morning air, and taking a breezy Alaska leak into the snow.

In the subsistence life-style, owning and feeding thirteen dogs is a real luxury, but Stan's got it down to an economical science. Still, it requires a lot more work than opening a couple of cans. Saturday morning we go outside, and he disappears into the shed. I watch as first the head, then the rest of a frozen caribou carcass emerges, followed by Stan, who's got it by the hindquarters. I peek inside the shed and there, stacked like lawn chairs, are three more caribou stiffs. He drags today's victim over toward the house, near the large oil drum and another one, cut down to about a foot high. He puts some logs into the small drum, douses them with gasoline, and throws in a match. Then he puts the big drum on top and throws in some snow. Using a chain saw, he detaches one of the caribou's hind legs, skins it with a knife, and cuts the meaty part into pieces with an ax. The frosty red chunks go into the drum, along with some sludgy orange salmon oil (all protein) from a can, cereal, and some beaver parts that were just hanging around anyway. The youngest dog, a fuzzy vanilla-colored pup who roams free, grabs the flappy beaver tail. It hangs from his mouth like a giant black tongue. He toys with it a minute, then begins eating it.

The dogs' stew will cook all day, so Stan and I go inside for our breakfast, which he also cooks (bacon and eggs). There's basketball on TV—up here there's only one channel, which comes from a satellite, and all it seems to carry is basketball.

Stan, you may recall, is the son of mystery man Jerry Ybarra, who one day just assumed the name Tonelli. I visited Stan's brothers, Paul and Brad, and mother, Dr. Mary Jo O'Dell Tonelli, back in Texas. Stan split that state and roamed awhile; he was working as a ranch hand in Nevada when he met Annie, who was the bookkeeper.

"By then I was burned out on Nevada," Stan says once breakfast's done and we settle in on the sofa. "It was economically depressed, and I liked to travel. I thought Texas would be too much of a culture shock for Annie. Too hot, too. So we drove this little Datsun pickup truck up to Alaska. We only had three hundred bucks on us, so she showed me how to do beadwork, and we did it on the way. When we got to Fairbanks, we sold the beadwork to pay for the airfare up to here.

"It used to be really rough up here. Used to be rampant binge drinking. I mean *weeks, months.* Yeah. And suicides. I didn't expect that. I'd never seen anything like it. I must have lost ten buddies. But then it just stopped, the binge drinking and the suicides."

Justin reaches over the back of Stan's chair and grabs his father's head.

"Hey, Dad, is it eleven yet?"

"Yeah—past."

"I guess I'll go, then."

"Get a good movie."

"Star Wars!"

"No!"

"OK—*Arachnophobia*!"

"Yeah!"

Justin runs out. "I was expert at hunting and fishing

when I moved here," Stan goes on, " 'cause I did a lot of it in Texas with my brothers. I was a good shot. But I'm still learning how to *live* here. Like you're twenty-five miles out and you cut yourself and you can't stop the bleeding. What do you do? So you have to learn there's a pitch from a certain pine tree that'll stop it. There are a million things like that you have to learn. How to dress—if it's forty or fifty below and you're dressed too warm, you'll start to sweat, and you'll freeze up. So that's the hardest part. See these? These are moccasins made of caribou. That's what you have to wear when it's real cold. We cut the fur, tan the hides, and sew them. I'm getting a master's degree in survival. I can survive in the woods. But it's *hard.* Every lesson is hard, and you have to go through a lot to learn it.

"Lucky for me, Annie's family is pretty mellow, and they took to me. Everybody here is like an extended family. But when I got here, I made it hard on myself. The way I grew up, success means having a good job, having money. Here, all that means *nothing.* Here being a success means you can hunt, you can fish, you can take care of yourself. I had to change my way of living and thinking."

There's something undeniably heroic about Stan, even romantic. He's kind of like the Tonelli Kevin Costner in *Dances with Wolves* as he honors the native ways and struggles to master existence. But all I can think is, Jesus, *what's the point?* Even Annie ditched this place the minute she could. "I went to the university, in Fairbanks," she says. "Then, on a lark, I applied to a college outside of Davis, California, so I just went down. I wanted to see a different part of the country. I didn't intend to come back—it was Stanford's idea. I liked it out there. You can travel just about anywhere by car. Here you have to fly everywhere. And I like the desert in Nevada. I was with some real good people there, who made it feel like home."

So why did Stan choose to live here?

"It's harsh up here," he says, "but out there it's like people are just *mean.* I watch the news, and it only confirms my belief, you know? Once you get free, it's just. . . . After I was here about a year, the old-timers said, 'You're never gonna leave.' They can see things like that. But I know it seems tough to you. When my mom came up here to visit, we were eating moose head soup—you make it with the tongue and everything, it's delicious. And she said, 'Boy, this is good, what is it?' When I told her, her spoon froze in midair. Once she wrote to the governor of Alaska and told him that I should have running water and indoor plumbing because it's so unsanitary this way. And I told her, 'Mom, I just don't want it. I think it's unsanitary to shit inside the house.' And she couldn't argue with that."

Stan remembers he has something he wanted to show me. A few years back he heard that he had a distant cousin living in Anchorage, "so I called him and said, 'My name's Stanford Tonelli, and somebody told me we're related. Does my name sound familiar to you? And he said, 'No.' So I said, 'Well, how about Ybarra?' And he said, 'Yeah.'" Then Stan's mother sent him photocopies of three long hand-written letters from a woman named Rufina Murillo of San Diego. The letters are family histories of three Mexican-American sisters born between 1878 and 1900. One of the women, Adelaide Rodriguez, took as her third husband a man named Arthur R. Ybarra, who was half-Mexican and half-Italian. They had three sons, one of whom, Jerome, was Stan's father. In the course of Rufina's family history, with no explanation, Jerome's last name changes from Ybarra to Tonelli. Stanford DeWitt Tonelli is listed as one of his three sons. It's a weird document, but it's all Stan has to explain who his mysterious father was and who Stan himself might be. I know that the main reason Stan called me on the telephone back in January was that he thought I might have some clues to share. But I don't, except for a few pages I tore out of the San Diego phone book, the pages that list column after column of Ybarras. So I hand them over.

The original plan for today was that Stan would take me out for a ride on the dogsled, but it's warm (about twenty-eight degrees) and the snow's too wet. So we decide to ride up to Graveyard Lake to see about getting some ducks, or maybe a moose. As we walk past the dogs, Stan points to one and says, "I'm gonna have to kill him."

"How come," I ask.

"He isn't working hard enough pulling the sled. He isn't giving one hundred percent. He's not worth the food I'm feeding him."

"Why doesn't he work harder," I ask.

"I don't know," Stan replies. "Bloodlines."

We take an uneventful trip to the lake. Nothing was moving out there unless you count me—I stepped off the snowmobile and immediately plunged into the snow, up to my ass and still I didn't hit bottom. We head back for dinner, a real Alaskan meal finally, roast moose (it's as dark and closely grained as walnut, and the meat is dense but neither tough nor gamy).

After that we polish off the last of the half-gallon of whiskey. Stan and I look at each other, at the empty bottle, and after a brief consultation we decide to go visit his neighbor, the only other white man living here (like Stan, he married into Allakaket). A man who *may,* in fact, have an extra bottle lying around the house. It is Saturday night, after all.

We get to his friend's big cabin, walk in, and find him and his wife curled up together, watching "Star Trek: The Next Generation" on TV. We have a drink or two, and Stan wanders over to the bowls of food on the kitchen table and makes himself a taco. It's the custom here—food's out, and help yourself. We talk about the usual subjects—dogs, fishing, hunting, fresh water supply. After a while, Stan asks his friend if he has any extra whiskey to sell—the going rate up here is fifty dollars for a quart bottle—but he doesn't, though he offers to give Stan a small juice bottle full of vodka. Stan accepts it, but he's determined to complete tonight's mission, so we hop onto the snowmobile and head back out into the night.

At our next stop there are several people but no whiskey at all; we visit a spell anyway. On the TV, "Star Trek" is ending and a call-in show, "Tax Talk," begins. Stan introduces me around, giving my three most impressive credentials (in order): I brought him a switchblade knife; I went to the Lonely Lady topless bar in Fairbanks; and I work at *Esquire* magazine in New York. One of the women there, Irene, hears that and says, "Holy shit! *Esquire?* I can't believe it. Hey, Bill, tell this to *Esquire:* We need more meat. We get plenty of fish, but we need to be able to get more meat." She's referring to the limits on shooting game that were implemented because of trophy hunters but that affect the locals who hunt to survive. "And tell *Esquire* the white man is trying to steal our land."

OK, Irene—I'll tell them to cut it out. Next we visit Floyd, his wife, and their brood, who are all cuddled under a huge blanket, watching the second half of "Tax Talk." A big, genial guy, Floyd brings out some homemade smoked salmon jerky, but he has no whiskey, so the three of us have a mix from Stan's little bottle. Now he has less than he had twenty minutes ago. We men sit at the table and talk for a bit. By this point in the night my memory has begun to fade, so I can't say what about, but it was animated and friendly.

OK, time to mush. We pull up outside the cabin of one of Stan's closest friends, Banjo, who might know some reliable sources of whiskey. But his snowmobile's missing—borrowed, no doubt, by a relative, a theft up here would be unimaginable. He takes Stan's fifty dollar bill and goes off on Stan's snowmobile, while Stan and I wait, have a mix, and watch the start of "The New Untouchables" on TV. Soon, Banjo comes back empty-handed. Resigned, we finish off the juice bottle. Then Stan rises from the sofa and goes outside for a cigarette. He comes back in a minute later.

"I ralphed," he announces, grinning and swaying in the doorway. "I blew chunks."

Goddammit! I was afraid of this. *I'd* be drunk by now too, if the idea of riding back to the cabin in that state hadn't scared me sober. But Stan has no such inhibition. In fact, he's suddenly in a hurry to drive home—he wants to catch the end of "The New Untouchables."

• • • Well, we made it back just fine, but next morning I step outside and there's an ominous sign: it's snowing. Annie hears from a neighbor that there may not be a flight out today. I'm going to be a weather hostage. I may never come out alive. Standing outside as the flurries fall, Stan and I have one last conversation; I'm still trying to understand what holds him here, and he does his best to explain, but I think I'll never get it.

Something *does* occur to me, though, thinking back to last night when Stan and I went so freely, amid such nonchalant hospitality, from cabin to cabin. I realize today what it reminded me of: When I was a little kid, I'd walk with my father the five blocks back to the street where he grew up, and we'd enter one house after another, never ringing a doorbell, seeing his parents and his sisters and his cousins and old friends (and the cousins of old friends, and the friends of old cousins). We'd visit his in-laws, too, my mother's relatives, since everybody lived within a block or so of each other. It was like a route my father was covering—it was like his rounds. It was a reminder, for both of us, that there was one place in the world where we unquestionably belonged. I'll never take that kind of walk again, it occurs to me this morning. Probably no American Tonelli ever will, save one: Stanford, a lucky man after all, who has found the traditional comforts and protections that go with membership in an ethnic group—the clannish Athabascan Indians, in the ancient village of Allakaket, on the vast, indifferent Arctic Circle.

• • • Fly over the frozen Yukon—God, I love the sound of that—into Fairbanks, where I return to the Wedgwood and proper plumbing. After a shower I collapse and watch TV, *The Robe* with Richard Burton and Victor Mature, the first reminder that today's Palm Sunday. I fall asleep almost instantly, and suddenly I'm at some kind of EST-like human potential event that's noisy with the most ridiculous psychobabble ever heard. All I want to do is split, but then I'm in a small room, alone. In walks a skinny, intense, angry little guy, obviously the boss guru. I think he's pissed because I want to leave. I stick my hand out and say, "I'm Tonelli, I guess you are, too." "No," he spits back. "I'm Spielberg. I'm Michael Jackson. I'm Einstein." *That* wakes me up in a hurry. I'm through with Alaska. I can't wait to get back—not to my home, to my car, to the road.

Look, *I* know it: As adventure goes, this is chickenshit. But as chickenshit goes, this is an adventure.

Paul Tonelli

Ron, Calistera, and daughter
Christine Tonelli

Paola
Tonelli

Dante Tonelli and
family

Dan Tonelli

Nancy Tonelli

Leroy and son
Stephen Tonelli

Restaurant
sign, Napa,
California

Mark Tonelli

Joe Kwong-Tonelli

Gina Tonelli

10.

The Passion of Santa Rosa

Even before I see him, I hear him. I'm stuck in traffic heading from San Francisco down to San Jose, trying to get to KSJO-FM's studio before ten o'clock so I can watch Paul Tonelli and his partner, Lamont Hollywood, finish their morning drive-time show. They're of the wacky DJ school: I learned of Paul's existence in a newspaper story about the time the station dangled him from a crane over a highway. On the radio I hear them announce some kind of regular feature, a battle of the sexes trivia quiz:

"It's pee-pees versus ta-tas!" says Paul.

"Bulges versus boobs!" says Lamont.

Who says we're not a highbrow family? Lamont announces, "Some guy from *Esquire* magazine is coming here today to do a story on Tonelli."

"Yeah, and I'll do him proud," Paul says. "Of course, if he's a Tonelli, he won't be here until ten-thirty."

He's almost right, but then this infernal California crawl eases, and I arrive at the station's corporate campus home just in time to catch their last five minutes. Paul's an athletic-look-

133

The Amazing Story of the Tonelli Family in America

ing guy with dark curly hair and a mustache, sweatshirt, jeans, and sneakers—he could pass for a gym teacher—standing at one microphone; his lanky, WASPy looking partner sits behind the console. There's something funny about two guys announcing at each other across such a small room.

A song comes on, and Paul flips off his headphones and says, "Here's my story. I applied, after college, for a job at UPS, which has a long orientation period that ends with a driving test. I knew a UPS supervisor in San Francisco, and I had him take me out so I could get a little practice driving the truck. And I did fine—no problem. Then they take me out for my official test, and I have to make a turn on this little narrow street in San Francisco. And I clip a parked car—dent the fender and smash the taillight. Disqualified. I'm out. That was on a Friday, and on Monday I got a call from a news director I had done an internship for, and he was offering me a ski report job, which eventually led to the job I have now. So it's funny—if I hadn't hit that car, I wouldn't have this job."

"Wait a second," I say, "do you mean that if you had been hired as a UPS truck driver, you wouldn't have taken the radio job?"

"Well, I couldn't really take another job on my first day at UPS," he reasons. "Besides, UPS was looking pretty good to me."

Paul switches back to his on-air voice—"Hi, KSJO, Lamont and Tonelli on the air, who's this?"—just as his brother Jerry shows up. Then the show ends, and we pile into Jerry's black Camaro and head out for breakfast.

Here's my first Tonelli joke, thanks to Jerry, once we're seated at a restaurant: "Guy walks into a bar when he sees a sign that says Gentlemen must wear ties. Except he doesn't have one, so he goes out to his car, gets his jumper cables out of the trunk, ties them around his neck, goes back in, and says to the bartender, 'Is this OK?' And the bartender says, 'Yeah, you can come in, but don't you start anything.' "

I had met their mother, Elsie, when I had dinner with Bill and Irene Tonelli the night before leaving for Alaska. Their late father, Dino, was Bill's younger brother. Bill and Dino were pharmacists, as are Bill's son Randall and Jerry—everybody but Paul.

"I thought it would be a good career opportunity," Jerry says of his decision to work at the pharmacy. "It was an established business. And I *liked* the business. The only other thing I was interested in was cars, but I didn't want to sell them. And fixing them didn't seem like much of a career. It's funny, you grow up with the normal father-son relationship, and you don't know when you start to work together how it's going to go. But it turned into a real good friendship. You know, when you're a kid your father just tells you what to do, and then it became more of a peer thing between us."

"So instead of telling you to do things, he asked you," Paul says.

"Yeah," says Jerry. "And I'd say no, and then he'd *tell* me to do it."

Paul had worked in the family pharmacy, too.

"The customers all still remember him and like him," Jerry says.

"But I just felt like I had to give radio one shot," says Paul. "And even then, it almost didn't work out."

"Did you tell him the UPS story?" Jerry asks.

Paul's partner Lamont shows up at the restaurant, and we're talking across the table when I hear Paul ask Jerry, "Is your wife any part Italian?"

"No, she's French and Portuguese."

"See," says Paul, "and if I marry the girl I'm with now, she doesn't have any Italian in her."

Jerry holds his fingers an inch apart and says, "Well, she has a *little* Italian in her."

Everybody laughs.

"This is a tough crowd," says Paul.

● ● ● For proof that I'm not the only one hung up on ethnic matters, try this any Sunday: Pick up the *New York Times* and realize that nearly every international story is about ethnicity. On today's front page Afghanistan is breaking apart, being partitioned into three autonomous nations. The Uzbeks and the Tajiks, who make up one-third of the population, will get their own chunk of real estate; a second piece will be run by the Pathans, half the population; a third region, to the west, will be ruled by Muslim Afghans with close ties to Iran. (Could *you* tell an Uzbek from a Pathan? Me neither, but don't say that to a Tajik.) It seems too obvious to mention that the Serbs and the Croats are still going at it, but of course they are. So are some rival Chinese clans: "Like many villages in China, Pan Shi is made up of a single clan, so all the men have the same surname and feel a sense of kinship that often extends into a network of connections that extends outside the village," according to the article. Pan Shi was founded two hundred years ago by the Mai family, who originally came from Xing, a neighboring town they shared with the Li clan. Of course, the Mai and the Li couldn't share peacefully, so some Mai guys fled and started their own village. And *still* they're fighting. "No one knows why it's this way," says a Li woman. "It doesn't make sense. Our life is better. It's stable. People are educated. Maybe we won't fight again." *Can't we all just get along?* Fat chance. Some villagers have hit on the one surefire way to escape the madness— they emigrate, to Macao, Canada, or the United States. That's why America exists: History *needs* America. The world would have blown itself up long ago without America.

One page later, I see that the cabinet of India has quit to allow the government to respond to something called "communal strife," which just means that neighbors with everything in common except for a little religious training are killing each other. Secular Hindi there allowed some religious zealots to raze a mosque, and the fighting that followed claimed more than seventeen hundred lives. How did these madmen get the reputation in the West for possessing vast spiritual enlightenment? Crazy. In the West, killing for God went out of style years ago. Same page, Sri Lankan rebels blew up their own weapon ship when it was surrounded by Indian Navy vessels. The rebels, who operate under a cool name, the Liberation Tigers of Tamil Eelam, have been fighting since 1963 to establish a homeland for the country's Hindu Tamil minority.

And that's just one day's paper. Multiply that by three

hundred and sixty-five, and throw in all the ethnic strife that doesn't fit into the *Times*. It's more common than rain, I bet, more common than love—ethnic hate makes the world go 'round.

● ● ● "We're muffin people!" Donna Black sings. Wait, how did she get in here? She's the Nebraska-born but quintessentially California (blond, sunny outlook, incandescent teeth and eyes, great body) girlfriend of Dan Tonelli, and we're discussing their culinary habits because we're headed out to lunch. "We're practically vegetarians!"

By contrast, Dan, who was born here in Oakland, is a fairly unimposing physical specimen (quiet, dark-haired, bony, eyeglasses, thirty-four years old). "But I'm going to tell you something about this man," Donna blurts once we're seated. "This man is an incredible bicycling machine! Did you show him the article from *Bicycling* magazine?"

No, he didn't, he admits, but it turns out the magazine featured Dan in an article titled "Mileage Junkies," commemorating his racking up twenty thousand miles in one year.

"In 1988, my best year ever, I put in twenty-one thousand three hundred and sixty-five miles," he says. "That's including riding New Year's Eve *and* New Year's Day. The weather was good that year—that was the peak of the drought."

"This man has legs you wouldn't believe," Donna says. "If you think Rudolf Nureyev had legs. . . . "

"In 1986, '87, '88, I was on the road three hundred days a year. Now, every weekend day is still only one hundred and four days a year, so, as you can tell, I was doing a *lot* of riding. I'd do five hundred miles a week for weeks on end, until I was exhausted, and then I'd do a four-hundred-mile week to rest up."

I ask him, "What must your social life have been like?"

"None. Zero. I was too tired. I *lived* on my bike. I'd work, ride, go home and collapse. Until I met Donna my social life was a dry spell. I'm not talking weeks, or months, I'm talking a *decade*. Sure it bothered me. But the more it bothered me, the more miles I put on." Lucky for him, Dan met Donna at his bicyclists' club, and now they ride together.

His grandfather came here from Italy, but Dan says he doesn't know why. "I imagine for better economic opportunity. They were starving to death, from what I understand." The family settled in Santa Rosa, up north, a Tonelli hotbed, then moved to the Bay Area. "But I don't know *who* my relatives there are," he says. "I don't know their names. I don't know what they look like. I've never met them. I think there was some kind of estrangement, if you know anything about Italian families."

The waitress comes by to get our dessert orders. We're having lunch in a restaurant owned by the ice-cream company where Dan works as the computer whiz and general-ledger man, so I ask him for a recommendation.

"Actually," he says, "vanilla is my favorite."

The ice cream arrives and reminds me of something Dan wrote on his questionnaire about the difference between Italian-Americans and everybody else.

"We're not at the point where the more recent immigrants, like the Vietnamese, are, like a distinct group," he says when I ask about it. "I'm speaking of California, now—we don't have distinctly Italian neighborhoods or any of that. I think most ethnic groups have pretty much—let's put it this way: If you can look down the street and you're unable to tell Italian-Americans from anybody else, they've *melted*."

• • • That same Sunday *Times's* first *national* news section story is also about ethnic strife, it turns out: Arizona is hoping it can improve its image by finally establishing a holiday for Martin Luther King. In 1990, people there voted against making the holiday official, and the state lost almost $200 million in cancelled convention business and another $150 million when the Super Bowl moved to Pasadena. In Sri Lanka, we'd be tearing each other's hearts out and eating them, but here—thank God—we inflict our injuries in dollars and cents.

American pluralism was not an ideal with which people started, Thomas Sowell writes,

> but an accommodation to which they were eventually driven by the destructive toll of mutual intolerance in

a country too large and diverse for effective dominance by any one segment of the population. The rich economic opportunities of the country also provided alternative outlets for energies, made fighting over the division of existing material things less important than the expansion of output for all, and rewarded cooperative efforts so well as to make it profitable to overlook many differences.

• • • "Women Who Have Extramarital Affairs" is the subject of the talk show that's narcotizing everyone in a hospital emergency room waiting area in Richmond, just outside San Francisco. Two days ago I saw a different talk show with the same theme, except on that show the panel had their faces disguised, and today they're out in the open, unashamed. Customs change *fast* on these shows. The waiting room's crowded, but nobody's in obvious agony; all the blacks are on one large semicircular couch, the one closer to the TV, and all the whites are on the other.

A young, clean-cut doctor pokes his head out and calls me into an examining room.

"I always wanted to get out of Denver," Dr. Mark Tonelli is saying. "Everybody knew, my folks always knew. And I think it's been good for my marriage and for our evolution, to be away. But still, it's a big pull—everybody's still there. My father left Joliet, Illinois, to take a job in California, so he understood the appeal. But when you meet him, you'll see that the hardest thing for him is not having all of his family around him."

When he hears I'm going to visit his folks and six brothers and sisters in Colorado, Mark suggests that I go on a Friday night—Pizza Night.

"Pizza Night is funny because it's a tradition that started a year or two before I left Denver," he says. "It only really started when everybody began moving out of the house. Then people would start showing up at my parents' house at random times to eat their food. So they decided not to cook on Friday nights and to order pizza for everybody instead. Now it's not *quite* as frequent as it was—my mom got mad because nobody else was paying for the pizzas. It was more informal when I was there, but then it got to where there was pretty good attendance, and everybody'd show up with spouses and girlfriends and grandchildren. And then we'd play cards or whatever. It got to be like six large pizzas every Friday night. They tried to do it at my sisters' houses, but basically nobody wanted to host it. Nobody wanted their houses trashed by my family."

"And your mother isn't even Italian, is she?" I ask.

"Nobody marries Italians in my family. The men tend to marry blond and Irish. My grandmother's blond and Irish, and so are my mother and my wife. I guess the Irish are the only other big group of Catholics. It's funny, when we're all together we tend to act the way you'd think Italians would act—loud and raucous and noisy and yelling and so forth. But my dad's not like that at all—he's very laid back, taking it all in. My *mother's* the loud one.

"When I grew up I always felt Italian—the name, and the big nose. People'd ask, 'Hey, are you Italian?' and I'd answer, 'Yeah, I am.' But only until I started to travel. When you meet people abroad, they don't care if you're Italian-American. They think of you as *American*. And you *are*. Being Italian-American is something I definitely feel proud of, but I no longer *feel* Italian. It's funny, because my best friend in Denver when I was growing up was Italian. I don't know why, I loved his family, and being with them was very comfortable. And I think I gravitate toward Italian-Americans as friends more than would be expected, statistically. I wonder, is it just because it's easy to break the ice with what we have in common? But with my friend and his family, it was fun, loud—they had a certain way of dealing with people. One thing that drives me crazy with my wife's family is that they're so polite and civilized that it's no fun.

"But I think the Italian part got watered down in me by going to other places and realizing it *did* mean something to be an American. That you definitely *were* different from the French, or the Italians, or the English. And it's not just the way you look, or the language. It's the way you behave. I think my own personal identification—I would always say that I'm Italian, but I don't anymore. I don't speak it—I *cook* it—but I'm *not* it. Now I'm an American of Italian descent. My grandfather always said he was a proud dago, but *his* father never even let them *speak* Italian. He was an American. He had to speak like an American. In a way it's sad to lose that part of your identity. It's definitely less fun, being an American."

• • • Anyway, as Sowell wrote, we overlook "many" differences, but not all, not always, not everywhere. I have a friend named Tom who grew up in South Philly, moved to New York, then moved back home. When he did, he was happy to see that there was an old lady living next door, the self-appointed block watchdog, who kept an eye on his car whenever he was away. Then one day, after several months had passed, he was cooking a steak on the hibachi in his backyard when the doorbell rang; it was the fire department, summoned, Tom felt sure, by the old lady. He believes she turned on him when she noticed (and the old ladies in South Philly notice *everything*—they're radar in baggy stockings) that from time to time he had visits from black people. Tom was a little stunned, but it was plain to me that the old lady was acting consistently—in watching his car and in punishing him over his choice of guests, her impulse was the same: To protect the block from outsiders, *all* outsiders. It worries me a little, that I can so easily understand how that old bitch thinks. I see the benefits of attitudes like hers a little too clearly.

• • • "Can I *cook*?" Gina Tonelli rolls her eyes. "Yes and no. I *hate* cooking." She's twenty-six, lives with her parents just south of San Francisco, pretty, with dark hair and eyes. "But I can clean real good." She works for Randy Tonelli, the pharmacist (I had dinner with him at his father Bill's house the night before I left for Alaska), but they're not related. "I went to an all-girl school, and we were taught that we were the women of the future. When I tell my grandmother, 'My husband is going to have to vacuum' and so on, she can't stand it. In my family, the men do the outdoor stuff, and the women do the indoor stuff. My younger sister, even though her boyfriend can do lots of

142

stuff, she's very domestic. She cooks dinner for him and brings it to him at work."

Gina's a restless, ornery mixture of fierce, modern independence and old-world family closeness (her father came to America when he was eight). Gina drives a black pickup truck—everybody in her family drives pickup trucks. "My brother, he's just *pampered.* He'll be watching TV at night, and he'll ask my mother to bring him ice cream, and she'll do it. My father asks me to do it, and I say, 'No way, get it yourself.' I was out with this guy and I told him, 'I don't cook and I don't do any of that crap.' I told my grandmother and she said, 'You don't *tell* a boy that!' But I don't play any games."

• • • Needing a break from all these Tonellis, I decide to visit my friend Joe Kwong, who works for Colossal Pictures, the famously cool video and animation company. I walk into his office and see that he's wearing a stick-on name tag that says, "Hello, my name is Joe Tonelli." He introduces me to a colleague, whose name tag says, "Hello, my name is Prudence Tonelli." Reeling, I stagger out of the room and come face to face with seventy or so of their coworkers—all wearing name tags that bear the name I thought (so long ago) was mine and mine alone.

• • • I can't wait to hit the Pacific Coast's Tonelli hotbed, Santa Rosa, but I have one more stop in the Bay Area before I can head north.

Paola Tonelli is not Italian-American—she's Italian, born in Parma, came here for school in 1966, studied physics and engineering. "When I first came, I didn't want to be associated with the Italian-Americans I saw, because they were southern Italians, and they spoke broken Italian and were uneducated. I didn't have anything in common with them, and I didn't want to have anything to do with them. Today, Italian things—fashion, cooking—have become fashionable. But when I went to the Milton Academy as a teenager, it was a very fancy place, and being Italian there did not make me feel very special. If I had been French it would have been different. But being Italian, I felt I was being seen as like one of the shopkeepers. Like I came from a Third World country. The bulk of the Italians I met here struck me as not being very Italian at all. They couldn't *speak* Italian. They didn't keep up with what was going on in Italy. They were true immigrants—they came here and never went back."

Paola is an executive for a cellular communications firm in the Bay Area. She's married to an American, George, and they live in an elegant house on the grounds of a country club north of Oakland. We three are in the living room, having polenta and white wine, and we're about to explore the difference between Italians and Americans.

"Well, for example," says Paola, "if you act American, when you're on the street or in an office and you cross somebody's path, you smile. Or if you make eye contact, you say hello. An Italian would never do that. An Italian just keeps going."

"And pushes right by you," says George.

"Well, *no,*" Paola says. "I can't tell you how many times I'll be out walking, not looking around at anyone, and some man will say to me, 'Why don't you *smile?*' I say, 'It's none of your business.' "

"Americans are friendly," says George.

"Well," Paola says, "friendly in a superficial way. Italians don't smile. Italians have sour faces. But that doesn't mean they're not *friendly.*"

"OK, what else?"

"Fashion," Paola says. "The way they dress."

"Can I give an example?" George cuts in. "An Italian woman will spend money at the most expensive store, even—"

"Let me give an example," Paola interrupts. "Two women meet, and one says to the other, 'Hey, nice dress.' If it's an Italian woman, she'll just smile. If it's an American, she'll say, 'Boy, you wouldn't believe how cheap it was on sale.' An Italian would *never* say that. To Italians, the more expensive, the better. And an Italian is never too casual in dress. Italian women would *never* be caught dead in sneakers in the street."

"They wear four-inch heels and two-inch skirts," says George.

"They're not *that* bad," says Paola. "On the other hand, I

think middle-aged American women take better care of them-selves in terms of exercise and health. But that's another thing I'll never understand, the issue of fat. Italians look at Ameri-cans and say, 'Why are so many of them obese?' And Americans look at Italians and say, 'They're so *fat.*' I think the difference is that here, they go to extremes.

"Another interesting difference, from a woman's perspec-tive, is that Italy is a lot friendlier toward women than America is. And that's because, in my opinion, American men don't know how to flirt. They are so worried about what you call sexual ha-rassment. On the other hand, Italian men are more sure of themselves, so they feel free to give compliments without it hav-ing to mean anything more."

"Can I give a rebuttal?" George asks.

"No," says Paola, "I'm not done. And men in Italy are more courteous than men here. Men in Italy *always* hold open a door and *always* stand up when a woman enters the room. But when you live in another country awhile, you lose your identity and you acquire one from the new country. And that's kind of scary. It's encouraging—to know you can change and develop. But it's scary to lose the things you were."

• • • The big story on the "Today" show this morning is Mario Cuomo's announcement that he doesn't want the Supreme Court job. I almost kick my motel TV when I hear the anchorman fill-ing in for Bryant ask the reporter, "Is there something in his background he doesn't want scrutinized?" (I'm so bitter I'll tell you the anchorman's name, it's Matt Lauer, L-a-u-e-r.) You know exactly what he's asking, but even *this* guy's not enough of a moron to think that Cuomo could have committed some impro-priety that's still waiting to be discovered. So his *real* question is, Does Cuomo have some relative or ancestor whose criminal past he doesn't want scrutinized? Of course, *that* wouldn't nor-mally disqualify a federal jurist, would it? No, but come on, let's face it, it's *easy* to picture Supreme Court Justice Cuomo making a midnight phone call to a police precinct in Queens, ordering them to go easy on some button man from the old neighborhood—isn't it, Matt, you chucklehead?

• • • Where I grew up, it was the custom on Good Friday to go to church and visit what are known as the Stations of the Cross, the wall reliefs that depict the scenes of Christ's bloody passion. No way did *I* ever observe that custom, but my distance from home on this holiday makes me sentimental enough to have arranged in advance to be taken on a similar tour—through the northern California city of Santa Rosa, from Tonelli to Tonelli.

First, though, I have to drive a hundred miles up the coast and find a motel with a coin laundry, to catch up on my housekeeping. When I finally make it to Dante Tonelli's house, it's after noon, the hour that custom has decided Christ's ordeal began.

Dante's a retired electrical contractor whose mammoth van is parked out front (his retirement plan was that he and his wife Marilyn would use it to travel, but they haven't yet). We climb aboard and begin our pilgrimage by driving to his cousin Leroy Tonelli's concrete plant (Dante's father and Leroy's grandfather were brothers). I meet Leroy and his wife, Verde; then we all settle in the office, which is lined with photos of Leroy taking part in various golf tournaments.

"Business been slow?" Dante asks.

"It's the shits," Leroy says. "Thirty-one years in this business and it's never been this bad."

I ask him, "How did you get your name?"

"My aunt—my godmother, my mother's sister, she picked my name. I asked my mother once, where did you get—how the hell do you name an Italian kid *Leroy*? It really dawned on me when I was about sixteen. I was, you know, proud of my heritage, and guys I knew would tell me, 'Guido, OK, but *Leroy*?!' "

"Hey, Leroy," Dante says, "do you still play the accordion?"

"I just went to an accordion festival," Leroy says, "and I saw all these paisans playing, and I said, 'Hey, I can play that song.' So I got it out of the closet and had it restored. I spent about four hundred dollars on it, got it back into shape, and I haven't touched it since."

" 'Lady of Spain'!" Dante says.

"Yeah, 'Lady of Spain.' I used to play it. People used to ask me to play at parties, and I would say, 'Look, before I start, I want you to know that what you're about to hear cost my father twelve thousand dollars in lessons.' "

Soon they're talking about the good old days, when everybody was poor, and I ask if either of them worked on farms when they were kids. They both look at me as if I suddenly turned stupid.

"Shit, *yes!*" Dante says. "We *all* did. The work the Mexicans do now, the Italians used to do. That was before welfare—if you wanted to eat, you had to work. I picked hops, prunes, . . . as soon as you were old enough to walk, you picked. You got your clothes to go back to school, and the rest of the money the family pooled."

The subject switches to family longevity; Dante says that his mother was over a hundred when she died.

"That's one thing about the Tonellis," Leroy says.

"They're short-livers," Dante finishes the thought.

"My dad died when he was fifty," says Leroy, "and he was one of the older ones."

"Yeah," says Dante, "heart attack and cancer. I'm sixty-eight. So I beat the odds."

"They had tougher lives back then, of course," Leroy says.

Just then their cousin Barbara (Tonelli) Torrance and her mother, Dolores, appear in the doorway.

Dolores says to me, "I'm going to stare at you awhile to find the Tonelli."

"Did you go to the cemetery yet?" Dante asks.

"No," says Barbara. "We're going to go. I told them to get her place ready." Everybody laughs.

"They're going to have to wait a long time," Dolores says.

Soon they leave for church, and Leroy gives Dante and me a tour of the plant. Then we climb back into Dante's van and head over toward his cousin Rose's house.

"See, Bill, this part of town, west of the tracks, used to be all Italian," Dante says. "Woptown, they used to call it. Now it's just everybody, Mexicans and everything else."

It's kind of run-down, more urban than the rest of Santa Rosa. We park, step up onto Rose's porch, and knock, and an elderly sprite dressed crisply in gray sweater, slacks, and turban opens the door.

"Now," she immediately barks at me, "who are your parents?"

I tell her.

"And where are they from?"

She doesn't mean where in America; she means where in Italy. I tell her.

"Well, we're not connected," she decides.

Inside, Dante and Rose ignore me for a minute so they can catch up on cousins, kids, and other relations. Then Rose turns to me and says, "My mother moved here in 1914. I was with her until I moved to San Francisco. But my mother always kept this house. We lived first on a ranch. And I *think*—I was only four when they bought this—I think my brothers convinced my father to trade some acreage for this house. And my father couldn't get used to living here. He felt penned in after being out on the ranch with the cows. And after nine months he died of a stroke.

"I moved away when I was sixteen. My brothers had stores in Richmond, and they convinced my mother to move there to keep house for them, but she didn't sell this house. Then I got married and I moved to San Francisco. Then my mother was alone, and I moved back here. That was in . . . "

She stops and squints hard. "You don't look like a Tonelli *at all*," she tells me.

"I went to the cemetery and brought flowers today," she tells Dante. "I went to all the graves—seven of them. Then I went to the drugstore. Then I went to the bank. Then I went to the church." She's got to be eighty, but she's as thin and lively as a girl.

"How old is Fred now?" Dante asks.

"My brother's eighty-four!"

"And how's his heart?"

"He's got a bum back! You should see how he walks."

She turns back to me. "I was thirteen when I went to work at the cannery. They employed all the Italians back then. They talk about discrimination now, but back then it used to be something else. They called them dago and wop and every other thing. You know, they had a lot of nerve back then, coming to this country, not even speaking the language. . . . "

"That's why, like the Mexicans now," Dante says, "they come here and don't even bother to learn any English. And they all live together and stay together. . . . "

"So did all the Italians!" Rose says. "They all lived in their little neighborhood. That's why they couldn't learn any English!"

We leave Rose and head back to Dante's house, where his wife Marilyn, daughter Dani, and son-in-law Jack are all waiting. Dante begins telling them how we spent our day together.

"Well, we went to see Leroy at his business," he says.

"What's Leroy's business?" Dani asks.

"Concrete. And we went to visit Rose."

"Who's Rose?"

• • • I wander awhile through Santa Rosa, a sweet little city where Luther Burbank once lived. The many Italians who came to this part of the country were drawn here mostly by farm work, which was what most of them did in Italy. Even knowing that, however, does nothing to diminish my astonishment at the thought of Tonellis on tractors. Downtown features lots of cafés and bookstores peopled with college types, teenage neo-hippies, diesel dykes, a kind of sunny bohemia—like Portland with better weather. People are just prettier in California—all that blood mixing evens out the grotesque faces you find back East.

• • • "I was doing a reading for a lady and I started to go into her past life—I don't know if you believe in that—but I saw her in ancient Egypt, teaching the people something the rulers didn't want them to know."

It's a gorgeous northern California spring Saturday morning, and we're just starting a tarot card reading by Nancy Tonelli, psychic.

"And they started stoning her. I saw her bent over and holding her stomach. And they stoned her to death. And this lady said, 'That's interesting, because I went to see the big King

Tut exhibit a few years ago, and when I got inside the museum, I got severe stomach cramps and passed out. So I left, but the next day I thought I should go back and try again, and I did, but again I got cramps. So *then*—' "

Nancy stops abruptly, like she's switching channels. "I'm going to see your face on TV, I know it," she tells me. "You should be prepared. Get a nice outfit." She's laid-back and sunny and sexy, lives with her boyfriend and her teenage son, who's having his cereal at the kitchen table. After a few minutes she gets out her tarot cards and spreads them out on the sofa cushion between us, the kings face up. "Pick the one you're drawn to," she instructs, and I obey.

"That's the King of Pentacles," she says. "That's the card that represents the monetary part of life. Before we start, remember, you can change anything that the cards see. You can use them as a guideline of what to watch out for. Now, think of a question and keep it in your mind while I shuffle the deck." If we're going to talk money, I figure, we might as well talk about this book. She mixes the cards then stacks them into a neat pile.

"OK, hand me the deck with your left hand." I do it, and she spreads the cards out faceup.

"I'm just going to tell you what comes to mind. If I had to look at the financial picture for your book, I'd say financially it's not a problem. It will be handled well. I *do* feel a real tearing problem with doing your daytime job while you're trying to write at night or whenever. I see a burden, and all your efforts going into this and maybe not so much of your effort and creativity going into your job.

"You've been at that job how long? Four years. Well, because of the book, another job offer will come, from another company, and you'll take it. When you take that job, it will involve a lot of travel. I feel the reason you're doing this book is because it will lead you to where you'll be for the rest of your life. It will open doors, shall I say? After the book . . . I don't see money flowing in right away. I see a delay. When the money starts rolling in, there will . . . I see you with two homes." She grins at me. "*That's* good. One is by the water—the view is absolutely beautiful. You sit in the living room with your coffee and the view is magnificent. Like any other book, its popularity will last for a moment, but it will remain on the shelves. And there will be some kind of spin-offs. And there will be a second book. Have you ever written a book? No. Well, there will be a second book. And it will have to do with travel again, and it will have pictures."

She changes channels. "In your past life you were a doctor, but you were a woman, too. It's funny, one thing about you that stands out is that your ability to listen has carried over from your past life. You *are* a good listener, and in the past people talked to you, but more as a psychiatrist than as a physician. You lived to an old age, people trusted you, but you had no children and no spouse. You were involved in people's lives, though. You were a helper."

A long pause. "Uhhh . . . wow. You're not married now, are you? The woman I see you'll end up with—when you're open to it, when you have that kind of energy—she'll be really beautiful, really classy. You'll meet her at some kind of cocktail party, some kind of function, but not for your book—it's some kind of art opening. Do you go to that kind of event? No? Well, you're going to meet a lot of people as a result of your book, not just Tonellis, so you should be open to that."

She picks up a card, the King of Swords.

"I don't know why this should be covering the card you chose. Is there anyone, kind of a stern person, a brusque person, back at the magazine, who is happy for you but wishes you'd hurry up and get back there already?"

"Very possible," I say.

"Anyway, I see you at a different job." She picks up another card, a lady with cups all around.

"See, this lady looks sad. She's looking at the cups that spilled, but she's not looking at the cups that are still full. Remember that change can be painful sometimes—it can be a pain in the butt—but that's how we grow."

She changes channels. "When I see you in two houses, I don't see a woman with you yet. I see her coming later. The house by the water I see you using for your work. Even though it's close to the water, it's close to where you live now. I see the number forty-five around the house. I can't tell what it means. It could happen in forty-five days, or when you're forty-five. When you go to Reno, play the machine that has the oval that says 'Wild Cherry' on it. I'll tell you an interesting story. Awhile ago four of us were going to Reno, and as we drove in I saw a big number four hovering over the city. I said, 'I bet that by four o'clock I'll have hit a jackpot.' Well, I hit a hundred and twenty-five dollar jackpot, and I looked at my watch, and it was four minutes to four.

"Anyway," she says, "what you'll get from doing this book will be so much more than money. A real growth in your spirituality. I don't mean religion, but your experience. You'll use what you learn in the future with people you interact with. You won't forget the people you're meeting, even if they're only a little sentence in your book. Whether you know this or not, and you'll say I'm crazy, but this is a spiritual journey for you. And the people you're in touch with now you were in touch with in your past life. That woman, that doctor, was a strong soul. And the soul *lasts*."

OK, show's over, we can both relax. Nancy's lived her whole life in Santa Rosa. "I'm born and raised here, and here I am, still. Is that sad or what? No, I do like it here, but . . . maybe it's a midlife crisis, but I'm saying to myself, 'Is that all there *is*?' " She's a bookkeeper for a children's dentist. "And I've been there for twelve years and I'm going *nuts*. I have to get out of that, and I know there's something beyond the dental world."

She looks up at the ceiling and smiles. "Hurry and get here!"

• • • When my friend Tom told me the story about his neighbor the sweet old lady racist, it reminded me of something else: The week my neighborhood was the site of a pitched ethnic war of its own. Nothing to rival the Liberation Tigers of Tamil Eelam, but still. It started with a rumor that a black teenager on his way home from the high school had stolen a bike from a white kid. I never found out if it was true, but I'm sure something had happened—something was *always* happening. The next day some white teenagers retaliated on the heads of some black teenagers. By the day after that, word of the exchanges had spread, and when I arrived at the corner where my friends and

The Amazing Story of the Tonelli Family in America

I normally loitered, more or less peacefully, I walked right into a mob of maybe fifty young white guys, most of them strangers, many of them bearing baseball bats, chains, etcetera. My friend Albert opened the trunk of his car so that his golf clubs could be loaned out, as weapons—it was the country club scene from *West Side Story.* Mainly as a show of team spirit, I carried the most useless weapon ever wielded—a thick railroad spike attached to maybe eight inches of chain. To use it, I'd have to be close enough to my victim to bite him. Of course, the police had gotten wind of all this, so they, too, were laying siege to our little piece of the promised land. It was a riot (almost).

Every day that week, at precisely 4:15 P.M., there would be a brief but spirited clash between the blacks on their way home from school and the whites who waited in ambush—trash cans hurled through windows, minor leg wounds, flying epithets, but mostly lots of trying to outrace the cops (unsuccessfully) to the moving battlefields. It was sick, but it was fun. Like a Spike Lee movie, only from the other side. One afternoon, a car filled with black men coming home from work made an unlucky turn and was instantly surrounded by our team. I was close enough to the action to be able to see inside, to the face of the middle-aged man in the front passenger seat. He looked out with an expression not yet of terror but of total, slack-jawed surprise. I felt sorry for him. Then the bricks flew, and the windows shattered, and the mob moved in. And I could see no more, until the cavalry came to the rescue. It didn't seem as bad then as it does now: Then it just seemed like the natural order of life. I know that because we were the white team it sounds like racism, pure and simple, but it never felt like the oppressors versus the oppressed. We were *all* oppressors; we were *all* oppressed. At one time or another in my neighborhood, everybody—the innocent in with the guilty—took their lumps because of who they were born.

• • • "Well, as far as my life's concerned, I wanted to be a fireman ever since I was five, and I've been one since I was twenty—that was twenty-six years ago. In 1999, I'll retire. I wanted two children, a boy and a girl, and I have that. I wanted that since I was small, too. I bought this house in 1970, and I added on that room there, and I'll die here, probably."

Hey, *that* was quick. We've been in Ron Tonelli's sunny kitchen in Santa Rosa for less than five minutes, and he's gone from birth to the beyond in a single paragraph. It's OK, though, because now we can watch the video a few of his cousins mentioned to me—all the family's home movies from the forties and fifties.

"It's basically the movies my Uncle Amos took on eight millimeter," Ron says. "Amos was my grandfather's wife's brother. I put them on video, and then I made copies for all the others."

Ron's wife, Calistera, and their teenage daughter, Christine, arrive home just in time for the screening. I assume they've both seen it, but when I ask Christine, she says, "Well, *parts* of it."

Ron's surprised. "Oh, come on, you've seen this," he says.

"Not *all*."

Grinning, Calistera asks her, "You mean you're not *into* this?"

But then, just as it gets going, Ron's mother, Maxine, shows up. She begins grilling me on what my book's *really* about. She can't believe anybody will buy it, a common worry even in the Tonelli Nation, but especially so in the Tonelli In-Law Nation.

Meanwhile, on the TV screen, a big, expansive-looking man is floating in a cloud of smoke.

"There's Vic," Maxine says, turning her attention away from me. Vic was her father-in-law. "Smoking his pipe. Loved to laugh. Loved women. Thought he was King Tut."

"Just like *all* Tonelli men," Calistera says.

The scene switches. "There's the church where we got married," Ron says. "St. Rose. And there's Leo, my dad."

Now it's a suburban street, just after World War II judging by the cars and the clothes.

"This is Tenth Street," Ron says. "And one of those cars is the car my dad was killed in. He died in 1950. My sisters, the twins, were just born. They weren't even home from the hospital yet."

"There's the car your dad died in," says Maxine. "It was your grandparents' car. It always stalled. And it did that night, too."

"That's how my father was killed," Ron says. "The car stalled, and a truck ran him over."

A small blond boy with a weird cowlick is being held up to the lens.

"There's Ronnie!" Maxine squeals.

"Hey, Dad," Christine says, "nice hair."

"I kind of like these movies," Ron says, " 'cause it's the only way I've ever seen my dad. I was five when he died. The only thing I remember about him was that he made me eat my spinach. And every time I try to eat it now, I get nauseous."

Once the room quiets down a little, I can hear that there's narration on the video—Ron and Maxine describing what's on the screen.

"I had to cut her off when she talked too long," Ron says.

"There were disagreements," Maxine allows.

Amos, the uncle who made the movies, finally shows up on-screen.

"Now, he never married," says Maxine. "That's another thing about Italians—they take care of their mommies and daddies, and if they don't want them to get married, then they don't."

Christine wanders out of the room.

Christine wanders back into the room. On the video, everybody's in a pool.

"And that's where the college was," says Maxine.

"High school," says Ron.

After Ron's father died, Maxine and her kids moved in with her in-laws on their ranch. Ron's grandfather served as his father figure even after Maxine remarried, when Ron was twelve, and they moved off the ranch.

"Yeah, my father figure was an older man," Ron says. "He spoke Pidgin English, but it sounded perfectly clear to me. One of my first memories was when he shot a mountain lion and he let me shoot it too. It was up a tree, and he shot it down, but he let me kill it, so when we went back the story could be that *I* killed the mountain lion. I worshipped my grandfather."

"This is interesting to hear," Maxine says, "your memories and your feelings about him. Because we had a lot of problems when I remarried. Your stepfather Dick didn't stand a chance with you."

"No, he didn't, I guess," Ron agrees.

"I used to stand up for you against him with all my heart," Maxine says, "but I see how you blocked him out. Now I finally know how you felt. And it really makes me sad."

"When I was kid," Ron explains, looking up at me, "if I wanted a hamburger and they were having something else for dinner, I'd just get up from the table and walk around the corner to my grandmother's house and say, 'Fix me a hamburger.' If my mother's husband told me to do something that I didn't want to do, I'd ignore him. If he told me to mow the lawn and I didn't want to, my mother would do it and *say* I'd done it."

"I didn't realize how indoctrinated you were," Maxine says.

"No," Ron cuts her off, "Dick just didn't fit my image of the perfect dad. The person I looked up to was my grandfather. He was to the point, very strong willed. He had good goals in life, and he knew what he wanted early. And I guess, now that I think about it, that I was the same way.

"Anyway," Ron says, unprompted by anything on-screen, "that's my life, pretty much cut and dried. Pretty structured. A lot of my friends are now changing careers, changing wives at forty, forty-five. And I say to myself, 'What the hell did I do wrong?' They're doing all that, and I'm looking forward to retiring. But then my mom reminds me, this must be the way I wanted it."

In the middle of all this, unnoticed, the video ends.

Ron goes on, "My son knows what *he's* gonna do with his life, too. He's always wanted to be a cop, and he's going to be one. And my daughter's *also* goal-oriented."

• • • Sunday morning brings to this trip a new sensation: Melancholy. The streaming sunlight is just barely sneaking around the edges of these motel-orange drapes; I lie in bed, flattened by gloom. Even bathing in the flicker and drone of some great white father delivering cable Jesus doesn't help; even dragging my unshaven, ill-groomed self to the empty coffee shop for Cheerios doesn't help. Today's Easter, I feel it like a pain; out there the entire Tonelli Nation is assembling for ravioli and I—oh, irony—I'm alone and far from anybody I love or even like a lot. Plus, I have no visits scheduled for today, and without a reason for being here, I'm just one more sucker, I mean seeker, who's run out of road at the Pacific. Maybe it's flight sickness. Maybe it's California-induced depression. Maybe I should begin upgrading my accommodations (*those drapes*). If it wasn't for self-pity, I'd have no pity at all.

What's *really* bumming me out, though, is how my indifferent tyrant, geography, will be sending me back home starting the second I step on the gas. From the outset, I believed that the point of this expedition was to visit lots of Tonellis, which I've done; by my rough computation I've already met fifty or so, in eight states. And there are plenty more to see between here and the Atlantic. Today it occurs to me that maybe what I really wanted was only to track Tonellis as far away as they went—to the extremes of the Tonelli Nation. And now I face spending another month on the road, a month that will only bring me right back where I began. At the halfway point, this trip feels *done*.

For this reason alone I dread getting in the car, but I promised myself I'd make Reno and do some gambling this afternoon, so it's time. The roads are holiday lonesome as I split Santa Rosa and follow Route 12's dips and curves through Napa Valley, which is slavishly gorgeous and sun-dappled, as subtle as a jigsaw puzzle. All I notice is how the wooden stakes holding up the grapevines look like rows of crucifixes. "Every Picture Tells a Story," Rod Stewart's epic road poem, is today's soundtrack. His voyage sounds more the way it's supposed to be: in one short song he's in Rome and Paris, broke, arrested for inciting a riot, seduced on a boat by an exotic older woman. . . . *She took me up on deck and bit my neck.* . . . Jesus, what have I missed? He crows:

If there's one thing I can say to you
To help you on your way down the road
I couldn't quote you no Dickens, Shelley or Keats
'Cause it's all been said before
Make the best out of the bad, just laugh it off
You didn't have to come here anyway. . . .

On Easter, I turned east.

Tony Bennett, for no particular reason, on my motel TV, Winnemucca, Nevada

Intermission

A Statistical Portrait of the Tonelli Nation

Hey, whatever happened to the results of the Tonelli questionnaire, I hear you not asking. Well, I got back around two hundred of them and hired the Beta Research Corporation, of Syosset, Long Island, which has conducted *Money* magazine's "Best Places to Live" survey among others, to crunch the numbers. Here are the highlights:

Only a little more than half of the Tonelli Nation (53.3 percent) is of full Italian ancestry.

At one point in my travels, it occurred to me that I could use lots of my interviews as research for a book about German-Americans, so prevalent was mixed parentage. Of those respondents under thirty years old, almost three-quarters have only one Italian parent, so the future is clear. It's also interesting to see that among Tonellis with postgraduate degrees, 52.6 percent are of mixed ancestry, as opposed to 47.4 percent who are of Italian-only background. Some of that's attributable to age,

159

no doubt, but it bears out a statistic I read somewhere: That Italian-Americans of mixed ancestry go farther in life than those who are Italian on both sides.

Most who responded (52.3 percent) are the grandchildren of immigrants.

Same as I am. It's noteworthy that only 9.2 percent of respondents from the Northeast are great-grandchildren of immigrants, compared with 29.4 percent from the South, 25.7 percent from the Midwest, and 21.1 percent from the West.

Most (57.4 percent) did not marry someone of Italian ancestry.

And while half of those age forty-five or older married Italians, only one-quarter of those under age thirty who are married did so. (Of course, many of those Tonellis are not of full Italian ancestry themselves, so their choice of mate doesn't even represent intermarriage.) Sociologists say that *endogamy—* marriage to someone of your own group—is the most important indicator of strong ethnic identity.

Forty percent of Tonellis speak a few words of Italian, 24.1 percent speak none at all, and 16.6 percent speak it fluently.

I'm with the crowd again.

They're more likely to spend several social evenings a week with a friend (29.6 percent) than with a neighbor (8 percent), a relative (16.1 percent), a sibling (18.6 percent), or a parent (16.1 percent).

The commonest answer to "How often do you spend a social evening with a neighbor?" was "Almost Never" (41.2 percent); with a relative, "Several Times a Year" (26.1 percent); with a sibling, "Several Times a Week" (18.6 percent); with a parent, "Several Times a Year," (19.1 percent). In 1991, the National Opinion Research Center, based at the University of Chicago, conducted a study of ethnicity and social contacts. It ranked fifteen ethnic groups by the frequency with which members spent "several" social evenings a week with friends, neighbors, relatives, parents, and siblings. Here's how Italian-Americans ranked:

With a friend: Fifth place. (Jews were most likely to say they spend several evenings a week with friends; Scandinavians least likely.)

With a neighbor: Eighth place. (Blacks were first; Asians were last.)

With a relative: Eighth place. (Hispanics were first; Jews were last.)

With a parent: Fifth place. (Hispanics were first; Jews were last.)

With a sibling: Sixth place. (Hispanics were first; Jews were last.)

The survey also asked if respondents spent at least one evening a year socializing in a bar. Italians came in first; Asians, last.

Back to the Tonellis:

Most (60.8 percent) haven't driven across America.

Ha!

An almost identical number (60.3 percent) have never been to Italy.

Most (70.4 percent) have lived in more than one city.

"Do you own more recordings by Frank Sinatra or Luciano Pavarotti?"

Sinatra: 43.2 percent
Pavarotti: 23.6 percent
No answer: 24.1 percent

The Amazing Story of the Tonelli Family in America

The most startling comparison on this question regards the difference between all-Italian respondents and those of mixed ancestry: Only 18.9 percent of the former chose "No Answer" (indicating that they probably own records by neither), as compared to 30.1 percent of the latter. Midwesterners were weighted most heavily toward Sinatra—51.4 percent versus 17.1 percent for Pavarotti.

"Can you recognize more songs by Madonna or Giuseppe Verdi?"

Madonna: 63.8 percent

Verdi: 28.1 percent

The only significant comparison is that Madonna fared worst in the Northeast (57.9 percent) and best in the West (73.7 percent).

"Have you spent more time reading books by Mario Puzo or Dante?"

Puzo: 45.7 percent

Dante: 17.1 percent

No answer: 26.1 percent

Neither: 11.1 percent

Because I don't wish to impugn the honesty of 17.1 percent of Tonellis, I'll skip to the next question.

"Are you more familiar with the movies of Sylvester Stallone or Marcello Mastroianni?"

Stallone: 73.4 percent

Mastroianni: 18.6 percent

Stallone did markedly better among the young (92.5 percent of those under age thirty), the less educated (76.8 percent of those with high-school diplomas or less), the less-compensated (76 percent of those earning under $30,000), the great-grandchildren of immigrants (94.1 percent), and those of mixed ancestry (80.6 percent). Women liked Marcello better (24.3 percent compared with 17 percent).

"Which of the Godfather movies was your favorite?"

I: 72.9 percent

II: 8.5 percent

III: 2.5 percent

There are no significant differences in preference for the more romantic vision of Italian-America, except that southerners are way out there in favor of the first Godfather movie (82.4 percent). Scary to note that 2.5 percent of Tonellis are insane.

"As a general rule, do portrayals of Italian-Americans in movies or on TV offend you?"

Yes: 25.1 percent

No: 71.9 percent

The more they earn, the more likely they were to say they were offended; great-grandchildren of immigrants were least likely to say yes. Biggest gulf: 39.5 percent of northeasterners are offended, as opposed to 5.3 percent of westerners.

"As a general rule, do you feel more comfortable with people of Italian ancestry than with those not of Italian ancestry?"

Yes: 33.2 percent

No: 49.7 percent

Don't know: 15.6 percent

This question and the next one were the most important on the whole form, to my mind, for the way they addressed the "us" versus "them" worldview so crucial to ethnic identity. The respondents who are younger and better educated are more likely to answer no to this one. Those of two Italian parents said yes far more often than those of mixed parentage, 41.5 percent compared with 23.7 percent. And 40.7 percent of children of immigrants said yes, compared with 23.5 percent of great-grandchildren of immigrants. Females say no more often than males, 63.5 percent compared with 21.6 percent. Midwesterners are most likely to say no (54.3 percent).

"How strongly do you think of yourself as an Italian-American?"

Very strongly: 46.2 percent
Moderately: 35.7 percent
Slightly: 10.1 percent
Not at all: 7.5 percent

Only 8.9 percent of those age forty-five and over answered "slightly" or "not at all"; while 28.6 percent of those age thirty to forty-four chose one of those two replies. Almost 23 percent of midwesterners chose one of those two replies, tops by region.

"When you have tomato sauce at home, is it . . . "

Homemade: 67.3 percent
From a jar: 27.6 percent
Both: 4.5 percent

About 80 percent of northeasterners make it themselves, compared with 42.1 percent of westerners. And 75.5 percent of Tonellis of Italian-only ancestry go homemade, compared with 58.1 percent of those of mixed ancestry.

More than half (56.8 percent) say they've never been discriminated against because of their Italian ancestry.

The predictable differences show up here. Children of two Italian parents say yes more often than those of mixed marriages, 27.4 percent compared with 10.8 percent. Northeasterners say yes more often than westerners, 23.7 percent compared with 13.2 percent. Children of immigrants say yes more often than great-grandchildren, 29.6 percent compared with 8.8 percent.

Their preference in 1992 was Clinton (49.7 percent), Bush (21.6 percent), Perot (12.1 percent) and No Answer (16.6 percent).

Income breakdown: Terrific—the commonest answer was "No Answer" (28.6 percent).

A Statistical Portrait of the Tonelli Nation

• • • Because I don't really trust myself around numbers, I contacted Dr. Richard D. Alba, a professor of sociology at the State University of New York, Albany, and a respected authority on ethnicity, as well as the author of two books that have been helpful to me on this quest, *Italian Americans: Into the Twilight of Ethnicity* and *Ethnic Identity: The Transformation of White America*. I commissioned him to read the questionnaire results and comment on what they portend. The following is taken from his analysis of the Tonelli Nation census:

> I note that the Tonellis, like Italian-Americans, are now primarily a third-generation group: a majority traces back the immigration of the Tonelli ancestor to the grandparents' generation. The typical generation will, of course, continue to shift, as members of the first and second generations, concentrated in older age groups, die off, and as the group more and more resembles its current young members, who come disproportionately from the fourth and later generations (half of the Tonellis under thirty have to look back to their great-grandparents to find the immigrant ancestor). The increasing proportion of the group that will belong to the fourth generation in the near future signals an important transition, because the fourth generation has little or no contact with the immigrants and thus is missing a set of experiences that can help to sustain a strong ethnic identity.

He also writes:

> The shift in the direction of mixed ancestry is another critical one, because the family context in which an individual is raised undoubtedly lays the groundwork for many adult ethnic traits. Note, for example, that there is a clear relationship between ancestry type and marriage to another Italian. Tonellis who are only partly Italian are markedly more likely to marry non-Italians. My research shows that not only is the prevalence of mixed ancestry on the rise, so too is the ethnic complexity (i.e., the number of distinct ethnic elements) of ancestry.

Three- and four-ethnicity combinations are becoming more common, and I would bet that they can be found among the children of the younger Tonellis in the survey.

Finally:

The ethnic dynamics visible in the demographic data for the Tonellis lend themselves to a "soft" form of ethnicity, quite consistent with what Dr. Herbert Gans has described as "symbolic ethnicity." In this soft form, people identify with their ethnic background in ways that are compatible with the multi-ethnic social contexts in which they lead their lives—signs of ethnicity tend to be muted and to be kinds that, like food, can be appreciated by, or at least do not give offense to, those who do not share one's background. Manifestations of ethnicity that are exclusive of others or that hold the potential to generate conflict tend to be avoided.

Also consistent with this soft ethnicity is an interest in food, which is the most commonly cited ordinary experience connected with ethnicity. In this light, it is interesting that two-thirds of the Tonelli respondents make their own tomato sauce, and the large majority of those who do use a recipe acquired from a family member. Nevertheless, there are differences in this respect, too, associated with ancestry type: Individuals with mixed Italian ancestry are less likely to make tomato sauce at home and also less likely when they do to use another family member's recipe (although the latter difference is too small to be statistically significant).

So it's obvious—we Tonellis have never been less Italian than we are right now, and we'll never be even *this* Italian ever again. The divisiveness of the "us" and "them" mentality will go, but along with it goes the idea that there's anything more meaningful than macaroni holding us together. And that's true not just for Tonellis but for all Italian-Americans. I'm sure it's true for Irish-, Polish-, Cuban-, Greek-, Chinese-, Danish-, and every other kind of hyphenated American, too. You're going to miss us Tonellis when we're gone. You're going to wish you had been nicer to us when you had the chance.

Terry Tonelli

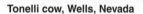
Tonelli cow, Wells, Nevada

11.

You Look Like a Mormon

I won't depress you by describing Easter in Reno. I made it worse when I pulled off the highway at a battered gas station that probably last saw use during a Hell's Angels run, maybe as recently as 1962. This is northern California, just before the Nevada border. So things were already looking grim when I got out of the car and discovered that up there in the mountains the snowbanks were as tall as I am. And that even the air had suddenly gone wintry. By this point I had become a cocky pilot on dry asphalt, but snow and ice were something else. Snow and ice were deadly for all I knew, never having driven on either. I remembered that in a skid, you must steer in the direction you're skidding. Or in the opposite direction. I had a feeling that if I went into a skid on an icy mountain road, it wouldn't matter which way I steered.

While I stopped, I figured I'd call my kin with Easter greetings. So there I am, shivering in a beat-up phone booth in a place I could not name, talking to my mother, my grandmother, my two sisters, my brother-in-law, my nephew, each in their turn asking, "Where are you?" and replying to each only

Dennis Tonelli

Tonelli Gibbs

Buick rear-view mirror, somewhere in Utah

this: "Someplace." All of which was conducted with the sounds of a holiday dinner shrieking in the background. And me, there—where?—like an exile. Like a dog on the run.

So I make it to town and stop at the $36.80 A Night sign at Circus Circus. (I know I said I wasn't going to describe Easter in Reno, but there's a navigational vignette that might amuse.) After I check in, first thing I do is take Nancy the psychic's advice and play the Wild Cherry slot machine. There goes fifty. Then I sit at a roulette table. I find that gamblers here are chattier than they are in Atlantic City or Vegas—and I hate chatty gamblers. There goes a hundred. I go to my room and, in an at-

The Amazing Story of the Tonelli Family in America

tempt to lift the day's dreary mood, I eat the remainder of my magic mushrooms. And decide to take in the sights of the town.

I'm fine on the streets—I remember all the turns I make, so it's a snap finding my hotel again. Addled, but only mildly, I see the Circus Circus sign and enter the doors. *Wow.* All casinos are designed to disorient, I realize that—if you lose your bearings maybe you'll lose everything else, too. But even as casinos go, this one is spectacularly discombobulating. I'm trying to situate myself, but there's a trapeze act swinging over my head, several distinguishable qualities of ringing and buzzing and clattering all going like mad, and the lights . . . it's like a parking lot for fire engines in here. Throw in the crowds—don't they have Easter in Nevada?—and I'm drowning. In the course of the next fifteen minutes, I ask directions to the hotel elevator at least six times, and each assist draws me further into a hellish maze. To show how far gone I am, my sole navigational landmark through all this, the rock I return to after each room-finding foray, is something called the Clown Bar. I finally ask the bartender for the easiest way back, and he looks at the passcard in my hand and says, "You're in the wrong building." *No wonder.* Now I just have to find the shuttle monorail, and after a total of forty-five minutes wandering through a maelstrom, I make it back to my wing and then my bed, vowing never again to roam. I may now know something about driving, I tell myself, but I still don't know shit about finding.

• • • I think this may be the coolest Tonelli occupation yet: Terry, of Reno, is an "electron-beam furnace operator"—he runs an oven that melts titanium scrap into ingots with 2.4 million volts of electricity. (He used to be a cook back home in Michigan, and he followed an employer out here for a restaurant job, ditched that, and became a chef of another sort.)

He shows me a souvenir he brought home from work yesterday, a bit of titanium spill that hardened into a long silvery strand of metal ending in a purplish-green, iridescent blob. It's weirdly beautiful, and I'm hitting him with questions about the oven, when his wife Blair, who is large with child, says from the sofa, "What he's *really* about is that he's a Civil War expert. He knows *everything* about the Civil War. This titanium stuff is just a paycheck. Terry, show him your little men."

He leads me into a small, cramped room, saying, "I'm about two-thirds through reproducing the army of northern Virginia, Robert E. Lee's army." Shoulder to shoulder, we gaze at the walls, which are solidly lined with shelves holding thumbnail-sized lead soldiers, horses, and weaponry that Terry painted.

"It's forty-to-one scale. I've got about fifteen hundred soldiers done."

"How many more to go," I ask.

"Oh, about a thousand, I guess. It depends on whether or not I'm going to attack the cavalry. Horses are a pain in the ass to do."

The soldiers who aren't on shelves are on dioramas Terry's set up on tables, battle scenes complete with little bushes, rocks, and grass. The room's only closet is stacked high with boxes. "Those are my war games. I've got about two or three hundred of them. My collection isn't nearly what it was, to my chagrin. Right now I'm fighting the battle of Waterloo by mail. I'm the Anglo allies—the Prussians, the British, the Dutch, and so on. So basically, the guy I'm fighting with is Napoleon, and I'm Wellington. And between you and me, I'm kicking his butt. As a matter of fact—"

He goes to a table and shuffles through today's mail.

"—here's his turn. I've been waiting about six weeks for this."

Next Terry shows me his one hundred thirty–volume history of the Civil War, a complete collection of both sides' officers' letters, reports, and other official documents. I ask if he's ever heard of Lieutenant Colonel Luigi Tinelli, and he hasn't, so we look him up. In the course of *my* research I stumbled over the Colonel—he came to America with Garibaldi and his brigade of revolutionaries during their exile, fought for the Union during the Civil War, then worked as a lawyer and businessman in New Jersey, where he established this country's first silk industry. Sure enough, Luigi is in the book.

"Why am I so fascinated by the Civil War?" Terry says. "I don't know. It was *American.* All these battles were fought in somebody's backyard."

Terry, whose sister Bobbie I had dinner with in San Diego, has been out here with Blair for several years, but he and his wife are planning on moving back to their hometown, Lansing, Michigan, as soon as she has the baby. Both sets of parents are getting old, and Blair and Terry want to spend time with them, which is one reason for the move.

"Plus," Terry says, "Blair was kind of a social queen there, and it's kind of isolated here."

"This is not exactly the intellectual Mecca here," Blair says. "There's a reason they want to put that nuke dump here. And my parents really miss me."

"Her mom's already picked out a house for us," Terry says. "Right across the street. But it feels good to know we're not going back because we couldn't make it somewhere else."

"Right," says Blair, "that we're going because we *want* to."

"It's a real feeling of accomplishment to be able to strike out on our own and find a job and a house and make new friends and build a life somewhere we didn't know anybody."

Terry's a reddish-haired man with not much about him that suggests his Italian ancestry. I ask, "Do you feel your roots at all?"

"No," he says. "My mom is Dutch and Scottish. In fact, we're like the classic melting-pot family. Her family came over on the Mayflower. So we were raised nominally Catholic. The only times I really felt Italian were when we visited my grandparents. But once we moved to California, I had no sense of it at all. I was just the all-American kid."

"What he hates," Blair says, "is when he introduces himself and people say, 'Oh, hi, Tony.' "

• • • Northern Nevada gives me the creeps. I've driven roads like this before, stretches of fried asphalt with not another traveler in sight to split the misery. But once you get east of Reno, it's beyond spooky—it's otherworldly. The combination of ego-shattering solitude and the lifeless land—no perceivable chlorophyll, nothing but dry, brilliantly beige grass, crust-brown mountains, a fish-belly sky—makes this road mind-bending: I'm driving eighty and it feels like twenty, slowed down like dope-time, the white lines crawl under the car. Feels like I'm losing speed, so I look at the dashboard and see the needle: pinned. Higher into the mountains there's a glittering skin of snow on the ground, like frozen milk, pierced by tufty bushes. Something skitters across the road—an animal? A tumbleweed! It cracks me up—the desert is hilarious; it's exactly like a Road Runner cartoon. But this part of the country gets to be an unfunny joke pretty fast; you could nuke it and not lose a thing. It's like the moon with an interstate.

Hold on—there's somebody walking along the shoulder, a man in a too-heavy tan corduroy jacket, like a mule with shopping bags slung over his neck. His back's to me, but he doesn't turn at the sound of my car. Can you even call him a hitchhiker? And where did he get on this road? The last on-ramp was maybe fifteen miles back, and he's got another twelve to cross before he can exit. How far can he travel in a day, I wonder, crushed under all those bags and the blazing, monotonous star? If anything happens to this hobo, only the buzzards will care. He could even be a Tonelli, but I'll never know.

Wells, Nevada, is like a ghost town—two-thirds of the dusty, beat-up old storefronts are vacant, and there's not a soul walking or driving around. I stop at a desolate café where the owner and the cook are arguing over the specials of the day, find the pay phone, and call Lana Tonelli Gibbs out at the cattle ranch where she lives. She thought I should call before I headed over there; if I got lost or my car broke down, nobody would find me unless they knew to look. Great.

"OK," she tells me, "cross the railroad tracks and make a left. The first eight or ten miles are paved, but the road's dirt after that. It'll be about thirty miles on the dirt road, and you'll see the sign for the ranch. You'll have to come through three gates before you get to the house."

For the first few miles, I can make out the railroad tracks through the scrubby bush that dwarfs the car, but after that I'm on my own. I've driven about nine thousand miles so far, but I didn't really know what *thirty* miles was until I did it utterly alone on a narrow, rutted, unmarked, dirt road. Since southern Texas I've had moments when I'd gaze at my surroundings and, stupefied by rough splendor, I'd whisper to myself, "This is like driving through a cowboy movie." I was wrong—*this* is like driving through a cowboy movie, nothing but sagebrush and buttes, highlands and badlands, and me, a cloud of dust wandering accidentally onto the set. After almost an hour, and several navigational alarms (all false), I come upon the first gate, a conventional affair. Five minutes past it I hit the second gate, but it appears to be just some barbed wire strung spring-tight between two posts. A large black cow ambles to my side, fascinated for the entire ten minutes it takes me to figure out how to undo the barrier and then replace it without perforating myself. A full eighteen minutes after I turned in at the Gibbs Ranch sign I find the ranch house.

Once we settle out on the porch, the first thing Lana's husband, Bill Gibbs, asks is if I saw any antelope herds on my way in. Suddenly I flash on Alaska, and not just because up there, Stanford's first question was if I had seen any caribou herds on my way in. It's the isolation and the ruggedness of the land, and what it takes for people to live with it. It's the scary sensation that there's nothing between you and the great whatever. Like Alaska, out here you either do or die (or move). It's not for everybody: Lana met Bill when her twin sister Donna and Bill's cousin Tim married and moved out here, but Donna and Tim have since moved on. Lana grew up in Santa Rosa (I visited her brother, Ron the fireman, there), but now she can ride, brand, inoculate calves, and handle the bookkeeping, too.

"I'm just a typical rancher's wife, I guess. My mom says, 'How can you live in this godforsaken place?' but I like it here. You can be just who you want to be. But you really have to *be* here. It's a twelve-month-a-year thing, farming is."

"Ranching," Bill says.

"Right, ranching."

Their daughter married and moved to town; their son, Matt, who's eighteen, is about to go to college in California. I ask if he'll take over the ranch someday.

"You *hope* they do," Lana says. "You don't want to work this hard just to sell it."

"There are a lot fewer people staying on the ranch," Bill says. His family has owned this spread since 1916. "A lot fewer families, and a lot fewer people of my generation."

"Why's that," I ask.

"I think a lot of it is because when you're here, you're here *by yourself.* There's not a lot of other people around."

"Yeah, not a lot of friends," says Lana.

"That's why I *like* it," Bill says. "But also, sometimes on a ranch you just barely scrape by."

"Yeah," Lana says, "the kids'll say, 'If I was working at an hourly job in town, do you know how much money I'd make?' But this is great for family life."

"It is, but we're fighting the government and the environmentalists out here," Bill says. "You ever hear the expression, 'Cattle-free in '93'? They don't want any cows out here at *all.*"

"That's why we tell Matt he'd better learn something else in school," Lana says.

"Yeah," Bill says. "This way of life might not be here for long."

• • • I make it back to Wells, where the only lighted signs on the main drag are for casinos, which are not the customary elaborate affairs—they're all ramshackle, lonesome saloons with two dusty card tables and three slot machines, one of which is invariably out of order. Men sit silently at the bar, pulling on Buds, shoveling quarters into the video poker machines set in the countertops. I leave one airless tomb many quarters lighter and wander into a cheap Mexican café, joining four teenage girls, six senior citizens, and a young couple with a baby. Dead quiet, except for the girls giggling over their French fries. In come a woman in her thirties, plaid flannel shirt and leather vest, shades, dirty hair, and a nice-looking, chubby kid, her son, maybe eleven, all smiles. She's grouchy as hell, studying her map in a booth. He asks for quarters for the video games, but she says, "No, we're in a hurry. Tell the man

The Amazing Story of the Tonelli Family in America

we want our cheeseburgers to go." Suddenly she looks up, catches me staring, and says, "Do you know what Wendover's like?"

"No," I say.

"I just have to get somewhere soon to sleep. We left Reno this morning—I woke up feeling like going to Casper, Wyoming, to see Mount Rushmore, so I packed some things and my kid in the car. 'Cept I get anxious on the road, so I have to stop every so often." Another victim of road psychosis, or maybe only psychos love the road?

After dinner I stroll, the only human in Wells so inclined. Across the railroad tracks, off in the haze, there's a tiny, blinking red light, like a beacon, towering over a cinderblock fortress with neon beer signs in the windows. Cars and pickups throw dust in the parking lot, the most activity I've seen all night. As I get closer, two barking hellhounds begin to circle me, so I turn back, to the right side of the tracks, to my chaste motel.

• • • Driving through northern Nevada has been so grim that the big, sweeping turn at Wendover makes my heart soar—compared with the rest of the state, this fried little burg looks as lush and fertile as Florida. Cross the border into Utah, and the landscape changes instantly—the highway is suddenly surrounded on both sides by strips of the greenest water I've ever seen, *way* too green to be real. The surreal effect is heightened by the way the road seems to shimmer and float, like a bridge that's barely clearing the water. On the edges of the green there's a brilliant white crust. Soon, a sign: Bonneville Salt Flats.

I follow my directions into town, exit the highway, stop, and . . . and I haven't felt this conspicuous since Alaska. I'm in a gentle, residential part of Salt Lake City, next to a picnic table in front of Franco's Burgers. School must have just let out, because the streets are swarming with Stepford Kids, sun-bleached, well-mannered, modestly dressed blond teenagers giving a wide berth to the spot where I loiter against my filthy Buick.

A sporty little red roadster zooms up, and a sporty little salt-and-pepper–haired guy hollers, "Hey, *you* look like a Mormon!"

Very funny, Dennis. He tells me to follow him, and a minute or two later we're in the sparely furnished suburban house Dennis Tonelli shares with his beautiful blond lady friend, Lonnie. Dennis brings out salami and bread and wine, and we settle in the kitchen. I'm still so disoriented that I begin babbling over how freaky Nevada seemed.

"I think Nevada's a cold place," Lonnie says. "People there just aren't friendly."

"Until you get to know them," Dennis says. "Until you live there. When I worked in Elko we had a little group we hung out with, and everybody got close. But the people there *were* more nomadic. They were there just for a few months, or just to get a divorce, or whatever."

"Well, it's not a home," Lonnie says. "It's a changeover place."

Salt Lake City has a special place in the Tonelli cosmology, if only because of the vast, world-famous geneology records kept by the Mormons. Back in New York, I visited the Mormon branch office and looked up my name: I was shocked to find more than a dozen of us listed, mostly nineteenth-century Brazilians, for some reason. The story behind all that record keeping is a little bizarre: The Mormons collect birth, marriage, and death information from all over the planet, going back centuries; then they use it to baptize the unknowing souls into the Mormon Church. Like soul-snatching, it seems to me. What if you didn't *want* to spend eternity in Mormon heaven? I figure maybe Dennis and Lonnie will know more about it, so I ask if they're any clearer than I am on the practice.

"You have to *live* here to understand it," Lonnie says, and they both laugh.

"When I came here I had absolutely nothing against these people," Dennis says. "I even knew some Mormons before I moved here, and they were fantastic. But here they run *everything*—the school board, politics, everything."

"The Mormons brought *my* Italian ancestors over here," Lonnie says. "The missionaries got them and brought them back. Then they changed their name. I don't even know my Italian grandmother's *name*. I was *married* before I even knew that I had any Italian blood *in* me. I'd always ask my mother, 'Who is this little old dark-haired, mean-looking lady on the piano?' And my mother would say, 'Oh, she's Italian, but don't you worry about it. We're Danish.' And I was like, 'Oh. OK.' The Mormons are *nazis*. If there are any Italians who are Mormons, it's a shame, but they'll lose their Italian identity. Because the Mormons are so racist.

"For instance, no blacks could become Mormon priests, right? Now, the Mormons run the Boy Scouts here, and there was one black kid who was ready to become an Eagle Scout. Except you can't be an Eagle Scout unless you're a Mormon priest. So the Mormons suddenly had a vision—*blacks could now become priests*. And now they take their ten percent tithe just like everybody else's. It's funny that the Mormons control the Boy Scouts but not the Girl Scouts. Women are *nothing* to Mormons."

"So how did a non-Mormon like you end up here," I ask.

"Well," she says, "I *am* a member of the Church. But I was not raised in the usual Mormon way. And I live in sin. I tried my best to get them to kick me out. But they won't. Ask *him* how he got stuck in Utah with the Mormons. He *hates* it."

"I got here in a strange way," Dennis begins. He grew up in Santa Rosa, part of the loose Tonelli clan there. "I was a musician. As soon as I got out of school, I started playing on the road. I went *everywhere*—Alaska, all the western states, the Midwest, the East Coast. I enjoyed it. I used my mother's house as my mailing address. You were *always* moving so you didn't have a place to call home. I *had* no home. I even did my banking through my mother. I would send her the money to deposit. And I did that for ten years.

"Then, after I got married, my wife started traveling with me, and it was a pain in the ass for her. I would try and get motel rooms that had a little kitchen in them, so we could eat at home once in a while, like normal people. I think it sounded glamorous to her—at first. But then you have to *do* it. And we did it for four or five years.

"When I got drafted, I did my time, and then I joined a reserve unit. I was working in a lounge act in Vegas. I was a drummer, singer, front man, whatever. But it was OK. I could travel with the band and then just do my two weeks of reserve duty every summer. But the army wanted to call me up for one more year and send me to Vietnam. I said no way to that, so I had to join a regular reserve unit and go to monthly meetings. I looked around in various places where I could live so I'd be able to play, and I ended up here because it's close enough to Vegas, Reno, and Tahoe. But it still didn't work out, so I told the guys in the band, 'Look, I'll see you in a year.'

"By then, we had a baby. And that was that. My wife was happy about it. She was a Mormon—not the best of Mormons, but you know how they are with home and family and all that stuff. So I got out of the music business for ten years. Totally. Not a note. I thought I'd try to be a family man. Go out on weekends with the wife. I don't know how to put this, but when I tried, the feeling I got was, Here we go with the rest of the sheep. Still, I thought, OK, I'm gonna try this. But I lost my whole identity. Then we got a divorce." By then Dennis had gotten a straight job, working for the federal government. He just took an early retirement, and now he's playing again, but only two nights a week, in a lounge in a Chinese restaurant.

Somehow, as happens so often on this trip, the subject turns to food.

"These Mormons," Dennis says, "they like *vanilla*. Nothing spicy. We went to a place called the Spaghetti Factory."

"Awful," Lonnie says, making a face.

"I would have been better off opening a can of Spaghetti-Os," Dennis says. "Lonnie's doing real good at that now. My mother taught her how, and she's making her own ravioli. And my mother's not even Italian! But *she* picked it up, too."

• • • I'm in my motel room in Grand Junction, Colorado, typing up my notes from Utah, when the phone rings. It's my friend Jimmy Slipcovers (that's his business, so that became his nickname) from South Philly. I've known Jimmy and his wife Monica since we were all teenagers.

Jimmy: Guess what? My brother's moving to New Mexico!

Me: Why's he moving?

Jimmy: He's a goofball.

Me: Why's he moving?

Jimmy: He's a *goof*ball.

Me: But why New Mexico?

Jimmy: Because his in-laws live there.

Me: No kidding, since when?

Jimmy: They retired there a few years ago. Everybody here's mad at him. They don't even care if he goes, just leave the kids. You should hear my mother, she's scream-ing, "You're gonna raise my grandchildren in the desert with the Indians?!"

Me: Why's he moving?

Jimmy: Who knows? *To start a new life.* Goofball.

Art and Flo Tonelli and family

Art's joke jacket

12.

Don't Call Me Dago

 More mountain torture on the road to Denver. I've been shadowed by looming geology since the Sierra Nevadas, in northern California, but once you see the Rockies off in the distance, you know by the lump in your stomach: you're *there.* First the highway twists low, plunging me into Glenwood Canyon. Sheer rock walls and skinny pines shroud the road in bluish gloom, casting dusk light even at noon over the Colorado River, which courses cinematically just beyond the guardrail. Then the road squirms high, crawling up to what must be the top of the world, Vail Pass, where the interstate gets swallowed up by a forest. At its peak (around eleven thousand feet elevation) all I can see is snow and trees, and the ghost of this brave little highway cutting through the wilderness. My fuel injector, not prepared for this altitude, is wheezing so badly that even with my foot nailed to the floor it barely injects enough to keep me going forty. Meanwhile, every eighteen-wheeler in Colorado is blowing by me like a rocket, throwing sheets of mud over my windshield. Between that and the snow whipping by in the wind, I can barely make out the ground—and this is the interstate! If I'd been on some lesser highway, I would have bought it, I have no doubt. On a curve, a tractor-trailer comes sliding

181

into my lane, and I perceive that in one motion I am about to be dead *and* buried. But, as the truckers say after moments like that, I just shook the piss off my shoe and kept driving.

• • • "We were going to put on our Italian act for you," Tom Tonelli says when I show up. "We were going to be as loud and obnoxious as we could. And we were all going to wear those undershirts, you know—"

"Guinea T-shirts," says his mother, Flo.

"Yeah."

Finally—Pizza Night is here. It takes place *every* Friday in Littleton, a Denver suburb, just like Mark, the surgeon now living in California, promised. The house is quiet now, but only because Tom, Flo, and I are waiting for the patriarch of this clan, Art, to show up with the pizzas and for the rest of the family to arrive.

Wait, here's Art now, bearing six large boxes—from Pizza Hut. And before long, the rest of the brood (Tim, Toby, Nancy, Chris, Beth, spouses, significant others, kids)—mostly fair, all clean-cut—show up, too, and swarm throughout the house. The pizzas are opened on the kitchen counter, next to a big bowl of salad and stacks of red plastic dishes and cups. As the boxes are being stripped, Art and I watch and talk.

"We, in my generation, never really thought that much about our Italian ancestry," he's saying. "Whereas my dad was like [stiffens], 'Don't call *me* dago!' And he was very proud of his background and felt bad when he heard about Italians who had—for instance, he didn't like Sinatra because he felt he had behaved badly. But then my kids, some of them at least, feel very strongly about being Italian."

From across the kitchen table, Tim's wife Angie says, "But don't you think it's because Italian is in vogue now? When I married Tim and changed my name, suddenly everybody I know was like, 'Ey! To*ne*lli!' "

Art's wife, Flo, says to him, "Don't you remember, when we got married I asked you to change your name to Tonell?"

"Yeah," Art says, "but you weren't serious, were you?"

"Sure I was. My parents were from the South, and when

they got married and were about to move up to Chicago, my grandfather told them, 'Don't go there or someday your daughter will marry an *Italian.*' He thought that's all there was in Chicago—Italians and gangsters. So I thought that Tonell sounded . . . *French.* You know—Toe-NELL. Sounds sophisticated. I mean, these people," she says, nodding toward Art, "he lived on the poor side of Joliet and didn't even *know* it."

"All my dad's brothers and sisters were forced to quit school at sixteen and go to work," Art says. "Even us—Joliet's a real blue-collar town, and we were not encouraged to go to school. The thing that was so scary about it was that if you stayed there, you were expected to . . . *bowl!* With your *parents!* You were *expected* to be in the bowling league—forever! It was expected that *everything* in your life would revolve around your family!" But Art found a way out—he had an older cousin who became an engineer and moved West, to take an aerospace job in southern California. "And my motivation, when we went out there in sixty-one, was to work in aerospace, too. I never thought twice about leaving Joliet. I just thought, 'OK, I guess I'll miss my family and friends.' And we really did miss our families—until we started having our own."

He and Flo have seven kids, and six of them still live nearby. Only Mark, the surgeon living in northern California, advanced Art's own leave-taking and moved away.

Actually, Beth moved away, too, but then she came back.

"She came back because she missed Pizza Night," Flo says.

"I came back because of my family," Beth says. "I just kept thinking I didn't want to raise my kids away from my family."

Nancy says, "*I* get the urge to move, now and then. Of course, I'm a single mother, so it's easier having my parents and family around. I'd *definitely* like to move away for a while. Then I'd move back."

"Tim feels the same way," his wife, Angie, says.

"Tim, *do* you want to move?" Art asks.

"No," he says. "Except for the weather."

"No," Flo says. "He'd miss his family too much."

"If everybody else moved away, then I'd go someplace warm."

"Why do you think Mark left?" I ask.

"We told him to," Beth says.

"He always thought we were just a bunch of ignorant, uh—" Nancy begins.

"Ignorant wops, huh?" Art offers.

"Mark was always independent," Nancy says.

"The thing about Mark is," Art says, "he'll never do the same thing everybody else does."

"He makes fun of all of us because we live in the suburbs," says Beth. "We all *love* the suburbs."

"He really was a jerk," says Nancy.

"Oh, no!" Flo says.

"He really was, Mom," Beth says. "Especially to us girls."

"Oh, you guys all gotta admit it," Nancy says. "He was a total jerk."

"No, no, no," says Art, shaking his head but smiling.

"He could make you feel really stupid," Toby says.

"Because he's really intelligent," says Nancy.

"But he could be nice, too," says Beth.

"We love him, that's why we can talk about him like this," says Nancy.

"He'll come home for a visit," says Art, "and he'll take on everybody—he'd throw you in there, too—and take on everybody by himself in Jeopardy, and he'll win."

"He has this *ego*," says Nancy.

"He got really mad the time Toby beat him," Beth says.

"I beat him, and he got so mad he threw the whole game over."

"He doesn't like to lose," says Art.

"In his whole life, the only test he ever flunked was his driver's test," says Beth.

"That's right!" says Nancy. "Because he insisted on using a stick shift. I told him, *'Don't use the stick shift!'*"

"So, did he talk about all of us?" Beth asks.

"Yeah," I say, "he gave me the whole rundown. He also told me that he'd never move back to Denver."

The table gets quiet a second.

"I'm surprised to hear you say that," Nancy says.

"No," says Art. "He'll never come back."

God, some gorgeous symmetry in that moment. Art escaped his kin to expand his horizons, so he knows exactly what drove Mark away. Art and Flo then proceeded to create their own big clan here in Denver. Now it's Art's turn to pine for the son who blew town; the pattern repeats, endlessly.

Pizza Night ends, for me, in the beautiful Oxford Hotel bar, in the company of a woman who's lived in Denver all her life. She's just getting over a guy—he was from Seattle, owned a coffee business there. They met on a vacation, fell in love, both went home, talked constantly on the phone. She flew to Seattle, they packed his stuff in a U-Haul, drove together back to Denver. Once they were shacked up, all they did was fight, so she finally kicked him out (her version). He's not going back to Seattle: "He said he had always *wanted* to live in Denver." End of story.

• • • Driving east out of the city next morning the land immediately goes dead flat, what a relief. By Nebraska, the farms and ranches are so friendly they come right up to the interstate and nuzzle your car. The terrain is softer, too—wide tan carpets of corn, grass as green as AstroTurf, ponds as blue and shiny as a K-Mart nightgown. It's easy driving—you just floor it and then look up every ten minutes or so to make sure somebody's cow didn't get out.

OK, now how noteworthy is it that on a Saturday night, at least half the men in the vast Desert Rose Dance Hall in Grand Island, Nebraska, are wearing cowboy hats? Not very, right, except show me another type of nightclub where anybody is wearing a hat of *any* kind, let alone one that belongs outside near cowshit. For psychic sons of Gary Cooper, these dudes seem awfully affected. Especially since most of them are the desk cowboy type, judging by the aviator eyeglasses, pencil biceps, and fleshy waistlines separating the hats above from the boots below. The women seem far less studied, and more plainly indigenous: The most beautiful girls in the Desert Rose are all tall and fat—gorgeous, heart-stopping faces above the sensuous curves of delicate double chins, broad, jutting torsos tapering to (relatively) tiny waists, then blossoming into firm but epic rumps. These heroines aren't soft; they're *fat*. They're cows, lovely, sexy, blue-ribbon cows.

They're also the only ones who look unself-conscious out on the dance floor, where only country line dances are being done. It really is the fashion out here, just the way those TV commercials show it: Row after row of cowboys and cowgirls shuffling and spinning and shaking in absolute unison. Instantly I am reminded of America's only true living folk dance—the hokey-pokey. When I was a kid, I went to weddings where people danced the tarantella with some authority. As I got older, they still played the song, but the dancers were clearly beginning to fake it. Now, I bet, even the wedding bands in South Philly have given up on it. There's nobody left who remembers how it's done—it's gone, gone, one more death in the family. Now, like all other good Americans, the people of South Philadelphia do the hokey-pokey, and that's what it's all about. It's the sweetest spectacle—the graceful sight of my mother, my sisters, my aunts, my cousins, all swiveling and hopping as one in their chubby stocking feet. Their movements, effortless and precise, express not prideful individuality but the group's yearning to create something beautiful from its tidy, coordinated will. Then the music gets faster, the motions become ragged trying to keep up, the older ladies surrender but the younger ones persist, valiantly, until soon the music must outrace them, too, and the dance dissolves into meaninglessness and sorrow. It's a ritual, a pageant, a morality play; it's a sacrament that first celebrates the value of conformity and cooperation, then plays out their inevitable destruction. The heartbreaking hokey-pokey has so much to tell us, it moves me almost to tears. "You put your left foot in . . . " And for *what*?

A song that could also properly be seen as having replaced the tarantella at Italo-American nuptials is the number first heard in the wedding scene in *The Godfather*. Such is the power of art over memory that when it's played in real life, wedding guests respond with a genuine tear, as though to a traditional tune rather than music created to portray one in a movie. What *High Noon* is to the patrons of the Desert Rose, *The Godfather* is to us, I guess—it's the mythological drama that turned every son and daughter of twentieth-century urban immigrants into heroes and heroines, struggling to resolve the clash of two powerful, conflicting forces of history. I mean, Michael Corleone is practically the Italo-American Christ—he's the son of God(father) who suffered and died for our sins. For three long movies he tried to do what this country demands of all immigrant heirs: to turn his back on the old ways and become a good American. But at the same time, he was helpless to resist the commands of blood and custom. In the last of the trilogy, he tears at his brush cut and moans that every time he tries to leave the family business, "they keep dragging—me—back!" In the end, his torn, anguished life has satisfied neither the old world nor the new. And unlike Christ—he ain't coming back.

Charlie Tonelli and children Cheryl, Joe, and Frank

Bob Tonelli

13.

Elvis Tonelli

I'm speeding down a lonesome country road in Iowa, on my way to meet a legend.

I first came across Charlie Tonelli in some Des Moines newspaper clips from back in the 1940s. Then he was young, and virile isn't the word—he had fathered ten children in eleven years and made the news because at age thirty-six he was challenging his draft classification (hardship) so he could enlist and fight in the Pacific. There was a picture of his wife, Gladys, and their brood with the story, which noted that Charlie's clan would receive the largest dependents' pay the Navy had ever shelled out.

The next news item found Charlie in trouble for falling behind in his child support (he and Gladys had divorced, and he'd an eleventh child by a second wife). In their randomly ordered way, the rest of the clips told the disorderly tale of Charlie's spawn, in and out of smallish scrapes with the law (stealing a car battery, hit and run, drugs, an assault at a party). I saw his daughter, Carmella, in that federal prison camp in Texas, and in a few days I'll meet his twenty-two-year-old son, Bob, who pleaded guilty last year to second-degree murder in the death of his girlfriend's infant son. When that happened, Char-

Todd Tonelli

Mike and Albert Clausi

lie was eighty-six and had just buried his third wife, Bob's mother.

Just after I sent the questionnaires I got a call from Charlie's daughter Cheryl, who said that her dad was sick but that I was welcome to visit when I was in the neighborhood.

There it is—an old clapboard farmhouse against a gray sky. Out back there's a young guy pulling an engine from a car, and a toddler with a face that's sugary-red with candy.

Now the screen door closes behind me, and I'm in the living room, where basketball on TV is the only source of light or sound. On the couch, almost invisible in the gloom, is a skinny old man, frail, with gray stubble and bright, cautious eyes. His look says *What now?*

"Are you Charlie Tonelli?" I ask.

"Yeah," he says. "Who are you?"

"I'm Bill Tonelli, from New York." He's waiting for more. I tell him I'm going to visit his son Bob in jail.

"Yeah, get him out of there. He's a good boy."

I say I visited his daughter Carmella in prison in Texas.

"Yeah, she got messed up with some fuckhead she was shacked up with. Something about booze or something."

I explain how I'm here because of a book about Tonellis.

"Dad came here to America to work the coal mines in Cherry, Illinois," he starts in. "I guess he had some friends there. I don't know. I spoke Italian. I don't do too good anymore. Put me in with some dagos and I'll do OK. Dad got killed in a mine explosion. Then my mother remarried, to a Lancelotti. We came here, to Des Moines. And goddam, I passed three grades in three months—that's how much harder the schools were there than here. But I think I went only about six or seven months. Then, as soon as I could lift a goddam shovel of coal, I went to work in the goddam mines. But we ate. I stole a chicken once, I remember. Another time I shot a turkey and took it home. Mama used to say I had it easy. In Italy she had to take the sheep up to the mountains every morning. Then I had a body shop, and a restaurant, too. Nothing fancy."

"There are a lot more Italians in Des Moines than I expected," I say, but his hearing's not so good—he thinks I said there are a lot more Tonellis.

"They all belong to me, I think," he says, grinning. "Yeah, they're all mine. These kids were by . . . gee, let me think. By three women. 'Cause I was a whorin'-around son of a bitch. But I always took care of my kids. But I had a lot of fun. I was always a hell of a dancer."

We stare at the TV awhile.

"I think I gave you all the dope I can give you," he finally says. "When you go back home, tell your dad—he still alive?"

"No," I say.

"Well, how about your mother?"

"She's alive—what do you want me to tell her?" But he's forgotten.

"Are they gonna pay you for this?" he asks me.

"Yeah."

"Well, goddam, I think I gave you some pretty good dope there."

I go find Cheryl, who's with her brothers Joe and Frank

and her babies in another room. We make a list of all Charlie's known children and grandchildren and get it up to eighty before we quit. And that's not including great-grandchildren too numerous and dispersed to count.

"I mean, can you imagine having a newborn when you're sixty-five?" Cheryl says as we go through the list. "That's how old Dad was when Frank was born. But he took care of us—still does. I mean, if we ever needed anything, he'd be there. He's a good man. He's got a lot of love."

• • • I never got a form back from Charlie's son Angelo, so I try him on the phone. I get him, but he doesn't sound interested in getting together.

"I don't think we have anything in common," he says.

• • • "I was always one step ahead of the law," says Todd Tonelli, Angelo's son. We're in the living room of his mother Sally's house in Des Moines. "But I was always the one who knew when to say when." Sally's here, too—she married and divorced Todd's father, and though she's an in-law, she's been of enormous help to me just in keeping all the Tonellis of Iowa straight in my mind. Todd's twenty-nine, tall and lean; he's in the car business now.

"We were all kind of wild kids, though," he says of himself and his Tonelli-side cousins. "Our early years, from about eighteen to twenty-two—"

"*Younger*," Sally says.

"Yeah, from fourteen to twenty-two were our defiant years."

"*Very*," Sally says.

"Yeah. *Very*. Tunner was the big influence on *all* of us," Todd says, mentioning his late uncle, a family favorite and, by all accounts, a genuine outlaw character. "Tunner was a bigger influence than my dad. Tunner hated authority, hated the law. He taught us *everything* about drugs, about doing them and selling them. *Encouraged* us to sell them. How to beat the IRS. I mean, we were smoking pot at twelve and thirteen, smoking with Tunner. And the funny thing is, his son's a cop."

I still have trouble imagining Italians in Iowa, but Todd says there are plenty in Des Moines. "I run with a lot of Italians on the south side—that's the Little Italy," he says.

"There's a very strong sense of ethnic pride there," Sally says.

"Yeah," says Todd. "They have their big Italian festival every year. And you don't go if you're not Italian. I like the fact that I'm Italian. I'm proud to be, for the most part. Much more than either my brother or my sister."

Sally says, "His sister Terry told me, 'My name's Italian, and that's where it starts and stops.' "

• • • Maya Angelou is on the "Today" show, talking about the poem she wrote for Clinton's inauguration. At the time, I read it in the paper with an avid eye—in a pluralistic pileup, she honored by name the Asian, the Hispanic, the Jew, the African, the Native American, the Sioux, the Muslim, the French, the Greek, the Irish, the Rabbi, the Priest, the Sheikh, the gay, the straight, the preacher, the homeless, the Pawnee, Apache, Seneca, Cherokee, Turk, Arab, Swede, German, Eskimo, Scot, the Ashanti, the Yoruba, the Kru. . . . What the fuck is a *Kru*?! Wait—*she mentions the dinosaur!* Everybody but the Italian. A few days later, an angry letter to the editor ran in the *New York Post.* An Italian-American reader suggested a link between Columbus's fall from grace in these politically correct times and Angelou's omission. Maybe it was a crackpot theory, but it was a good one.

Now she's admitting that her poem wasn't *all* all-inclusive: The original text included the Italians and the Poles, she says, but then she forgot—*forgot*—to put them in the version she read at the inauguration. How do you remember sixty-two Pawnee and forget twelve million Italians? I can just see her on the morning of the inauguration, frantically searching her hotel room on hands and knees, muttering, "Now where did I put those guidos?"

● ● ● I mention to Mike Clausi that tomorrow I'm going to Anamosa Men's Reformatory to visit his cousin, Bob.

"*I* was at Anamosa, too," Mike says. "For armed robbery. It's pretty mellow there. There's a lot of kids. It's almost like a country club prison—racquetball and all that stuff."

I like Mike right away—he's got an unmistakable rough-and-tumble air about him, but he's an open, friendly guy who smiles a lot. And he's had it rougher than most (his mother, Carmella, is in the prison camp in Texas for drugs; his father killed himself when Mike was a teenager). We're at his job, at the trucking company in West Des Moines owned by his pretty wife Tracy's father.

"Yeah, they were wild young times," he says, grinning. "I'm glad I got caught when I did. You know, you get used to that easy money, and then it's hard to stop. There was lots of times before that one when I *didn't* get caught. But the last time there was some gunplay, so I was lucky I didn't get my head blown off."

The plan was that I'd meet him and his two brothers here today. But we're still waiting for Albert and Dom to show up.

"I see my brothers at least once a week," Mike says. "Mostly to work on cars together. Me and Albert, we used to like to drink a lot. Never Dominic, though—he was always the one getting us out of trouble."

He checks the time, picks up the phone and calls Dominic, but gets his answering machine.

"Dom, it's me. We're down here at the office. It's eleven-thirty. Call me." He hangs up, but a second later his wife calls from the next room, "It's Dominic on the phone."

"Hey, Poky, what are you *up* to?" Mike says. "We're just—oh, wait, I can see Albert coming in now. OK, well come on over."

Albert walks in. He's twenty-eight and has the same friendly, roguish manner as his brother. He's on his way to his job pouring concrete. First thing, I tell him about my trip tomorrow to see Bob in prison.

"*I* did three years up there, for defending myself," he says. "I was at a party, and a guy hit me on the head with an

A&W Root Beer mug. Hit me three times before it broke. My brother Dom pulled him off me, and I was on the floor—everything went black. Then I saw Mike and I said, 'Man, that dude fucked me up.' And I looked over and saw a big crowd, and I thought that the guy was beating Dom up, so I pulled out my knife and pushed through the crowd, and I saw the guy who hit me and I poked him. In the stomach."

"Then," Mike says, "me and Dom put the boots to him."

Only Albert was convicted of willful injury, but Mike and Dom got thirty days each for assault.

"Good thing you guys had each other," I say.

"Yeah," Mike says.

"Definitely," says Albert.

"We're brothers and best friends, too," Mike says.

"In fact," Albert says, "somebody once told me we were the closest family he'd ever seen, us three and our mom. That came mostly from our dad's values. Don't let anybody hurt your brothers. If your brother's in trouble, help him. But our dad wasn't around a lot when we were little. So we had to work things out ourselves."

"*Young*," Mike says.

"First thing I remember was when Dad was beating up Mom," Albert says. "I must have been eight or nine. We started plotting and we said, 'This is just not right.' Then we found out about the drugs. And that's what was making him do this shit to our mom. And we thought, There's something wrong about this stuff. We couldn't really do anything about it, but we talked about it a lot, and that's what started bonding us together."

"And we all lived together," Mike says, "even after we left home. We had apartments together."

"Yeah," says Albert, "you can see other people with their brothers and sisters—they're not nearly as close. So I'm glad. I feel fortunate."

Dom calls back—he's running late, so he'll have to skip the visit (they don't call him Poky for nothing).

"Our kids are a lot different than we were at their age," Mike says. "When I was thirteen I was already into drugs and booze and all that. My son's thirteen, and he's not even into girls yet. He's into Michael Jordan. And I'm glad about that. He's got eighty-five acres to play on. Got a motorcycle. Yeah, he's got it easy, but that's not a bad thing. Prison and all, that's not a life."

"I consider myself lucky today," Albert says. "Back then, because of drugs, I lost everything I had. I lost *vehicles.* But all I lost was my stuff. I didn't have to go out and steal from people I know."

"Like stealing from your own mom," says Mike.

"Yeah, and fucking over your own family," says Albert.

• • • On the corridor wall of my cheap Des Moines motel there's a faded sign that says Lounge pointing down a shadowy flight of stairs. Can't be anything decent down there, I think as I descend. At the bottom of the steps I find a door, and behind it there's a subterranean room with a jukebox and two pool tables; it's like somebody turned their grandparents' basement into a cocktail lounge. There's a gorgeous, sassy Ethiopian bartender named Mulu, obviously on very familiar terms with her cast of regulars—Gary, the fiftyish wiseguy; Chester, the mild and laconic prematurely bald guy; Donna, the spry, silver-haired grandmother in peppy sportswear; and the bashful, heavy young woman with a blond shag whose name I never hear.

I'm the silent, unknown presence at the end of the bar until two more women come in, and one of them, feeling boozy and frisky, puts some Patsy Cline on the box and asks me to dance. "Sure," I say, and we do, and before the third verse she's inviting me to accompany her and her sister's kids to Mount Rushmore in the summer. What the hell, I say sure to that, too. Our twirl more or less breaks the ice, and before long somebody asks why I'm in town, and I tell the truth, and it strikes everybody funny for about a minute. Lucky for me, just then a noisy group enters, including a woman named Janet whom everyone seems to know.

Chester leans over from the next stool and tells me, "That's Janet Tonelli."

Donna is saying it's her son's birthday and she has to send him a card, "but I'm so upset with him. He's pissed at me because I'm going with a black man. But since my husband died, *no* man has treated me better. It's time for me to think of *my* life, *my* happiness." We all agree and order more beers.

My dance partner calls down from the other end of the bar to re-extend her invitation to see Mount Rushmore.

"You should go," Chester says. "You can see George Tonelli."

Now somebody is at the jukebox, and "All Shook Up" comes on.

"Elvis Tonelli," Chester announces.

• • • It's still dark when I leave Des Moines for the three-hour drive to the middle of nowhere, to Anamosa, where Bob Tonelli pays the price. It's dark and cold and snowing, wet flakes.

The prison—what else do prisons do?—it *looms*. It's about a hundred years old, built in the days when public buildings were as temples to the state. It looms not grimly, but grandly. The office of Warden John Thalacker has a fireplace and ceilings that must be fifteen feet high.

To get to the narrow, airless conference room where Bob will tell his tale, I pass through two grim sets of barred thresholds. This is nothing like the bucolic prison camp where his half-sister Carmella is held. This is the worst.

"As I remember it, it happened at approximately eleven-fifteen, eleven-thirty at night." Bob and I are face to face across the table. I asked how he ended up this way.

"I laid him down on the floor to change his diaper, and I went into the other room to get the diaper and baby wipes.

"When I came back, he had pooped on the floor, so I cleaned him up and cleaned the poop. Then I tossed him onto the—the papers say I hurled him, that was his mother's mother's word. I wouldn't so much say that I hurled him, but I tossed him on the couch. By no means did I mean for this to happen. I can't really tell you how much force was involved, but he hit an ashtray. He hit his head on an ashtray. Then he got up, and he walked around the room once, and then he fell down and went into convulsions.

"And I called 911. Then I called his mother, who was my

girlfriend at the time. And I tried to get him to breathe. He was breathing, but he was breathing hard, and he, uh . . . I was trying to give him CPR. His mother got here, and she called the ambulance. She had to look up the number in the phone book. And then the ambulance got there and took him to the hospital. She called me from the hospital and said, 'Did he hit his head?' And I said, 'Yeah, on the ashtray.' Then she said, 'Well, he's in a coma.' He went on for a day and a half, responding to her, she said. She called and said, 'He moves, he opens his eyes when I call his name.'

"But then the day after that, the sheriff showed up at my house, and he said the baby had just died.

"If I could change things, I'd rather I was dead than that little child. I wake up at night . . . *sweating*. . . . I guess you'd have to go through it yourself. But it's bad thoughts, bad dreams. *Bad* dreams. Ohh . . . I don't know. . . . "

Silence.

Since I first learned of Bob, I'd been looking forward, in a blackish way, to finally meeting him, the most notorious Tonelli in the world. Now here I am, having just encouraged a soft-voiced, visibly shaken twenty-two-year-old kid to describe the bleakest, most shameful moment any living being can imagine. I feel sick, and we still have a few minutes left. What can I possibly say now?

I ask, "What would you be doing if none of this had happened?"

"I'd probably be in my own apartment," he says. "Close enough to my dad's house so I could go over there to visit him. Go fishing. Hunt. Sit at home. Basically, that's it."

• • • I head east from Anamosa, feeling too shitty to even pretend otherwise. Only one thing occurs to me after meeting the Tonellis of Iowa: tough times make tight families. When you're in a jam you can't buy or force your way out of, all you have left to depend on is kin. So there's this thought about family values: There's nothing like suffering to make you value family.

Kitchen wall hanging, Joliet, Illinois

Mario "Motts" Tonelli

Sister Theodore Tonelli

Michelle Tonelli

Mario and Stella Tonelli

Tom and Antoinette Tonelli

Restaurant sign, North Brook, Illinois

Irene Tonelli, Norma Ceci, and Lea Luchini

Kathy Tonelli So

14.

Guidos on
Harlem Avenue

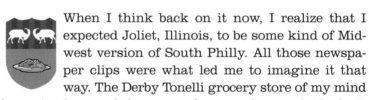

When I think back on it now, I realize that I expected Joliet, Illinois, to be some kind of Midwest version of South Philly. All those newspaper clips were what led me to imagine it that way. The Derby Tonelli grocery store of my mind could have stood around the corner from my house. And when, during Pizza Night in Denver, Art Tonelli described the multi-generational family bowling teams. . . . Anyway, I drove east with a picture in my head.

When I hit town, my directions brought me to a suburban-looking setting, but even then I didn't question it. After all, my first Joliet Tonelli lives in a necessarily gentle locale, Our Lady of Angels retirement convent.

"Now, are you connected to our branch of the family?" Sister Theodore Tonelli asks me. She's seventy-six, short and round and fair, and bears a strong resemblance to my own grandmother (who was, I have to remind myself, a Tonelli by marriage, not blood).

"No," I tell her, making the usual explanation for why I'm

here in the first place. I mention that I've just come from visiting a Tonelli in an Iowa jail.

"He's not from our branch either," she says, and I laugh. "Not that I'd feel any repugnance for a person in prison," she adds, shutting me up. "I spent twenty years working at Stateville prison. When I first started there, all we did was prepare the men for Sunday Mass. Singing and such. Then, my real ministry started. For about twenty years I'd go up there four days a week and have one-on-one conferences. With the men. We'd sit and talk, and I'd try to help them with any problems they had. I often wondered who got more out of it. They were all very respectful. I also went into the cell houses. I learned a *lot* on those visits," she says, laughing. "I'd see how they would provide for themselves, fix things, invent what they needed. They were . . . ingenious. One man told me they could blow up the place anytime they wanted. And then he told me *how.* Another man there taught me how to open a locked drawer. The men used to ask me, all the time, 'Why do you come up here with all us bad guys?' Well, it was not for *them,* that's for sure. It was for the love of God. But I guess I helped the men, indirectly. A lot of things I do without thinking about why. I see a need and I fill it. Stateville was not a very pleasant atmosphere. But it was not the fault of the men."

She's been a nun for sixty-one years, since she was fifteen years old, when this life called to her as it had to her older sister.

"We often debate about why it is that the girls don't come today. *My* idea—it's just my idea, now—is that they have about the same life out there as they do in here now, so that's why they don't come. When I started, we had *lots* of rules. Today, we are allowed to wear whatever we want—the full habit, or the slight change, like I'm wearing, or street clothes. We don't keep our salaries. We turn them in. But we *do* have a budget. So you see, the only real difference is that we live in community and the girls out there don't. What the girls fail to realize is the strength and support you get from living in community."

I ask, "But don't you have to give up a lot for that community?"

"Oh, yes," she readily admits.

"So do you still feel the calling as strongly as you did sixty years ago?"

"Maybe stronger."

• • • I had intended to catch up with Ernest Tonelli at his Little League team's game tonight. But then it poured, and the game was called, so once again, it's dinner talk.

Ernest, you may recall, first turned up in my clip file from the Joliet paper. He and his brother, A. Duane, were the first Tonellis to lodge in my imagination. (A. Duane, the elder, split Joliet and found success in the aerospace industry in San Diego; while Ernest stuck close to home, served on the school board, and coached sports.)

Once we're settled into a chain restaurant in a strip shopping center—still this gnawing suburban motif to Joliet—the talk turns to baseball anyway.

"We've got red jerseys—Modern Builders, that's our name—and on our team we've got a couple of real super studs and some average ballplayers, just real good kids. We have not always drafted the best players in the league. We try to draft the kid who's going to give us one hundred percent. And sometimes we stay away from kids if we don't feel their parents have the right attitude, to tell you the truth. We always, at the beginning of every year, have a meeting with the parents and the kids, and we tell them—I've umpired baseball, basketball, and football—and we tell them that we don't want the kids complaining to the umps. If something has to be said, we'll say it, because first of all, I think I know how to say it. And secondly, I know half of the umpires anyway. But we don't want the kids or the parents yelling at the umps. And our real goal is . . . I would certainly like to win a lot more than I lose, but, hey—we play thirty-two games, and I could go thirty-two and zero and—Bill, if I win thirty-two games every year for the next five years, I'm *still* never going to get an offer to coach in the majors. So my goal is to play about five hundred ball or better, because I do enjoy winning more than losing. But we try to stress to the kids—and we tell the parents that we need their help with this—that we *win* with class, and we *lose* with class, and we *play* with class. And that's it. If a kid throws a helmet or a bat, he sits down. We'll yank him out of the game right away. And I'll let him sit there a little bit, and then I'll go over and sit and ask if he knows why he's there. And that's the way it goes. We shake hands afterwards.

"I like Mike Ditka as a pro coach, and there are a lot of other people I like, and I like them because of their intensity. But they send the wrong—I shouldn't say that—people *pick up* the wrong message. And that's one reason I don't referee football anymore. I didn't like the language. I didn't like coaches telling kids, 'You gotta kick their ass.' That's contrary to what I believe in, so my son and I both quit doing football. With basketball, there are more technical fouls now than ever. There are more rules to avoid technicals than ever. And I think that when kids see that, they see the coaches and the adults challenge the authorities, and then *they* do it. And then we wonder what's the matter with our society. In high school sports? Very often, the teachers who complain the most about kids not respecting authority are the ones who go out there on the field and make asses of themselves. Disrespect the authority figure out there on the field and then wonder why the kids do it in their classrooms. Or anywhere else. I think we send so many mixed signals and mixed messages, and—jeez, I'm pontificating. That's not how this started. But our motto is win with class, lose with class. If I teach the kids that, teach them how to be gracious and enjoy themselves—it's a *game.*"

Great guy, right? He's the Tonelli contribution to America's game.

• • • "There's a lot of Tonellis in Joliet, but we're not related to one of them." We're in Stella Tonelli's sunny living room with her and her brother Mario, who lives with his wife a few blocks away. They're both retired. "Though everywhere I go, people say, 'Are you related to so-and-so?'"

"Maybe we're hundred-and-twenty-fifth cousins," Mario says.

They're actually from Cuba, Illinois, originally. "I was working in a job at a garage in 1936, in the Depression, and they told me they'd have to lay me off," Mario says. "Our cousin Attilio was with a roofing company, and he said that if I'd drive him back to Joliet, where he was living, he'd get me a job. I was twenty-one. I told Mom, 'I'm going to go,' because there was nothing there for me in Cuba." Mario married an Italian girl he met in Joliet. Stella, a beauty-shop owner who followed her brother to Joliet in 1958, never married.

"My two kids did not marry Italians," Mario says when I ask. "My one married a German, and the other married I don't know what."

"Once you get down far enough, everybody's mixed up with everybody else," Stella says.

"Ninety percent of the Italians, I think, have forgotten the past," Mario says. "But there's one group that'll *never* forget it—the blacks."

• • • Last stop in Joliet and I still haven't found anything remotely resembling an urban Little Italy. In fact, twenty-year-old Michelle Tonelli, who's a psychology student, lives with her parents in an area that borders on farmland. I ask if she'll stay in Joliet once she graduates.

"You know, I'm not sure," she says, sitting at the kitchen table. "After I go to graduate school and stuff, I'll go wherever I can establish a practice. So probably around here, maybe Chicago—at least for a while. But eventually I'll go to a warmer climate, like Florida." She lets that hang in the air then says, "But I'll probably end up staying here. Like everybody else."

"What's it like," I wonder, "growing up in an area where there are so many people with your name?"

"Everyone always asks me, are you related to Art or to Ernest? And I'm like, 'Yeah,' but there hasn't been a family reunion for a long time."

"About the only time we see anybody is at a wedding or a funeral," her mother says. "The reunions used to be once a year. But the old ones die off, and they're the ones who organized it."

I pick up Route 30 east, a rutted two-lane heading toward Chicago. Almost to Joliet's city limits, I come upon its hard urban core. It's as gray and gritty and familiar as anything back home. I realize that *this* is where the Joliet Tonellis of yore most likely lived. What must I have been thinking, what time warp must I have been in, to expect that they'd still be here?

• • • It is only thanks to modern ways of thinking about family and name that I even discovered Irene Tonelli and her sisters, Norma Ceci and Lea Luchini. They're all grandmothers, but Irene, once she divorced her husband, a Mr. Botkin, then reassumed her maiden name.

"She had enough of him," Norma jokes as Irene sets out the vast selection of take-out food she'd picked up on her way home from work. We're about midway between Joliet and Chicago now, in Irene's apartment.

"No," Irene says. "I just wanted to be Tonelli again."

"My daughter did it, kept her maiden name," Lea says.

"And she's still married," says Norma.

"Her husband and their kids have one name," says Lea, "and she has another."

Puccini's on the stereo in the other room, and once we're all at the table and digging in, I ask, "Do you think the women of your children's generation are upholding the old traditions, the food and everything else?"

Irene: Well, when we got married we started cooking the way Ma did, all of us.

Lea: I still do.

Irene: Well, you're still married to a nice Italian guy. But my husband was a meat and potatoes man. He didn't want polenta—that's *mush* to him. He wouldn't eat chicken. On Thanksgiving when we went to Ma's, he wouldn't eat turkey—

Lea: No fowl?

Irene: No—what did he used to have on Thanksgiving?

Lea: *I* don't know.

Norma: Ham.

Irene: I used to fix a ham, with the corn pudding because he wouldn't eat what Ma had. He didn't like fowl. That's because his mother killed a chicken every Sunday. And so he got fed up with chicken.

Lea: Well, Robert still eats his chicken.

Irene: And he didn't like spaghetti. He wanted it on the side. But I like spaghetti *here,* with my salad and vinegar and oil running into it.

Norma: My girls, they have their spaghetti once in a while, but I don't think they cook like . . . they cook the way their husbands like to eat.

Irene: Yeah, they change.

Lea: It changes you.

Norma: No, my Roseanne cooks like I do. I told you, I don't make *sugo** anymore. Her kids like my daughter's *sugo* better than mine.

Me: What are some other differences between your daughters and you?

Norma: Well, now we're looking at the nineties housewife.

Lea: Yeah.

Irene: My oldest daughter used to do a lot of cooking, but now . . . I think, my oldest daughter, she's gotten away—they eat out. She still cooks, but not as much.

Norma: I'll tell you what's different—

Irene: They're all a little lazy.

Norma: Come the holidays, we're still *cooking*! And that's *wrong*!

Lea: Right!

---

*Sugo (SOO-go) is the Italian word for tomato sauce. But most Italian-Americans, myself included, grew up calling it "gravy," which is confusing to outsiders, who imagine spaghetti topped with gelatinous brown gunk. For the sake of simplicity and clarity, in this book I have used the term *tomato sauce* even when Tonellis called it something else.

Norma: And they come over just in time to eat!

Irene: Not me—mine don't come home! One's way out in Florida. One's out in Seattle.

Norma: No, when Ma used to cook for Easter, or any holiday, we were there the day before, *and* that morning, to help her. But not now. Now they come in time to eat!

Lea: Uh-huh.

Me: Is that because they don't know how to do it?

Norma: No, they *could* do it. But they go either to their mothers-in-law or to their mothers. Mostly to their mothers. Now, when Ma—how old was she when we split it up?

Lea: I don't know.

Norma: It was getting to be pretty hard for Ma to do it all, so the night before, we'd go over to help her, to set up the table, or sometimes we'd cook the turkey the night before, and then we'd all bring something.

Irene: Then it got to the point where we'd let her cook only once a year—I think it was Easter. Then Norma took Thanksgiving, Lea took Christmas, and I took New Year's. We split the holidays up. We each took one. Then our daughters started bringing boyfriends, and it started growing, and then the kids got older, and then there were sons-in-law, so we thought—of course, Ma was gone by this time—so we said, oh, forget it, everybody take care of their own.

Lea: It gets to be too much. I have sixteen people to feed. I have to put the extension on the table—

Norma: No, you have to do what other families do: They rent a hall. . . .

Lea: Oh, Jesus.

Norma: They *do*! And everybody brings something. Or they have it catered.

Irene: But Lea, I think Ma was *your* age when she quit doing it.

Lea: I *know*!

Irene: So how come *you're* still doing it?

Lea: I'm seventy and I'm *still cooking*! [Everybody laughs.]

• • • I'm strolling (*zoom*) down Imperial Road just northwest of Chicago, killing some time before a lunch date, but believe me, this is no place to (*zoom*) stroll. There's barely a sidewalk, and there's nothing and nobody to see. It's not meant to be experienced on foot; it takes forever to get from one thing to the next. And the traffic (*zoom*) is (*zoom*) real (*zoom*) close. For six weeks I've been driving like a trucker, and it still hasn't curbed my geographic instinct to walk, which means I've eaten a lot of exhaust lately. In Nereto, where my grandfather was born, you can walk. In South Philly you can walk. In New York you can walk. But America is about transportation, about *moving*—first boats and horses and stagecoaches, then trains and Model Ts and planes, rocket ships, satellites, fiber optics, faxes. Movement is what transported Americans even across the intangible barriers of birth and blood. To us, movement is magic. Where would we be if the pioneers sucked at driving? Stuck in New York. We still wouldn't know what the Pacific looks like. Every time we drive, we worship our American ancestors by re-enacting their brave, restless impulse. Every quick run to the 7-Eleven for charcoal briquettes is an homage to Lewis and Clark. Which makes walking (*zoom*) (*zoom*) (*zoom*) un-American.

But I'm (*zoom*) walking.

• • • "I wanted my husband to meet you, but he wasn't able to. He's kind of a hermit. He's been in this country for ten years now, and he just became a citizen, but he feels uncomfortable still. He's self-conscious about his accent. He's still uncomfortable driving, too. He got his license a few weeks ago, but he still takes the bus."

I'd also hoped to meet Kathy Tonelli So at home, if only because she's married to a Korean and they have two kids—the only mingling, to my knowledge, of Asian and Tonelli blood. But our schedules didn't work, so I find her at Beltone, the hearing-aid maker, where she is a programmer/analyst. We get into her new Tempo and head out for pizza.

"I seem to be in most places about three years, then I move on. I was born in Battle Creek. When I was a kid, the whole family moved to San Diego, and we lived there for eleven years, until I was in college. Then we moved back to Battle Creek—my mother hated California, she thought it was fantasyland, she missed the changing seasons. I went to Michigan State—that's where my brother Terry was going—I kind of followed him. [Her brother is Terry the Civil War nut of Reno. Her sister is Bobbie McNichol from the dinner in San Diego.] Then I moved to Washington, D.C., for a job. But I really missed California, and it took me three years, but I got back there, to Long Beach. I took a government job, but I hated the office where I worked."

The pizza shows up, divided in the odd Chicago way—a round pie cut into small squares.

"So I applied for overseas jobs with the Department of Defense, and they sent me to Korea. A coworker of mine had worked there and really liked it. And I thought, Why not? I was single, and I thought, Why not break the tie? I had been having some problems with my boyfriend at the time, so it was easier to break it off by going to Korea. I thought it might be exciting. I might see something. And being there under the auspices of the army, it wasn't too much of a risk. If you stayed on the army base it was like being in Kansas. But I lived in Seoul, and it was exciting. I had never lived in a big city before. It was . . . wild."

Chan So, her husband, worked in the same office as Kathy, and they dated for about a year before deciding to get married. "I was surprised that his parents didn't kick up a fuss—he's the only son. But they didn't. Then my job was abolished, so we came back to Washington." Because she had a pretty good career going, she says there was never any thought that they'd settle in Korea. "He had always wanted to come here. *Everybody* does, at least to visit. When we came back, I was still working for the government. My husband was working for the post office, but he's a volatile person, and he got into a fight and quit. We were in Washington at the time, and it was expensive to live there. So I looked into moving back to Battle Creek, where my parents live. We even moved there for two months, but there were no jobs. So that's why we're in Chicago. We've been here three years, but now we're considering moving back to the Coast. I still miss it. And the weather's better. And my husband would be closer to Korea. He hasn't been back since we left, in '84. And the kids have never seen Korea, and they need to."

Her husband is studying to be an automobile mechanic. "He comes from a scholarly background, and it was a little difficult for him to make the decision to get a skill. He worked in sales and was very good at it, but he hated it. It took him awhile to wise up. He had always wanted to be a writer, but it's hard for him to do in English. So meanwhile, he can have a vocation, if not a career." When he became a citizen last year, he changed his first name from Chan to John.

"So what does all this make your children?" I ask.

"They're *American*. My daughter asked me last week, 'Mom, am I Oriental?' I told her, 'Yes and no. You look Korean, and you *are* half-Korean, but you're raised, and you think, as an American.' My son, he's more sensitive. He was three before he'd even admit he was part Korean. And he always resisted speaking any Korean. He has always been very concerned with being seen as 'normal.' "

I ask if their home feels multicultural, if, for instance, she does any Korean cooking.

"I make something called *bulgogi*. It's kind of like Korean barbecued beef," she says. "But other than that, we eat American food—a lot of spaghetti. . . . "

• • • A dream dashed: All along I've been thinking that I had a physically challenged Tonelli to add to my culturally diverse nation, and today I learn otherwise. One of my newspaper database searches turned up Jerry Tonelli, star player of the Toronto Spitfires, a wheelchair basketball team. I finally track him down via telephone and discover that while he does play on the team, he is actually able-bodied. And, his name's Tonello.

The Amazing Story of the Tonelli Family in America

• • • I'm heading north of Chicago, to Skokie, and the greatest Tonelli of them all.

From the start, one of my goals was to see what Tonellis had contributed to America, and as soon as I found Mario "Motts" Tonelli in my newspaper clip searches I knew he'd be our shining star.

He first made the papers in the thirties, when he was a star running back for Notre Dame, a two-year starter who once scored a game-winning touchdown against Southern California in the final minutes. He played with the old Chicago Cardinals pro team until World War II started, at which time he shipped out to the South Pacific. There, he was captured and survived the unspeakably brutal Bataan Death March and almost four years of captivity in a Japanese prisoner of war camp. That would have been plenty, but there's more. After he returned home from captivity, sick with malaria and dysentery and weighing ninety-eight pounds, he whipped himself back into shape and played two more seasons of pro football, before getting into politics. He was a Cook County commissioner, and later, the county's top environmental protection official.

His lady friend, Mary, lets me into the house, and a minute later Motts strides in, a seventy-six-year-old man still in fighting shape, with a shock of white hair and an energetic bounce to his bearing. He leads me into a back room to show me something—the medals he brought home from the war: the Bronze Oak Leaf Clusters, an American Service ribbon with bronze star, a Philippines Defense ribbon, and more. Then we're all walking out to the car, headed to dinner.

"We're going to a restaurant called Tonelli's," he says, giving me a deadpan look. "I hope you don't mind."

"Great," I say.

The conversation starts off in kind of a weird direction—all I have in my notebook is the word *phonies,* but as I remember it, he's complaining about the state of the world in general, and especially the failure of leaders to be forthright and brave. But he's doing all this in a Socratic mode—Motts asks me slightly leading questions, trying to solicit my views first, then weighs what I say with a serious look on his face. I can't figure out what exactly is going on. But it goes on this way for a while.

"Let me ask you another question," he says, glancing over at me while he drives. "Do you think I'm an oddball?"

"No," I say, but I'm thinking: *Where's this going?*

"Motts," Mary says from the backseat, "I think you should tell Bill the story about your class ring."

He looks me in the eye and flashes the old Notre Dame ring at me.

"When we started the death march," he begins, "we weren't thinking about our rings or anything like that. We were thinking about the guys getting killed, getting their heads ch—— getting tortured. Wait. Let me tell you something. When I've told newspaper reporters this story, I get calls from Japanese people who say, 'Why do you have to talk about this? It makes it hard on us, hard on our kids.' I tell them, 'Look, I understand how you feel, but it's all true. You *were* brutal.' Anyway, on the march, at the first stop, an enlisted man came up to all the prisoners and took from us anything he could find— watches, ballpoint pens, everything. So he comes to me and says, 'I want that ring.' And I said, 'No,' and he said it again, 'I *want* that ring.' Finally I said to myself, I'd better give it to him, but I felt bad about that, so I kept my eye on him. I watched him give all our stuff to his officer, and the officer went through it all, and then he started walking toward us. He walked up to me and asked—in English, in *excellent* English—whether his soldiers had taken anything from me. So I said, 'Yeah, they took my Notre Dame ring.' Well, it turned out he had gone to school in America and knew all about Notre Dame. And he said to me, 'I'm going to give you your ring back. But if I were you, I'd hide it, because more soldiers are going to want to take it from you.' And then he wished me luck, and I wished him luck, and that was it."

He's silent a second, then he says, "I hid that ring a lot of places."

"Like where?" I ask, not meaning it as funny as it comes out sounding.

"A lot of places."

Mary giggles in the backseat. But Motts doesn't crack a smile.

"Hey, Motts," I say, "where'd you get that nickname?"

"I don't know," he says. "In high school. And it's not for Motts Apple Sauce. Evidently, they say I was a pretty rough kid back then. I never got in trouble, but I was probably tough and had a chip on my shoulder. *I* thought I was kind and gentle and treated people with loving care. You know, somebody once told me that *motts,* in Italian dialect, means 'killer.' So maybe that's where it came from. Though I never killed anybody, except maybe in the war."

"*I* can tell you one of his accomplishments," Mary says. "He was the *only* Republican ever elected county commissioner of Chicago. Back in the late forties he was a county commissioner for eight years."

"How'd you manage that?" I ask him.

"His charm," Mary says.

"No," Motts says, "I knew a lot of the kids who were precinct captains. I had played ball with them. Also, the war had just ended, and I was a vet, so that helped."

We fall back into small talk for a minute or so, and then Motts picks up where he left off before.

"I love America, but I think we better wake up and take care of things if we want them, rather than just take them for granted, like they're always going to be here. You know, in the *next* war—I think in twenty years we're going to be at war with Japan again. They've never accepted what we did to them. Say, did you ever stop to think, to visualize, what would happen if a bomb was dropped on the city of Chicago—what would happen? You know, people think a nuclear bomb has to come out of an airplane, but it doesn't. It could be in a suitcase. If Chicago was bombed, people would all run out of their offices to drive home. Then the fire engines couldn't get in, and people would have to abandon their cars. It would be a mess. Don't you think we should be better prepared?"

"Like how?" I ask.

"By not letting people use their cars for work—to take public transportation. But we talk about this and we talk about that—remember how we used to talk about air-raid shelters? Do you ever think about the things I'm telling you?"

"No," I reply.

"Why?" he says. "Why do *I* think about them?"

Before I can think of an answer to that one, he's pulling into the restaurant parking lot. As we get out of the car he's saying, "Can you picture the average American woman surviving a war? Can you picture them going out and chopping wood for a fire? Could they go without their dishwashers and washing machines? Could they survive and keep a family together? I'm not saying either way, I'm just asking you."

"Well," I say, "I guess if they had to they would."

"Would they? I don't know. I think they're too used to having everything. Where would they go to get firewood?"

"Maybe they'd just burn their furniture," I say.

"And where would they burn it?" he says. He's grinning now. "Right in the house?"

We walk inside and slide into a booth, he and Mary on one side and me on the other. They're sweet and fond together; he's unassuming, but he carries himself gallant and strong and straight.

"Another thing," he starts, right after we order dinner, "Father Scanlon was the pastor at Our Lady of Lourdes Church, which was right down the street from us. Now, every day my mother made soup, and my father ate it at noon, and every Monday we got the bread delivered. So of course, every Monday Father Scanlon would stop at my parents' house, and he would eat soup with us. He would always be carrying the bag full of donations to the church, carrying it down to the bank. And after he left us he'd walk down the alley a couple blocks to the bank. Now—do you think he could do that today?"

I can see where this is going.

"Walk around, even down an alley, with all that money?"

"Oh, I guess not," I answer. There's something absolutely riveting about conversation with Motts—every single subject leads him to fret over the dangers in life; the moral of every story is that our sense of safety is an illusion. Perfectly understandable, considering where the forces of fate once carried him. But even as he follows his thoughts to their gloomy ends, his manner remains unfailingly solicitous and outgoing, even cheerful. He's an enigma—there's a mystery, something huge but tender, inside him. What he wants most to say is unsayable, except in his roundabout, gently probing way.

"And then," he goes on, "when I was an altar boy, I used to get the favored spot during Mass because of Father Scanlon, and everybody wondered why. But I never told them. Now—was *that* right?"

"Motts," I tell him, "I can't believe you can find an ethical dilemma even in *that* story."

"Well, *kind* of," he says.

"But the priest was just returning the favor," I say.

"You know, when Mayor Daley—you've heard of Mayor Daley? When reporters came to him after they found out he'd given some of the city's insurance business to his son, he said, 'Well, if *I* don't give him business, who will?' And he was right. It was a stupid question."

"Motts," I ask him, "what made you wonder about how American women will manage during a war?"

"Because they're spoiled," he says. "Not that they shouldn't be." He pauses a second and looks straight into me.

"Did you expect me to be talking like this?" he asks. "What did you expect?"

"I didn't really have anything in mind," I say. I must have had *something* in mind, I'm thinking, but it wasn't this.

"I just think the American people should know these things in case they ever happen. Don't you? Because someday they're going to happen. Don't you agree?"

"It's kind of hard to imagine," I say.

"Not for me," he replies.

He's got me there. But I push on. "Motts," I ask, "do you really worry about *all this stuff*?"

"Yeah," he says, "but don't you think the government should be worrying? Don't you think the government knew the Japs were going to attack? They cracked the codes. *They knew.* But we don't want to face reality. I don't worry about it, because I won't be around that long. But people should worry about it.

People should know these things. Did you ever hear that the U.S. was bombed during World War II?"

"No," I say.

"Would you say I was goofy if I told you that?"

"I'd never call you goofy, Motts."

"Well, we were. Balloon bombs. They landed as far east as Iowa. Mostly along the coast, though. It's true. I think the people like me—I was in there for forty-two months—things happen that you can't *believe* would ever happen. Maybe that's why I think these things. I *do* wake up at night thinking, What if? I don't think I could live through that again, but I'm glad I lived through it. Because it made me a different man."

Dinner's over. As we leave, I stop to take some pictures of the restaurant's sign, then catch up with them in the parking lot. We ride awhile in silence, then Motts smiles and says, "She gave me hell before you got in the car."

"I just said you were being too negative," Mary says. "He's really not like that."

"The reason I'm negative is I'm concerned that the younger generations don't have to go through what we went through in World War II. And that's why I hate to hear anybody say, about *anything*, 'Well, that can't happen.' That *can* happen."

Back home, the night ends as it began—Motts has something he wants to show me. This time, though, it's not war related; it's old family photos and snapshots of his trip to Italy. As we're plowing through souvenirs and memorabilia, he tells me that he's been approached about writing his life story, and that sometimes he wants to, but he doesn't want the story to center on his football and wartime exploits.

"I want it to prove that America had to depend on immigrants, and how they came here and did a good job and didn't demand everything, didn't demand that everything be printed in their language and so on," he says. "And that was the old America, the real America. And we're losing that."

Motts, I guess that if we're losing it, then we'll lose it. But I hope people will remember that when we had it, you—a Tonelli—were there, giving everything to keep it safe.

• • • As I'm writing this, a debate on a related subject has broken out in the nation's egghead journals. In *Commentary,* conservative think-tanker and author Francis Fukuyama published an essay, "Immigrants and Family Values," in which he argues against the charge that today's newcomers from Asia and Latin America are ruining the country with their inability to act like all-American self-sustaining nuclear families. A position that, serendipitously, feels like it has everything to do with my cogitations on the Tonelli Nation—that the more successfully you master America, the less bound you need be to your kin.

Fukuyama writes:

> The notion that non-European immigrants are a threat to family values and other core American cultural characteristics is, in a way, quite puzzling. After all, the breakdown of traditional family structures, from extended to nuclear, has long been understood to be a disease of advanced industrial countries and not of nations just emerging from their agricultural pasts.
>
> Some conservatives tend to see the third world as a vast, global underclass, teeming with the same social pathologies as Compton in Los Angeles or Bedford-Stuyvesant in Brooklyn. But the sad fact is that the decay of basic social relationships evident in American inner cities, stretching to the most intimate moral bonds linking parents and children, may well be something with few precedents in human history. Economic conditions in most third-world countries simply would not permit a social group suffering so total a collapse of family structure to survive; with absent fathers and no source of income, or mothers addicted to drugs, children would not live to adulthood.
>
> But it would also seem a priori likely that third-world immigrants should have stronger family values than white, middle-class, suburban Americans, while their work ethic and willingness to defer to traditional sources of authority should be greater as well. Few of

the factors that have led to family breakdown in the American middle class over the past couple of generations—rapidly changing economic conditions, with their attendant social disruptions; the rise of feminism and the refusal of women to play traditional social roles; or the legitimization of alternative life-styles and consequent proliferation of rights and entitlements on a retail level—apply in third world situations. Immigrants coming from traditional developing societies are likely to be poorer, less educated, and in possession of fewer skills than those from Europe, but they are also likely to have stronger family structures and moral inhibitions. Moreover, despite the greater ease of moving to America today than in the last century, immigrants are likely to be a self-selecting group with a much greater than average degree of energy, ambition, toughness, and adaptability.

He's saying that America transforms your attachment to kin—it goes from being a practical dependence to a sentimental one. And sentimental is the last stop before nonexistent. Quayle and Buchanan had it completely wrong: America is *hell* on family values. America *destroys* family values. Everything about this country, from its founding principles to its size to its romance, encourages you to strike out on your own, independent and unencumbered by the past. And that's what your family *is*: History on the hoof.

• • • On his questionnaire, where I asked for three things that make Italian-Americans different from others, Tom Tonelli wrote: "Poor diction, I-ROC Camaros, and the need to grab one's balls while talking." He went on to describe Tonellis generally as "Hard-headed, talk extremely loud, bad-tempered." And at the end, he included this note: "I would like to add that although I am one-half Italian and less Native American, I am proud to consider myself a Cherokee."

OK! The Cherokee Tonelli! Had to meet him. When we spoke on the phone, he promised that if I visited on a Friday night, we could witness together the amusing spectacle of young Italo-Americans and their ritual cruising along Harlem Avenue in Chicago.

"Did you see all the signs on Harlem Avenue—Chicago's Little Italy, No Cruising?" asks Tom's wife, Antoinette.

We're in their apartment, which they share with a cockatoo.

"Yeah," Tom says, "they'll be out there tonight. It's nice out. Just driving up and down, radios blasting, going nowhere."

"The latest thing they have now is neon tubes up and down the body of the car, or around the license plates," Antoinette says.

They're in their early twenties, together for eight years already, sweet and funny.

"There's so much neon, it looks like Las Vegas," Tom says.

"Or they park in a parking lot. At the White Castle. They leave their lights on and their music playing."

"And they'll drive like this," Tom says, slumping in his rocker so that his neck is practically on the seat, one arm stuck straight up, hand like a claw over an imaginary steering wheel. "It's pretty funny."

"They're all ages, from like fourteen to even older than us," Antoinette says.

"Oh, yeah, there's guys in their thirties out there all the time. In Eldorados."

"Guidos."

Tom's sweatshirt says American Indian Movement: Free Leonard Peltier. I ask if it mattered to him that Antoinette is also half Italian.

"No," he says, smiling. "Does *anybody* still think that way?"

"It never crossed my mind either," Antoinette says. "Do you know who still thinks that way now? The Greeks."

"Yeah," Tom says, "like Phil. He was really hot and heavy with this girl, but he wasn't Greek, so she broke up with him. Then, didn't we just read that she married a Greek dentist? I never even *heard* of a Greek dentist."

We leave for dinner. (Everybody eats dinner, I realize, but

the frequency with which my talks with Tonellis occur over food no longer strikes me as coincidence.) On the way, Tom points to a car ahead of ours and says, "See, there's one. Look how slow they're driving."

We pull up at—surprise—a typical Little Italy kind of restaurant, The Villa. Once we sit, Tom and Antoinette begin talking about a wedding they recently attended, somebody from her mother's side.

"You don't go to a Luciano family wedding and bring up Lucky," Tom says, laughing. "Especially once I looked around the room and saw all those pinky rings."

Using her index finger, Antoinette pushes the tip of her nose to one side. "They all went like *this*."

"Yeah," Tom says, "I figured it was time to leave before somebody kissed me."

The waitress comes and we order a pizza.

Tom spent most of his life in this neighborhood, "but my aunt lives fifteen minutes from me, and I haven't run into her for five years. My cousins, they all live just a couple minutes from us, and I haven't seen them for five years, probably. We're not a real close family. I'm much closer to my mother's side." (His parents are divorced.)

Tom's mother taught him to make lasagna. "It's killer," Antoinette says.

"Yeah," he says, "people have actually offered me money to make it for them. Every other layer is spinach noodles, and the secret ingredient is the fifth cheese. My grandfather on my mother's side was almost but not quite full-blooded Cherokee. And my grandmother was half Cherokee. My father's parents were full-blooded Italian."

So does he feel at all Italian?

"No, I really don't. Like my doctor'll say, 'Oh, Tonelli, you're Italian,' and I'll say, 'No, I'm American.' But the part of my background that interests me most, that fascinates me most, is the Native American."

"Probably because you know more about the Italian side," Antoinette says.

"Maybe, but see, in my family, we never pushed the Italian background, or said, like, 'We're *proud* to be Italian.' I don't have one of those Proud to be Italian bumper stickers."

"Or a Kiss Me I'm Italian button," Antoinette says, laughing.

As they talk, I can hear an old man at the next table faintly crooning some obscure Neopolitan song to his dinner companions.

"I'm really just *me,* you know what I mean?" Tom says. "I *do* have several tattoos, and they're all Native American designs. And I *do* like to tell people that Columbus didn't discover America—we already knew it was here. I know a lot of stuff about that culture—from things I've read, from going to pow-wows. I like to go to them."

He stops a second to think about that. At the next table, somebody else is singing a different old Italian tune—I haven't heard these songs for years.

"So," Tom says, "I guess maybe I *am* proud to be a Native American."

• • • Here's all you need to know about ethnicity in America. In 1973, the National Opinion Research Center (NORC) conducted a survey that asked a thousand people how they identified themselves ethnically. The answers were recorded, and then a year later the same people were asked the question again. During that year, *26 percent of those surveyed had changed their answers.* Blows *my* mind. Their ancestries hadn't changed, needless to say—only how they thought of themselves. The respondents rediscovered their German-ness, for instance, or decided that being Irish was suddenly uncool, or just felt so distanced from *any* ethnic background that they disconnected from anything predating their own birth. They were—has this term *always* meant this?—all-American. Puerto Ricans were least likely to have switched (3.5 percent), and those of English-Scottish-Welsh ancestry were most likely (45 percent). Italians were least likely of all white ethnics to change their answers, but still, 12.2 percent had switched. I learned about that startling survey in *Ethnic Options,* a book by sociologist Mary C. Waters. She conducted her own study, in which she asked people this: If given a choice, which ethnicity would you choose for yourself? The number one answer: Italian.

The NORC study prompted me to look for some universally accepted definition of ethnicity. The one sociologists quote most frequently was devised in 1922 by a scholar named Max Weber: He said an ethnic group is one whose members "entertain a subjective belief in their common descent because of similarities in physical type or of customs or both, or because of memories of colonization or migration. . . . It does not matter whether or not an objective blood relationship exists." They share, he wrote, "a consciousness of kind."

And I just assumed from the start that ethnicity was something scientific and measurable. Once I finally got around to finding a definition, I see that it was never any such thing. It has always depended on people believing that they have something in common. Which means that if something else intervenes—time, experience, a more stylish consciousness—then you lose your belief.

Joe and Mike
Tonelli and
family

15.

Fear of
Victor Sparducci

*If the traveler expects the highway to be safe
and well-graded, he might as well stay at
home. The little roads without numbers are the
ones I have liked the best, the bumpy ones that
lead over hills toward vicinities unknown.*

Or so Charles Kuralt states in his memoir, *A Life on the
Road*. I don't know—I've grown to love the broad, monolithic in-
terstates. There's something monumental about them, like the
Grand Canyon. They're true expressions of democratic geography—every one is exactly the same, the signs and the general
layouts are all identical, so there's no hometown-driver advantage. The side roads are for locals and tourists; these big dudes
are made for *voyagers*. You hardly even have to pay attention—
many times I'd be motoring along and suddenly wonder: Which
route is this? What state am I in? And believe me, after a while
all those little bumps and hills get annoying. Of course, the side
roads sometimes lead to high adventure, as in Kuralt's first
made-for-TV expedition, in New England:

Reverend John and Valentino Tonelli

A shower of lemon and scarlet and gold washed across our windshield. In every town, people were out raking leaves and children were playing in piles of leaves. We got the camera out and did our first "On the Road" story just about how pretty it all was.

Maybe he's onto something. I decide to see the real people on the real roads too, so I shun the interstate and take Route 20 east from Chicago through Indiana and Ohio. Here's my journal:

- Miles of farmland (air smells like cowshit).
- Tiny, forgettable town.
- Miles of farmland (air smells like pigshit).
- Tiny, forgettable town.
- Miles of farmland (air smells like sheepshit).
- Motel.

On a two-lane in western Ohio, I begin to pass a pickup truck with a slatted wooden enclosure on the bed. As I pull up alongside, I look over at the cage and am startled by the view: Right up a pig's ass. Spectacular.

• • • "Hey, are you William Tonelli?"

Jesus, does it still show? I'm wandering around in the mist of a gray Sunday afternoon, trying to find the right door to knock on to get inside a farmhouse in Monroeville, Ohio, when the voice comes from across the road. He's a short, slender man in a plaid flannel shirt, black hair, and a huge black beard, biblical even beyond anything grown in Alaska.

I nod.

"I am, too," he says. "But I go by Mike."

Oops, I was prowling around the wrong house. Inside we go, to the cozy living room with Mike and his children, Matt, Melissa, and Heather, and grandson, Tyler. His wife's out shopping with his sister, but his father, Joe, who would be working if not for the rain, is on his way over.

"My dad came from a town in Italy called Calabrese, I believe," Mike tells me. I ask what brought his father to America, but he says he isn't exactly sure. "Just came over to get work, I think."

Just then his father, a dapper soybean farmer, walks in.

"Dad, you're from Calabrese, aren't you?" Mike asks.

"No, I'm from a little village in Tuscany, Fivizzano."

"Oh. I thought it was Calabrese."

"My brother followed the family tree once," Joe says. "He said one of our ancestors was in the second crusade, unfortunately. He joined the army of the king of England, Richard the Lion-Hearted. That was the crusade that didn't accomplish much. I came here in 1935." Joe's father had died in World War I, and his mother remarried, to an Italian whose family owned a tombstone business in Sandusky, Ohio. She came to America, leaving Joe, who was an agriculture student, behind, "and she wasn't very happy here, with her two children in Italy. So I came.

"If I had stayed in Italy, I would have graduated, and then I probably would have been some kind of agriculture aide in the Italian government. I wouldn't have had much of an opportunity to farm there, unless I farmed for someone else. We had gotten away from the land by then, we were living in Genoa. I came here and worked in Sandusky for a while, in a washing machine factory, and then I went to work for my stepfather in the tombstone business. I married my wife in 1939. She was a widow. And she owned this land, and she wanted me to farm the place, so I quit a good business and went farming. She's Pennsylvania Dutch."

Did he mind moving to America?

"I really didn't care. I was very happy in Italy. But my

mother kept asking me to come, so I said 'All right, send me the ticket and I'll come.' And when I got here it was fine. I got acquainted real easy—it was very nice for me. I'm an Italian, but I feel just as American as if I was born here."

Since when? "Ever since I got married. Because after that, there was no more speaking Italian at home."

Joe works a medium-sized farm, soybeans and wheat, with his wife's son from her first marriage. Mike's a car man for the railroad. "They didn't really need me on the farm," he explains, "and I didn't want to go into debt to buy land. So right out of school I got a job at an auto-parts store, then I worked a grain elevator, and I was a gunsmith for five years."

"Matt's the one with the future," Joe says, nodding toward his grandson.

"He's about to graduate from college," Mike says. "He's majoring in business management. He can coach, too. He can get into sports management with that, that's what he wants to do."

"I want to be a head football coach at a college," Matt says. "I'll probably work construction after I graduate until I find a job in my field. I'd like to stay around here—I could probably coach at my high school—but the money won't be so good. So it's hard to say *where* I'll end up. Probably right here."

I ask Mike, "Did you think of moving away when you were young?"

"No, I really didn't. Just wanted to get a job and start working."

"Boy, *I* do," says Melissa, who's in high school.

"Why?" her grandfather asks.

"I want to go to college, to study forensic psychology— *the study of criminal minds*," Melissa says. "And I'll probably have to go to a city to do it."

"There's no better life than the country," Joe says.

"What kind of job could I get in the country?" Melissa asks him. *"Housewife?"*

• • • I'm still in Ohio, but now at a place that brings me back to the genesis of this entire expedition.

"I was in the pension and profit-sharing consulting business in '67, '68," says Dennis Haslinger, owner and president of Numa Corp., which is based in suburban Akron.

"Fellow by the name of Gary Halbert called on me. He was selling Pitney-Bowes postage meters. We were talking one day, and I asked him how he liked selling, and he said he hated it. He wanted to go into the direct-mail business. He said he wanted to start a little company he could run from his dining-room table, and he needed a partner. A few months later he had obtained a large mailing list, and he asked me if I'd help him put together a mailing, a catalog to sell personalized items—dog collars with the dog's name on it, stuff like that. And he had one item, it was a plaque showing a lion rampant, the heraldic symbol. And when you bought it, we'd put your name on the plaque. Well, it was our most successful item. People liked that one but we didn't know why.

"Then we noticed that we had a lot of people named Miller on our mailing list, so in our next mailing we included a letter to all the Millers offering them a history of the Miller name and a line drawing of the earliest Miller coat of arms, and a list of all the famous Millers throughout history. Well, the Millers out-responded all the rest by two to one. We thought, Gee, there must be a demand for this kind of information.

"So we put together a parchment scroll of information on various last names—we did it for about a dozen names. We got them from phone books for the twenty-five largest metropolitan areas. The average response to a direct-mail solicitation is about one, one and a half percent. But that mailing got a six percent response. And I was a history major, so all this was interesting to me. I left my other business to devote myself full-time to this, and in 1972 I bought Halbert out. In the seventies, we ended up mailing the entire population of the United States three times over—two hundred million American households got our mail in that decade. Then we started our international business, and our products are just as well received abroad as here."

That's right—it's the amazing story of the company that suckered me into buying *The Amazing Story of the Tonellis in America*.

"At one time we had about eighty people here who did nothing but research into various family genealogies. And we have all that information on computer now. And essentially, what we've done is add value to the information by organizing it and putting it together," Haslinger says.

Here's how they operate: They start with a list of all the surnames in America. Then they figure out how many people have a particular last name and check to see what information they have on the name and how recently they solicited that clan.

"Wait a second," I interrupt him "—how do you know how many names there are in the United States?"

"We've counted them," Haslinger says. "There are about one million eighty thousand surnames in America. Then the computer sorts all the surnames into what we call frequency ranges. It goes through about ninety-two million household files, which come from phone listings, drivers' license records, census information. And we buy information from the large compilers. We bought our East German names from the Stasi, the Communist secret police. They were the only ones who had *everybody's* name and address. The really high frequency names, like Jones or Smith, are not interested in our books, though we do have the information. There's something like four hundred fifty-four thousand households in the United States with the Smith surname. If we did a book for them, it would look like this," he says, holding his hands about four feet apart. "They're not interested because their name is so common. Whereas somebody named Tonelli, or Haslinger, is interested to see who else out there has their name."

They won't do books for names with fewer than thirty households or more than ten thousand, which still leaves a lot of potential customers—about two hundred million households worldwide (they sell here and in England, Ireland, Scotland, Wales, Germany, Austria, Switzerland, Australia, and along the Pacific Rim). They get takers for about thirty books per surname, which sounds low, but they don't even print and bind the book until it's ordered, so there's no inventory to pay for or store. They sell around a million books a year at thirty bucks a pop, and that provides about 80 percent of the firm's income. The rest comes from "heraldic items"—shot glasses and other stuff with your family crest and name—and the new "Heritage Travel" division. "We invite people of the same name to go on a reunion tour in, say, Ireland," Haslinger says. "We've taken thousands of people to Europe on our heritage tours. I went along on the Joyce family trip to Ireland, and James Joyce, the grandson of the writer, came around. We saw Joyce Mountain and Joyce River and had a party for the Joyces of Ireland and America."

So, by my calculation, figure around thirty-eight million dollars gross, 15 percent profit tops, say somewhere around four or five million dollars a year for Haslinger, the company's sole owner. As I leave his office, he says, "So you'll send us a complimentary copy of your book, right?" Right, Dennis—I'm going to charge *you* $30.

Next I'm in the company of Bill Forman, Numa's vice president, who's giving me the plant tour, and the thing that strikes me is this: It's all on the level. There really *are* two mainframe computers plus lots of PCs with millions of bits of family information. And the description of the Tonelli family coat of arms *wasn't* spurious, and it wasn't even crossed goats on a bed of linguini—I think I made that up. No, it's a simple red and silver geometric pattern with a red rose in the middle, and it comes from *Rietstap Armorial General,* an ancient, crackling book that gets a lot of use here. We visit the high-speed copiers that print the various books as they're ordered, and the work stations where the wall plaques and T-shirts are manufactured. As we're touring, it occurs to me that Bill's name sounds familiar, and I finally realize why: On the last mailing I got from Numa, the letter was signed, "Bill Forman, Tonelli Family Director." We're practically *related.*

Usually, he explains, they'll pick somebody from the list of a given surname and ask that person to lend his name to the direct-mail solicitation in exchange for a percentage of the take. Since the Tonelli pool was so small—373 U.S. households, we looked it up—Forman did the honors. The first Numa mailing I received, I tell him, was signed by Sharon Taylor, a phony if ever there was one.

"Dennis and I came up with that name on a flight back from Atlanta," Bill admits. "It had the right ascenders and descenders, and how could you not trust *Sharon Taylor*?"

You'd trust her, but you wouldn't *fear* her, apparently.

Numa sells a lot of books on credit, and "Sharon Taylor" used to be the name signed to the dunning letters that went to deadbeats. Now, Bill says, "We get a lot better response from people who owe us money by signing our collection letter with the name *Victor Sparducci*. We get twenty-five percent better response from Sparducci than we do from Sharon."

You should see how the imaginary Mr. Sparducci carves his signature into the letter—it looks like he has a thirty-pound hand. Was the intention to evoke in Numa's deadbeats the name of Sparafucile, the hired assassin in *Rigoletto*? Or should I be offended by the implicit ethnic slur? And if the latter is true, why do I feel proud that Mr. and Mrs. America believe it's unwise to fuck with Italians?

• • • Although there's a sizable pocket of Tonellis in Cuyahoga Falls, near Akron, I got not one questionnaire back from here. Strange, so in my motel room I pick up the phone book and call one, just to see what happens. He says I can't drop in because he's leaving town tonight.

"Just out of curiosity," I say, "why didn't you return the form?"

"I don't know," he snarls. "I'll have to ask my wife."

• • • What do I want? "Just water would be great."

"How about some grape juice?" Valentino Tonelli asks, his head inside the refrigerator.

"No, just water."

"How about some apple juice?"

"Water's great, really."

"How about some spinach lasagna?"

"Nah . . . "

"Can't handle that, huh?"

Tino's a high-energy guy, a widower in his sixties. First thing in the door he asks, "So, where are you from?" I'm about to say New York when he finishes his question, " . . . Abruzzo?"

"Good guess," I say.

(Invariably on this trek, older Tonellis ask where I'm from, but what they mean is What part of Italy was your grandfather from? Younger Tonellis *never* ask that. *They* invariably ask, "So, do you think we're all related?" The questions come from completely different directions, but I think they amount to the same thing—*are we connected*?)

"I'm from Fano," Tino says. "My dad was. I visited there when I was stationed in the army in Europe, in the fifties. It was like going home! It's like . . . *blood*! You know, cousins and hugging and kissing and all. Praise God."

Oh, right, this is the Tonelli family that single-handedly started an evangelical church in Buffalo. Tino's son Mark, who lives next door, sneaks away from his bank job and shows up at the kitchen table a few minutes after I arrive.

"Well," says Tino, "we had this Bible study group right here. Mark taught, my son Johnny taught, we had the whole house filled with kids. Then it got too big, so we moved it to the Howard Johnson's, we rented a room there. And they helped us, gave us two free rooms for the children's church. By then Johnny had gone to Rhema, the Bible college in Tulsa, Oklahoma, and we were holding services."

"It's a nondenominational Bible training school," Mark explains.

"And John was pastor starting at the Howard Johnson's. We stayed there for two years, then we built our first building. It seated about two hundred and eighty people."

"Now, the second building seats about twelve hundred," Mark says. "It's *huge*. And people just keep coming. We were all born and raised Catholic, but it just wasn't enough for us. God was very impersonal, and we went to church because we *had* to. My mother wanted to get a Bible study group going for us kids, and it all actually grew from that. I don't know how to explain it except to say it's the hand of God. Our church is nondenominational but very much a fundamentalist one. Very Bible based. So we do things God's way. We don't presume to say what God meant. We don't think we're smarter than God, so we do things His way."

"It's the personal relationship with Jesus, right?" Tino says.

"Yes," says Mark. "Now I can speak to him every day. It's the sensation of opening the Bible and realizing it was written for *me*, not just for some Bible scholars."

"You dedicate your life to the church," Tino says. "Monday is prayer night. Wednesday night is service. Sunday's a service. Then they have the young people stuff."

"Youth groups, you know," Mark says. "The typical Protestant church stuff."

"To keep the kids off the streets and out of trouble," Tino adds.

"Italians typically have close families," Mark says. "And there are so many people who have never had that kind of closeness. And they can draw off *our* togetherness."

"I wanted it to be a family together," says Tino. "That's the name of the game. Hey, let's take a ride and go see John."

In the car, Tino says, "I'll tell you the truth: my wife found the Lord first. Actually, it was Grandma, my mother-in-law. And then my wife went to a couple meetings and she came home and said, 'Tino, I found something that I can't believe.' My good little Catholic girl, I could never imagine her leaving the church. But *I* decided I didn't want to leave the church, so she had me read some of John, and I learned there's supposed to be just one mediator between you and God, and His name is Jesus Christ, Jesus being His earthly name and Christ His deity name, praise God." He turns up the tape deck a little. "As you can hear, I've got the Christian music on."

"How did your break with Catholicism go over with your parents?" I ask him.

"We had just gotten into it when my mother passed away," he says. "But we got her saved, so we know where she is. My dad," he laughs, "he wasn't even a good Catholic, poor man. He was one of those guys who worked twenty hours a day his whole life. He was a *worker.* I was the same way, worked crazy hours building houses, then we'd quit at five and go build a garage or something small, at night, work until midnight at a side job trying to make some money, trying to get ahead. I'd come home numb. My wife raised the kids. Hey, Bill, is your family in New York? No family? Just a wife? *No wife?* God, we've got to get you started! Greatest life there is. Kids are love. We're in Cheektowaga now. That's Indian for 'Land of the Crabapple.' "

We pull in at the last developed lot in a mostly barren

strip of suburb. There's a brand-new building, not landscaped yet, with a big cross on the lawn. We go inside, and the first person we see is the assistant pastor, who Tino greets with a hug. Then Tino's daughter-in-law Carrie appears, and she greets Tino with a hug. Then John emerges and everybody hugs everybody (except me).

"Hey, Dad, the pulpit came today!" John says, so we all go down the corridor to see it. It's a handsome one, carved of pale wood, but no more impressive than the room itself—it's suburban majestic, vast and telegenic, with a yawning ceiling and rows and rows of chairs.

We all settle down in John's office.

"Of all the things I love about being Italian, what I love best is the feeling for family," John says. "Not that other people don't love their families. But Italians are very huggy people—one guy'll kiss another guy and nobody wonders what's wrong with Uncle Harry. And we're even that way in this church—we have a real teddy-bear mentality here, and that's one thing, not to denigrate other nationalities. . . . "

"It's *them*," Carrie says. "It's the fact that they're Italian. My family, not that we're cold, but we're not as huggy. And I used to have to remind myself that I'd be offending John's family if I didn't hug and kiss them hello *and* good-bye."

"That's the thing I miss," John says, "that I wish I could have for *my* children. Some of my fondest memories are of sitting in my grandfather's yard, sitting around surrounded by family singing the old Italian songs—I didn't even know what the words meant, but after you heard them enough times—and eating peaches you grew in your own yard. And it was just *wonderful*. And I feel sad for my children, because our family is a lot smaller now. We have relatives, but they're in Florida and Canada and Virginia. And for me, there were people—I grew up on their *knees*—and I don't even know their names, but—"

Tino says, "They went to Florida once to meet their cousins for the first time—"

"—and it was just *instant!*" John says excitedly. "Like we'd known each other all our lives! And when the vacation was over, we were like, 'You're not gonna take us away from our cousins, are you?' I get teary-eyed just thinking about it." He stops a second. "Anyway, it was a wonderful culture. And I hate to see it diluted by America."

It's time to leave. We three men walk out to the parking lot. John hugs me. Tino hugs John. John hugs Tino. Tino and I head back to my car. When we get there, Tino hugs me. I hug Tino.

All along I've been wondering what, if anything, the citizens of the Tonelli Nation have in common, and listening to Rev. John in his office, it dawned on me: When called upon to talk about ethnicity, everybody speaks only of the past, either their grandparents, or their parents, or their childhoods. Never the present.

Another thing they have in common: They're sad. It's like the phantom pain that amputees feel: the Reverend aches for something he lost as a child, the sense of being surrounded and protected by his own kind. He longs for something else, too, something he never even experienced: a world where that kind of connectedness was the constant, reliable state in which life was lived. He can function perfectly well in this world, just like all the other Tonellis I've met. But they're sad.

• • • In a bar that night in Niagara Falls, drinking beer and shots of a 107-proof cinnamon liqueur with real gold flakes in it, with Nan, who's local, and Paul, a trucker from Tennessee. Nan's holding forth on the merits of various saloons in town.

"Look," she finally says, "you can have fun wherever you go. You can have fun in a shoebox. It's all up to you."

"Well, I don't necessarily agree with that," Paul replies.

"How do you mean?" Nan says.

"If, let's say, I go into a bar where I'm the only white face, I wouldn't have any fun."

"But you wouldn't go *into* a nigger bar," Nan snaps. "Just like you wouldn't send a dago into an Irish bar. But other than that . . . "

Lisa Tonelli Gentile and
Virginia Tonelli Green

Arthur Tonelli

16.

The German Side
Holds Me Back

I leave Niagara Falls early in the morning and
drive east toward Massachusetts. Upstate New
York surprises me—it's as fertile and bucolic as
the Midwest, with fuzzy brown hills for topo-
graphic variety. If it's any comfort, a lot more of
the air in America stinks of cowshit than stinks of chemical
plants.

• • • Here I am—in Massachusetts, the Tonelli capital of America. There are more of us here than in any other state, way more
than I could ever visit even if I wanted to. Which, maybe, I *did,*
back when I started, but now I'm too road weary to even fake the
effort. I can feel my home down there, pulling me like a magnet.

But I push on. First stop is West Springfield, in the spa-
cious living room of Lisa Tonelli Gentile, daughter of Albert and
Pearl of Florida and sister of Dee Dee of Los Angeles. With us
are her sons Christopher, age fifteen, and Alan, age eleven. The
question before the panel is this: To what degree is this particular extended family's closeness the result of being Italian, and to
what degree is it just *them*?

234

Chris and Alan Gentile

Backyard tombstone,
Shrewsbury, Massachusetts

Lisa: It's, it's . . .

Chris: She doesn't know.

Lisa: It's part of the Italian heritage, I guess. They feel
very much a part of this. My husband is Italian, on both
sides, and the family, I think, is very important to them.
Am I saying the right thing?

Chris: Yeah.

Lisa: Well, what do *you* think about it?

Chris: I don't know.

Lisa: Yes you do. You *like* being Italian.

Chris: Yeah, I do.

Lisa: Part of being Italian is respect for family, ethics,
values. My kids—I could take them anywhere. (The
phone rings, and Chris runs to answer it.)

Lisa: Chris is like—he's kind of obsessed with the mafia,
isn't he, Alan?

Alan: Yup.

Lisa: And all he can say is that it's because they get respect. They earn respect. But our *families* taught us to
be respectful of other people's property, of other people's

thoughts. And I see kids today who have none of that respect. And it bothers me. I took fifteen years off and raised these kids, and I could take them anywhere. The Tonellis are bonded. Hey, the Tonellis always fought, but when there was trouble, we're glued. It's caused a lot of problems in my marriage, because we are so close that when you get together with another family, they just don't understand it. I've been a little subdued because of my mom, she's German. We talked at work about that. I have a friend there who's all Italian. A lady who works with us said, "I figured out the difference between you two—she's emotional Italian and you're controlled Italian." The German side holds me back a little bit. It's tempered. If I were all Tonelli—I mean all Italian—I'd probably be very emotional and speak without thinking. Chris, what do *you* think about—

Chris: Keep going.

Lisa: No, *talk!* The Tonellis are very loving. Nobody can love you more. Nobody can hug you more. *But.* When they get angry, they're stubborn. They *demanded* respect from the children. I married an Italian, and we have the same ethics, morals, and feelings about family, and that's what's held us together. The difference is my husband's family let him go more—they were looser with the kids. My family held a lot tighter.

Chris: Your family wanted you to stay with them and not leave and become your own person. Maybe that was different for Dad.

Lisa: Right! I think they held us tighter. And expectations were very high. The thing about my dad—when we were young he was not available to us emotionally. But he gave us things—music lessons, horses. He gave us outlets, and they were wonderful. I could play the organ, and it was wonderful. But then he made us play for him at *his* restaurant. I loved having a horse. But then he made us enter *shows*. So it had to be *his* thing. My dad bought me an organ, but he put it in the restaurant. When I practiced, I had to practice in the restaurant.

People heard me and asked where the music was coming from. So my dad said, "They like what you play, why should I pay somebody when I have *you*?" I'll tell you something—my husband was like my father, working nine to nine when his kids were growing up. My husband's a psychologist, and he said to me, a child's personality is formed by the time they're two years old. And I felt great, because he was never *there* during those years. And these are *great* kids. And they *love* being Italian. (Lisa leaves the room for a moment. I ask Chris why he's obsessed by the mafia.)

Chris: She *told* you that?

Me: Kind of. (Just then Lisa's sister Ginny arrives from rehearsing with her vocal group. We five are now together in the living room.)

Lisa: OK, now ask my *sister* about our family.

• • • Driving back to my motel, I end up more lost than I've been yet—so spectacularly misdirected I'm not even in the right city anymore. I steal a tip from John Steinbeck's road book, *Travels with Charley*: Once when he was hopelessly lost, he paid a cab driver to lead him to his destination. When he did it, it sounded resourceful; when I do it, it feels pathetic. The cabbie's happy for a painless fare, but he looks at me like I'm retarded.

• • • Weeks ago, when I first called Ramon Tonelli, he was mysteriously reluctant to see me, which was surprising. This is, after all, according to a newspaper item, a man who once sang in nightclubs while drawing caricatures of audience members. He also turned up in my search of copyright applications, as coauthor of a song titled "Pledge Shalom." But instead of being genial, he was guarded; he interrogated me about my intentions and then finally allowed that maybe, if I came to town, we could meet. So as soon as I pull into downtown Worcester I call from a pay phone, but he starts grilling me again, asking if this has anything to do with his "invention," and saying that maybe the time isn't right to talk about it. And come on, really, what's my book about, because *surely* it can't be about Tonellis— who would buy such a thing? A total pain in the ass, in other words, and as I listen I'm figuring screw shalom, by now one Tonelli more or less won't make any difference.

So I give him one last shot: How about just meeting me somewhere for coffee, I ask, and he caves in and says, "OK, be at the downtown McDonald's at two."

I've been on the road almost sixty days now and never once entered a McDonald's, a blow against corporate food that I was proud of, but I'm long past caring. I tell him I'll be in a blue shirt; he says he'll be wearing dark glasses and sitting in front.

I arrive at the appointed time, buy two coffees, and take a table near the door. There's no man alone in sight, so I nurse my cup of mud amid the elderly, the unemployed, and the vagrant. It's as cheerful as it sounds. At a table nearby there's a couple in their sixties. She's nondescript, but he is by far the most dapper McDonald's diner I've ever seen: bohemian longish hair and droopy mustache, a snazzy blue double-breasted suit, yellow shirt, blue polka-dot tie. Aviator sunglasses. Suddenly he says, in a loud voice, "Anybody here waiting for Tonelli?"

"Are *you* Tonelli?" I ask.

"Yes, I am," he says as his companion solicitously jumps up and guides me into her seat.

Doesn't it just figure that my road snobbism gets punctured during the next two magical hours spent drinking coffee and smoking cigarettes at a corner table under the Golden Arches? I wish I could describe it all exactly as it happened, but I can't—Ramon wouldn't let me take notes, use a tape recorder, or even take his picture.

Anyway. The first thing he told me: He's blind. Hence the dark glasses. (How funny did it strike him when I described the shirt I'm wearing?) His eyes were injured in World War II, he says, and his vision gradually deteriorated; he was able to continue working as a muralist and art restorer until almost 1977, when he was judged officially sightless. Then, a year ago, he had an operation on one eye, and miraculously, inexplicably, vision began to return to the other one! Not a lot, he says; he can see fuzzy shapes if the light's right, but it's *something*. So he's kind of nonspecifically ecstatic these days. He's seeing a lot of the people and things in his life for the first time. He says that when he was sightless, living in the sighted world was a drag, that he never felt truly at ease there, but he didn't belong in the isolated, protected enclave inhabited by the congenitally blind either. He felt like a man without a country, he says. But now!

And finally—once I convince him that I'm not here on a mission of industrial espionage—I get to hear about his invention. Several years ago, when he still had some sight left, his art studio, by coincidence, was in the same building as an organization that serves the blind. So, preparing for a sightless future, he requested Braille reading lessons, and a woman instructor was provided. The sessions were free, but he wished to pay her somehow, so he asked if there was anything she wanted.

"What I want," she replied, "you can't give me."

"Well, tell me what it is?" he said.

She told him: "I know there's a window in this studio because I can feel the air come in, but what I want is to see what's outside that window."

Being a creative man, he gave her impossible request some serious thought. Back when he painted, he had thought of himself mainly as a colorist. And he knew that color defines form: if you can see the color of an orange car, for instance, then you can see the car. His musings led him to devise a Braille-like system for colors, each shade assigned to a different tactile pattern (raised horizontal lines for blue, say, or dots for red). The darker the color, the more crowded the pattern would be. His subject, the view from his studio window, was a tree between two small hills. So, on a flat surface, he created a tree shape with aluminum foil and then imprinted the foil with the pattern he had chosen for brown. Then he did the same for the leaves, and the buff-colored hills. Next time he saw her, he explained the code and led her fingers to the rendering.

"*That's* a tree?!" she exclaimed.

"Yes," he said. "How did you think it would look?"

She told him she thought it would be like a large limb with leaves—her only knowledge of trees had come from touching them. Then he moved her hands to the hills, and the leaves, and then he let her roam over the whole landscape. She took the picture home, he says, and later reported that she spent an entire week studying it.

And that's the big secret, what Ramon calls the "Touch Color" system. He says he gave the patent to a group that helps the blind, but that there's at least one commercial concern that's nosing around. Hence all the mystery.

Have I done justice to all this, to the mingling of a loner's eccentricity and high passion with which Ramon told his tales? Or even to the dizzy marvel I felt at hearing them spun in such grubby surroundings? These are the moments that pass every day, undetected, in the Tonelli Nation, but have I revealed the wonder of that?

• • • I show up at the Westborough, Massachusetts, Toyota dealership that serves as the nerve center of an entire clan of Tonellis—Arthur, the boss; his brother Ed, the retired State Police official who I caught up with in Florida; their brother Chick; Arthur's sons, Peter and Charlie; and Chick's son, Rick. I'm reminded of Rabbit Angstrom once again, and the car dealership—Toyota, too—that held his clan together.

I follow Arthur from the dealership to his home, where first thing, he pulls from the refrigerator a huge wheel of imported Parmesan cheese. No one else is here now, but two of his four grown children also live on the big spread, which holds the large main house, a smaller guest house, a pool and tennis court. Next to it, his brother Ed lives on his spread. Arthur's son Peter just bought a house on some nearby acres.

Arthur pours two glasses of his homemade red wine, then some olive oil into a black cast-iron skillet.

"She came over here—imagine that, a young girl, sixteen, coming here alone. My mother said she wanted a better life. But she was an adventuress. She was a *strong* woman. Everything had to be done *now*. Hated lazy people. She used to say, '*Dessa!*' *Now.*"

He slices some garlic as thin as he can and throws it into the sputtering oil.

"My father was a hard worker. A carpenter. He was doing well building houses on spec, until the Depression. I remember when I was a kid, how hard it was for him. He would have to go out and *search* for just one day's work. I remember once he found *two weeks' work*! That was really something—two weeks."

He opens a can of imported tomatoes, pours the water into a bowl, puts the tomatoes into the blender, and turns it on for two seconds.

"But even in those tough times, my father used to make his own wine."

He dumps the tomatoes into the skillet.

"And we always had fresh-squeezed orange juice, even in the heart of the Depression. But we had no money. My father was a proud man, though. I remember once a fellow had some money and he wanted something built. And he told my father he wanted to do it on the cheap. So my father said no, he wouldn't do it that way. He turned down the job. When he told my mother, she said, 'What do you care?' And he said, 'Two years from now, somebody will look at it and ask, "Who *did* this?" '

"My father wanted me to be an architect, but he couldn't afford college. You know what Worcester Tech cost back then? Four hundred dollars. Anyway, I went out after high school and got a job. My father thought the coming thing would be air conditioning and refrigeration. My brother Chick was working for a company as a foreman. He was getting fifty cents an hour. And I was going to get twenty-five cents an hour."

He pulls some herbs and parsley out of the refrigerator, chops them all up, and tosses them into the pan.

"My first week, the boss underpaid me—he said it was because I was still new on the job. But I was a hard worker. So I told my father, and he said, 'Quit!' And after a while he got me a job building army barracks, I was getting a dollar seventeen an hour. Then they wanted me to work Saturdays, too. I remember one day I told my mother, 'Hey, Ma, guess how much I made today? Twenty dollars!' And I'd give it all to her, and she'd give me an allowance."

He pours more olive oil into the pan.

"Then, after I came home from the service, my father was unhappy with me. He was a little mad. Because I had started my own business—roofing and siding. Cold calls, you know. And he said, 'That's no business, any fool can nail a roof!' "

He slides a dozen or so clams into the simmering tomato sauce.

"But we made money at it, my brothers and I. Then we went into windows, too—you know, like 'Tin Men.' And eventually we manufactured windows. *Then* I had a restaurant and motel, too. I would work all day at the window business, take a shower, and go to the motel and restaurant and work until I went to bed. I did that for ten years, then I got out of it and went into the automobile business. I built this house, and I built my mother's house, and I built my brother Eddie's first house, and I built my brother Chick's house. Eddie was in the State Police by then."

He stirs the tomato sauce, then pulls out a roaster pan and begins quartering potatoes.

"I learned to cook from my mother. She gave me the basics. I can make ravioli, pasta, from scratch. Every Sunday morning, early, I make my bread. I make the soup—my mother used to make a lot of soups with rice. I make a lot of soups my mother never made. You know—you watch, you try, you pick it up. See," he says, spooning the clams from the sauce, "you don't want these to overcook. I'll put them in again later."

He rinses a bunch of carrots and puts them with the potatoes into a bowl.

"It's funny, I have a cousin in Italy, she uses very little garlic—almost none. I asked her why, and she said they use it for medicine. Funny. I have to buy my carrots fresh, but I used to leave the stalks on until I was ready to use them. And I noticed they would always get soft. So I read that if you leave the stalk, it draws all the best out of the carrots. So now the first thing I do is chop off the stalks."

He pours olive oil into the roaster pan and places the carrots and potatoes in it, then he puts it into the oven.

"I cook every night. Well, every night since my wife passed away. I cook for my kids. Even if it's just two of us, I still cook a full meal."

He takes a veal tenderloin from the refrigerator, salts it, grinds fresh pepper, and puts it into a frying pan to brown. Then he begins slicing tomatoes.

"When my mother cooked, I was the helper. She chose me. She wouldn't even send my brothers to the store."

His daughter Larri, a lawyer, who arrived a few minutes ago, says, "You were the worker."

He pours olive oil over the sliced tomatoes, then goes into the other room and returns with basil leaves he's cut from a plant. The veal goes into the oven with the potatoes and carrots. The water boils, and the macaroni goes in.

"Larri can cook," Arthur says. "Dana, my other daughter, can cook. My son Charlie—nothing. If my son Peter was here, he'd make you a Grand Marnier Soufflé that would knock you out. Unbelievable."

Dinner is ready—linguini and clams in a light red sauce, veal with potatoes and carrots, a salad, homemade bread, homemade wine. Arthur, Larri, Charlie, and I sit down to eat. It's fantastic. When we're through, Arthur washes the dishes by hand.

"I won't use the dishwasher," he says. "I won't let them use it either. I don't know why. My mother never used one. I do my own shirts, too, wash and iron them. In fact, when it's nice, I hang them out to dry."

He glances out the window.

"The year before last, I was going to Italy, and I wanted to visit my grandmother's grave. I always go whenever I'm there. But my cousin told me that they were going to have to move her grave. It was a law. After so much time you have to empty the grave. I said, 'Bullshit, I'll buy the land.' But my cousin said, 'No, you can't.' So we were going to put her into one of those vaults, in a different cemetery. I told my cousin, 'OK, take her out, but I want the stone.' He thought I meant the photograph on the tombstone. I said, 'No, I want the stone.' He thought I was kidding. But I said, 'I'll pay for it.' And there it is, out there."

He points out the window, to the expanse of green rolling toward the pool, where his grandmother's tombstone rests against a tree.

"Now, when I go to visit my mother's grave, I tell her, 'Hey, Ma, *your* mother's here too.' When my mother died I thought, 'Well, that's the end of it.' But I didn't want it to end."

Paul Tonelli

Welcome mat, North Brunswick, New Jersey

17.

He's a Pagan Baby

I'll stop, I won't stop, I'll stop, I won't stop. This is the debate in my head while I'm driving down I-95 from Massachusetts into Connecticut: Do I or do I not pay a visit to Alexander Tonelli? On the one hand, by now I've had enough Tonellis. I want it to be over. I feel like I'm trapped in a cheap trucker lament: "Sixty days on the road and I'm gonna make it home tonight. . . . " On the other hand, Alexander is the uncle who Rick Tonelli of Lithonia, Georgia, paid that emotionally charged visit to a few years back, and I want to know how it felt from his end. Stop, don't, stop. I see the sign for Milford and think, What the hell, I'll stop. I'm running early for my afternoon appointment anyway.

I pull off the highway and call from a pay phone, and he's home, and sounding reluctant, but if I hurry he can spare a few minutes. I zoom over and into the driveway, which is just like Rick described it, two cars sticking out of the garage, TONEL-1 and TONEL-2.

"Yeah, Rick called me on the phone and said they were going to take a trip, and I said, 'Well, come on up,' " Alexan-

244

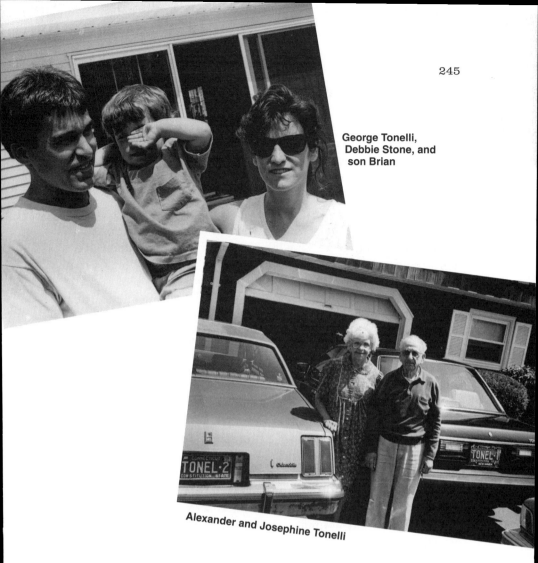

George Tonelli,
Debbie Stone, and
son Brian

Alexander and Josephine Tonelli

der—Uncle Lolly—says. He's seventy-seven, a retired gunstock maker, sitting in the dining room. "And he was tickled pink when he got here. I hadn't talked to him or seen him for thirty years, since his father died. In fact, he had to say his name twice on the phone—it caught me off-balance. I wasn't expecting him. And then he came over and we reminisced, and he met all my kids and their families—I've got seven grandchildren— and he met so many people in such a little bit of time. We took him to see the house where he used to live. He was only about two years old when they moved. His father, my brother, moved away right after our mother died. He said, 'Well, I don't have anybody here, and I want to go and try and live in Miami.' And now we're—I've got two sisters left and myself. One sister's in Florida, and the other one's in, uh . . . "

"Indiana, last we heard," says his wife, Josephine, who's joined us at the table.

"Yeah," says Alexander, "we think she's still in Indiana. See, we don't see them much. Once in a while we'll get a visit. Now, *I* have four sons. One who lives around the corner, one we lost—he got electrocuted—one who also lives here, in this town, and one lives about twelve, thirteen miles away."

I ask him, "What do *you* think the trip meant to Rick?"

"That's a good question. But there really isn't much I can tell you," he says with a shrug. "It was a pretty short stay."

• • • My disinclination to wander off the most direct route has finally caught up with me: All trip I've been cruelly prompt for my appointments, but this is ridiculous—I'm three hours early.

So when I exit 95 in Bridgeport, I'm grateful to find a ramshackle barbecue stand, serving what turns out to be the best road eats I've had east of the Mexican food belt. After two awesome pork shoulder sandwiches, I read the newspaper clippings that hang on the wall and discover that this joint is owned by an Englishman who fell in love with the food of the South and attempted to re-create North Carolina barbecue here.

Lucky for me, Paul Tonelli's home earlier than he expected, and he doesn't seem to mind finding me on his doorstep.

"Well, I really like the Northeast. I could *never* live in Florida—maybe when I'm old." He's an athletic-looking twenty-nine-year-old, still living in the city of his birth. He's the youngest in his family, but although his parents retired to Florida, and his brother Ed moved to Disney World, and his sister Debra landed in L.A., he's stuck it out here. We're in his kitchen, on bar stools.

"I love the change of seasons. And I love my job, and I have a decent future there." He's an electronics technician at a research lab. "As far as Bridgeport's concerned, I'm just stuck here. But the neighborhood doesn't bother me." It's mostly black and poor outside and menacing looking. "And I have low overhead here, so I can travel a *lot*. I live real good. I own a boat. I own a dirt bike. I have a lot of cousins that still live here, so they have become kind of my family. I see them quite a bit. Which is kind of strange, because a lot of people I talk to, I'll say, 'Oh, I did this or that with my cousins,' and they'll say, 'I don't even *know* my cousins.' We've gotten closer now that our parents have all moved away. But I'm *really* happy for my parents. They're living a good life now, and they deserve it."

• • • I'm home and I'm *still* not home. I make it back to Manhattan for a one-day layover in my apartment, though I still have a final visit to make tomorrow before I return the car to the Avis office in Philadelphia, never to drive again. I spend an hour sitting on the steps of my brownstone, reacclimating myself to the urban jangle. I could live here the rest of my life and I'm never going to know this neighborhood as well as I knew the turf of my youth. Which is no surprise, since I rarely sit here, whereas from age fifteen to twenty-five all I did was sit on one particular street corner in South Philadelphia. I didn't learn much that's practical during those years, but I was a student of the street, a Ph.D. of pavement. I saw it in every kind of light, at every hour, in every season. If you could grow anything in concrete, I would be a hell of a farmer, so well do I understand that land. It may have looked as though my friends and I were loitering our lives away, but we soaked up a lot of lessons out there. You'd see people get born, grow up, get old, go downhill, die, you'd watch them get beautiful, or ugly, or weird, you'd see every manner of human interaction, from murderous to amorous. We became scholars and philosophers—you get to know one really small patch of the planet *really well,* and in that way you gain a deep and knowing grip on everything surrounding it. In a year here I won't learn as much as I did in a week there. All that education—gone to waste. As I'm thinking this I witness a common sight in this city: A white infant being pushed in a stroller by a young black woman. Today, it occurs to me that this is connected to an equally common sight here: an elderly white person being led by the arm by a young black woman. In the former instance, both parents work at good jobs,

The Amazing Story of the Tonelli Family in America

so they can afford to pay an economically disadvantaged stranger to play the part of the doting mother. In the latter, that kid grows up and gets a good job, so he can afford to pay an economically disadvantaged stranger to play the part of the doting child. It's capitalistic domesticity, the free-market family—you pay somebody to assume your blood responsibilities. That's American family values, too.

• • • OK, last call.

"You just tend to think Italians are very religious." This is Debbie Stone speaking—she's Jewish and married to George Tonelli. They're a young, handsome, happy couple with a two-year-old son, Brian. I liked George, who's a contractor and an unpublished writer, since the moment I became aware of his existence—when he returned his questionnaire he included a proposal for an article he wanted to write for *Esquire.*

"He even went to Catholic school for ten years," Debbie says. "So you relate that to yeshiva and you'd think he'd be superreligious." It's Sunday, late morning. We're all out on the back deck of their North Brunswick tract house, on an outrageously sunny, clear day that makes this suburban Jersey setting seem even more glorious than usual. "By the time the baby was born, I realized that neither one of us was that religious. So we decided he'd get a little bit of both—more from the cultural point of view than anything else."

"And I said I'd never do that," says George. "Before he came, I thought that was ludicrous, church *or* temple, so I said he wasn't going to get either one. But then he'd miss out on a lot of family stuff and tradition. I can't wait to get into *that* issue—your mother's going to make him recite those funny prayers—"

"She won't *make* him do anything," Debbie says, grinning.

"Her sister married an Italian guy," George says, "and their kids are older. And on holidays her mother made the kids say the prayers, and her sister's husband flew off the handle. Everybody said, 'What's the big deal?' But I could see his point. He was consistent—neither one. They're divorced now."

"I was bat mitzvahed," Debbie says.

"So when did you lose your religion?" I ask.

"When I was thirteen—as soon as I was bat mitzvahed."

"As soon as the checks cleared," George says.

"What happens when you have to fill out some form that asks for the baby's religion?" I ask them.

"I would make up a hybrid—Judeo-Christian," George says.

"I wouldn't fill out the form," Debbie says. "I'd be offended."

"He's a pagan baby!" says George, laughing.

"*That's* what we'd put down!" says Debbie, laughing too.

Statues of Christopher
Columbus, Rocky Balboa,
and Guglielmo Marconi,
South Broad Street,
Philadelphia

18.

Ich Bin Ein Tonelli

Is it really over? It's really over.

Zooming Sunday afternoon down the Jersey Turnpike, and then I lean into the big turn just off the Walt Whitman Bridge, onto the ramp for Broad Street, and down there, to the right, it rises in my window like it might from a plane: *South Philly*. As a kid, this was always the exquisite moment—rumbling back from the seashore in some uncle's car, squirmy for the entire hour or so it took, swallowing back the hot urge to puke, searching the horizon for our harbor: Sweet chills. And then I'm back on rutted asphalt, the hero's homecoming, up Broad Street in a motorcade of one filthy blue Buick Century.

For years, and more often than I've liked, people would fix me with some smug look and say: "You can take the boy out of South Philly, but you can't take the South Philly out of the boy." Today I finally understand what that means: The more one place fills your head, the less room there is for anyplace else. Which means that to feel at ease everywhere is to belong nowhere. I left South Philly and went to see America, and I don't care what it says about me—it feels good to be back.

As soon as I park, I wet a handkerchief and rub it all over the Buick, on the headlights, the hood, the license plate, the hubcaps. Not once on this trip did I wash my car, and not out of laziness, either—I had a plan. This cruddy cloth will be my souvenir of earth, a little bit of every place that Tonellis call home. I know, I really am losing it. All this traveling has unhinged me like an out-of-body experience. But with that comes the shock of understanding, too.

OK, let's get it over with. Here's what I learned:

There really are Tonellis all over America.

Which, granted, I already had cause to believe, but now I *know*. And their forebears all started at roughly the same place, and they all got to their current addresses for all the usual reasons (familial precedent, economics, wanderlust, climatic comfort, bad directions).

They really are a diverse bunch of people.

What, I wonder, would Edith the psychologist and Carmella the drug dealer have to say to each other? Or even Dr. Alan in North Carolina and Dr. Mary Jo O'Dell in Texas? Maybe lots, or maybe nothing, but the coincidence of surname would exhaust itself as a subject of conversation real quick, I feel sure.

They really were happy to see me.

I know, partly because it's flattering to be the object of someone's curiosity for *any* reason. But my visits touched something genuine in these people, I could tell, some desire to connect with history, or blood, or experience. They had lots of questions about their namesmen; their imaginations, like mine, were poked by the vast mystery that there could be so many of us in so many different forms. Sometimes I felt like a Graham Greene character, a minor diplomat cast out in a strange land, conducting a census for an odd government-in-exile.

But they really don't think much about their ancestry.

Surrounded as Tonellis are by Americans (and even non-Americans) of every stripe and flavor, their pasts just don't have much to do with their presents. The tie has been severed; no aspect of their lives speaks to their sense of themselves as creatures of history. At some unobserved point, they (or somebody before them) made a crucial transfer—they stepped out of the story of their blood and into that of their country. That's mostly the work of real estate, the great transformer, for if they limited their associations to individuals of similar provenance, they'd be *very* lonely people. They're *Americans,* and that's why their ancestors came here in the first place, I guess. Those brave old greaseballs in the great beyond should be happy—they wouldn't be able to recognize (or even speak to) their own flesh and blood.

Just before I left on my voyage I read a book called *The End of History.* The title was what caught my attention, though it turned out that I misunderstood how the author meant it. (But that won't stop me from connecting his grand theorizing with my own cruder ruminations.) Francis Fukuyama's main point was that humanity's barbarous past has come to some kind of peaceful resolution in twentieth-century America—that history itself has been nothing but a long, drawn-out search for the enlightened, tolerant, bureaucratic democracy that finally took hold here.

The thought that sticks in *my* mind is that *histories* end in America, too—that for America to succeed, ethnic identity had to go out the window. This country isn't dedicated to blood or even to shared memories: it's dedicated to a proposition. Imagine the titanic struggle for something so ephemeral to glue beasts like us all together. No wonder the bonds of family and tribe, which have proven their savage power since before history *started,* had to be dissolved.* I laugh when I read about

---

*I know what you're thinking: *He's making this stuff up.* And maybe I am, but there are thinkers of proven wisdom and reliability who say the same thing. Like Christopher Lasch, for instance, in his 1991 book, *The True and Only Heaven,* who wrote about what seemed to many smart people (not him, though) to be social progress:

> They cited the abolition of slavery and the emancipation of women as indisputable evidence that the ideal of universal brotherhood was closer to realization than ever before. Its realization was chiefly impeded, it seemed, by the persistence of tribal loyalties rooted in the patriarchal stage of social development. The ties of kinship, nationality, and ethnic identity had to give way to "more inclusive identities," as Erik Erikson used to say—to an appreciation of the underlying unity of all mankind. Family feeling, clannishness, and patriotism—admirable enough in earlier days—could not be allowed to stand in the way of the global civilization that was arriving just in time, in fact, to save the human race from the self-destructive consequences of its old habits of national rivalry and war.

fancy Europeans criticizing us for being apolitical: they practice political science, but we *perform* it. That's what's amazing about the story of the Tonelli family in America: For the good of mankind, we had to try and obliterate centuries' worth of memory in just two or three generations. And we *did* it, too. (We forgot so well we don't even remember forgetting.) Now we're fit to live nowhere but here. That's what's amazing about *your* family, too. Go ahead, say it—*Ich bin ein Tonelli!*

So do you see how this country happened? It's like algebra:

> Ethnicity equals history.
> History equals memory.
> America equals amnesia.

Not that *I'm* complaining. "When it comes to externalizing evil," Nobel Prize-dude Joseph Brodsky wrote in this morning's paper (of the Balkans, but also of everywhere else), "few things can rival geography or, for that matter, history." So I guess we should all be grateful for our forgetting—in the end, it's a blessing. Because let's face it, the world is sick from memory, sick and tired. The world doesn't want to hear who hit whom first, six hundred years ago. The world's not a kid anymore. The world's not getting any younger. And if there's a trade-off, it's our job to accept it like adults—if we have to live with a little anomie, a little alienation, a little isolation, loneliness, existential anxiety, rootlessness, then *fine.* At least the world will get some peace and quiet and not so much remembering, not so much butchery and savagery.

(What will we get instead? Who knows? Believe me, it'll be just as horrible, give it time.)

And where does all this leave yours truly? Hey, don't worry about me. By the year 2040, I just read, only 5 percent of Americans of Italian ancestry will be Italian on both sides. Let them worry about all this stuff. (They won't.) Meantime, as throwbacks go, I'm doing fine. As dust goes, I'm OK, too. It's true, I have to wake up every morning knowing that sociologically speaking, I'm dead—I've gone from evolving to extinct in my own lifetime. But I've known that for a while; the trip only confirmed my suspicion. Maybe that's why I undertook this project to begin with: I wanted to be excused from history, too, just like everybody else. History can be a drag.

So I've lost my fundamental metaphysical certainty, but to be honest it never did me much good when I had it. By the end there it was getting to be a crutch, I think. And anyway, being extinct doesn't hurt a bit. When I come back to South Philly, I don't even notice that I'm a dead man. Here, we're *all* dead. We're just too stubborn to admit it. We're history's last good soldiers, fading away.

Because I'm a sucker for symmetry, I end this trip where it began—at Holy Cross Cemetery. If I get a say, this will be my real last stop, someday. I'll be back where I started, a collection of cells named Tonelli, surrounded by my family. I won't be pretty. I won't be good for much (I almost wrote *mulch*). But, as the elements work their magic on me, I'll become indistinguishable from the earth, and in that way—more literally than I ever imagined until just this second, honest to Christ—*I'll be home.* I feel a little weird because of what I'm about to do, but I do it anyway, take my final Tonelli portrait, a picture of my father's grave. I'm waiting to see if this strikes my mother as odd behavior, but then she asks me to take a picture of *her* father's grave, and of course, I do.

Epilogue

Anyway, that's all of it—my only true story.

I know it was just a trip in a car, meeting ordinary people, but it feels like a miracle happened to me. I drove twelve thousand miles in two months without killing anybody! Plus, I met more Tonellis than I ever thought I'd meet, in more places than I ever thought I'd see. As I met Tonellis, I felt as though I could claim them, and as I claimed Tonellis, I claimed America, too. Everything finally all came together. It really was a hell of a drive.

People who write for a living tell me there's always a gap between the way things seem at the time and the way they come out on paper, and this book is no different. The more I thought about everybody I met, all at once, the harder it became to express what I was feeling. Thomas Sowell, the economist, wrote: "The peopling of America is one of the great dramas in all of human history." It's easy to forget that, or to never see it in the first place, but it's so true. Nearly everybody I met comes from identical origins: They are the children, grandchildren, or great-grandchildren of poor, ignorant, early twentieth-century immigrants to America. But today, just two or three generations later, the circumstances of their lives—where they live, what they do, how they think, what they believe—are all so different. Most of what they have in common they also share with

The Amazing Story of the Tonelli Family in America

every other American. Of course, they *do* still have a special bond. But it has only to do with the people they might have been.

History, though, had other plans for them.

Bibliography

Alba, Richard D. *Ethnic Identity: The Transformation of White America.* New Haven, Conn.: Yale University Press, 1990.

——. *Italian-Americans: Into the Twilight of Ethnicity.* New York: Prentice Hall, 1985.

Allen, James Paul, and Eugene James Turner. *We the People: An Atlas of America's Ethnic Diversity.* New York: Macmillan, 1988.

Battistella, Graziano, ed. *Italian Americans in the '80s: A Sociodemographic Profile.* Staten Island, N.Y.: Center for Migration Studies of New York, 1989.

Belfiglio, Valentine. *Italian Experience in Texas.* Austin, Tx.: Eakin Press, 1983.

Bell, Rudolph M. *Fate and Honor, Family and Village: Demographic and Cultural Change in Rural Italy Since 1800.* Chicago: University of Chicago Press, 1979.

Darwin, Charles. *Darwin, A Norton Critical Edition.* Edited by Philip Appleman. New York: W.W. Norton, 1979.

Fukuyama, Francis. *The End of History and the Last Man.* New York: Free Press, 1992.

——. "Immigrants and Family Values." *Commentary* 95, no. 5 (May 1993): 26–32.

Gans, Herbert J. *The Urban Villagers.* New York: Free Press, 1982.

Greeley, Andrew M. *Why Can't They Be Like Us? America's White Ethnic Groups.* New York: Dutton, 1975.

————. *Ethnicity in the United States: A Preliminary Reconnaissance.* New York: John Wiley & Sons, 1974.

The Italian-Americans: Who They Are, Where They Live, How Many They Are. Torino, Italy: Fondazione Giovanni Agnelli, 1980.

Kerouac, Jack. *On the Road.* New York: NAL, 1958.

Kuralt, Charles. *A Life on the Road.* New York: Ballantine, 1991.

Lasch, Christopher. *The True and Only Heaven.* New York: W.W. Norton, 1991.

Least Heat Moon, William. *Blue Highways: A Journey into America.* Boston: Houghton Mifflin, 1982.

Mangione, Jerre, and Ben Morreale. *La Storia: Five Centuries of the Italian-American Experience.* New York: HarperCollins, 1992.

Shoumatoff, Alex. *Mountain of Names.* New York: Random House, 1980.

————. *Russian Blood.* New York: Coward, McCann & Geoghegan, 1982.

Smith, Tom W. *A Portrait of Italian Americans: 1972–1991.* Chicago: National Opinion Research Center, University of Chicago, 1992.

Sowell, Thomas. *Ethnic America: A History.* New York: Basic Books, 1981.

Steinbeck, John. *Travels with Charley.* New York: Viking, 1962.

Veronesi, Gene P. *Italian Americans and Their Communities of Cleveland.* Cleveland, Oh.: Cleveland State University, 1977.

Waters, Mary C. *Ethnic Options: Choosing Identities in America.* Berkeley, Calif.: University of California Press, 1990.

Acknowledgments

First things first: In the course of writing this book, I flat-out stole two lines from the works of other authors. Now, overcome by guilt, I wish to confess.

In chapter 1, I paraphrased a lyric from a song titled "In My Family," by brothers Ron and Russell Mael and their brilliant band, Sparks. The original line was "Gonna hang myself/from my family tree." One particular line of that song captures the joyous mystery of kinship better than anything in these pages: "Well, you've got your Rockefeller/and you've got your Edward Teller/J. Paul Getty is a splendid fellow/But none of them can be in my family . . . "

In chapter 18, I lifted a concept—that of man having lost his "fundamental metaphysical certainty"—from an essay by Václav Havel that ran in *Esquire*. The entire passage in which the line appears seems relevant to these proceedings, so I'll quote it all:

> I've always been deeply affected by the theater of the absurd because, I believe, it shows the world as it is, in a state of crisis. It shows man having lost his fundamental metaphysical certainty, his relationship to the spiritual, the sensation of meaning—in other words, *having lost the ground under his feet.* [Emphasis added.] As I've said in my book *Disturbing the Peace,* this is a man for whom

everything is coming apart, whose world is collapsing, who senses he has irrevocably lost something but is unable to admit this to himself and therefore hides from it.

Now, time to pay the rest of my debt to society.

In the spring of 1993, then *Esquire* Editor in Chief Terry McDonell, a cool dude in a loose mood, gave me the encouragement, slack, and time off that I needed to research and write this book. Without his generosity, it would not have happened. Will Blythe, *Esquire*'s Literary Editor, kindly read this book while it was in progress, and his impeccable taste and soulful enthusiasm gave me guidance and courage to go on. I also am grateful to the rest of the people I love and like at *Esquire* for giving me a safe harbor to return to now that this ball-breaker is done.

While I'm assigning blame, this book wouldn't have occurred if not for the sunny visions of literary agent Richard Pine, of Arthur Pine Associates, who looked at a goofy whim and saw a world.

This book also owes its life to its editor, the incandescent Liz Perle McKenna, who staked her hopes and high reputation on the sketchy promise that I might be a writer, and whose love sent me into the teeth of destiny, a realm I had always been happy enough to duck.

Speaking of love and destiny, I owe big-time the oceanic devotion and endurance of Lisa Mansourian, a queen among women, who made my efforts infinitely more memorable than they would have been without her in my life.

In the realm of research, thanks to Richard D. Alba of SUNY Albany, Sam Register of the New York Public Library, Father Lydio Tomasi of the Center for Migration Studies, Joseph Velikonja of the University of Washington, Alfred Aversa, Jr., of Fairleigh Dickinson University, Herbert J. Gans of Columbia University, Father Andrew M. Greeley of the University of Chicago, Furio Colombo and Franco Zerlenga of the Italian Cultural Institute, Alfred M. Rotondaro of the National Italian American Foundation, Francis X. Femminella of SUNY Albany, Fred Gardaphé of Columbia College, Chicago, Rudolph Vecoli of the University of Minnesota, Dominic Candeloro of Governors

Acknowledgments

State University, Valentine Belfiglio of Texas Women's College, journalists Alex Shoumatoff and Randy Rothenberg, and Paul DiLillo of Beta Research Corp.

Texas Congressman John Bryant and Texan Mark Warren of *Esquire* combined their efforts to get me into (and out of) the federal prison camp there when the prospect looked dim.

During my travels I lodged with Tonellis on three occasions: Alan and Beth, of North Carolina, Stanford and Annie, of Alaska, and Arthur, of Massachusetts, took me in like one of their own. So, too, did my pal Michelle Nader. Thanks, everybody.

John Aiello, of Philadelphia, showed me new ways of thinking about ethnicity and culture that got me started down the road that led to this book. Thanks, John, and thanks also to my Italo-litero heroes and heroines for being there a long time ago when I needed you, especially: Pietro DiDonato, Mario Puzo, Anthony Valerio, Gay Talese, Camille Paglia, Richard Gambino, Frank Lentricchia, Albert Innaurato, Barbara Grizzuti Harrison, Don DeLillo, Nick Pileggi, Phil Caputo, Ken Auletta, Jerre Mangione, Jerry Della Femina, Nick Tosches, Gaeton Fonzi, Jim Riggio, John Lombardi, Nick Virgilio, and Frank Rossi.

I owe various tangible and intangible debts to: my philosophy coach Dr. Andrew Pessin, Jean Seal, Michael Ian Kaye, E. Jean Carroll, Susie Bright, Alix M. Freedman, Joe Kwong, Marisa Acocella, Monica Oberthaler, my accountant Judith Hirsch, Ed Kosner, Guy Martin, Rachel Clarke, Mark Jacobson, Beverly Xua, Jess Brallier, Marianne Duldner, Alan Halpern, Carol Saline, Carlin Romano, Stephen Bruccoleri, Wendy Hickok Robinson, Maria Massi Walker, Lori Andiman, Mary D'Anella and Michael Mercanti (and Madelaina and Isabella), Dennis Caporiccio, Tom DeFelice, Jill Tonelli, Larry Venuti, Sandra Scandiber of Trattoria Dell'Arte, and my barbers John Pastino (Philly) and Sam Wong (New York).

After all this, do I really need to acknowledge my family? Nah—but I *do* owe my Aunt Marie and Aunt Jo, who were generous with their time and memories. And if I'm going to name names, I have to include my sisters, Lois Tonelli and Cindy Di-Menna, and my brother-in-law, Robert. To be fair, I should also

The Amazing Story of the Tonelli Family in America

name my Tonelli-side cousins: Pat, Dan, Tom, Joyce, Louis, Linda, Louis, Leona, John, and Barbara. But I can't name them and leave out my mother's side: uncles Dominic and Onorato, aunts Rose and Rita, and cousins Carmella, Pat, Dom, Robert, and Joseph. Because I know we'll meet again, I'll thank my ancestors, Luigi and Lena (Peca) Tonelli and Pasquale and Millie (Sinatra) Funaro. For posterity's sake, I'll say hello to my sister's offspring: Bobby, Laura, and Allison DiMenna. Yo, kids: You rule.

Hello to the boys from 15th and Moore.